Dear Colin and Noreen:

This is a token of my appreciation for many kindnesses and much friendship. True friends are rare jewels. It is also an attempt to introduce you to these chaps. If you look closely in these pages, you will see Australians as they (wish to) see themselves. Many thanks, especially for the most memorable party.

R W Marsh p.e.
May 20, 1994

A LITERARY HERITAGE

'BANJO' PATERSON

A LITERARY HERITAGE

'BANJO' PATERSON

Selected and with an introduction by
Rosamund Campbell and Philippa Harvie

WELDON

Permission to reproduce the Browns of Melbourne cover pattern entitled "Australian Parrots and Wildflowers" has kindly been granted by Austin Morgan Australia.

Designer: Elaine Rushbrooke

A Kevin Weldon Production
Published by Weldon Publishing
a division of Kevin Weldon & Associates Pty Limited
Level 5, 70 George St., Sydney 2000, Australia
First published Lansdowne Press 1988
Reprinted Weldon Publishing 1992
© Copyright in this selection Retusa Pty Limited 1988

Poems and prose by A. B. Paterson first
published prior to 1 May, 1969 — Copyright
Reserved — Proprietor, Retusa Pty Limited

© Copyright design Kevin Weldon & Associates Pty Limited 1988

Typeset in Australia by Savage Type Pty Ltd, Brisbane
Printed by Griffin Paperbacks, Watson Avenue, Netley, South Australia

National Library of Australia Cataloguing-in-Publication Data

A Literary Heritage: 'Banjo' Paterson and Henry Lawson

Includes Indexes.
ISBN 0 7018 2011 X (set)
ISBN 0 7018 2009 8 ('Banjo' Paterson)
ISBN 0 7018 2010 1 (Henry Lawson)

I. Paterson, A. B. (Andrew Barton), 1864–1941.
II. Lawson, Henry, 1867–1922. III. Campbell,
Rosamund. IV. Harvie, Philippa. V. Kiernan,
Brian. VI. Title.

A828'.2

Contents

Contents

Contents

Introduction

"So you're back from up the country, Mister Lawson, where you went," ...

With these words Andrew Barton Paterson commenced his defence of the Australian bush, in reply to a poem of his contemporary, Henry Lawson, and so began the 'feud' between the two well-known poets. Writing some personal reminiscences for *The Sydney Morning Herald* in 1939, Paterson recalled the encounter:

"Lawson was a man of remarkable insight in some things and of remarkable simplicity in others. We were both looking for the same reef, if you get what I mean, but I had done my prospecting on horseback with my meals cooked for me, while Lawson had done his prospecting on foot and had had to cook for himself. Nobody realised this better than Lawson, and one day he suggested that we should write against each other, he putting the bush from his point of view, and I putting it from mine.

'We ought to do pretty well out of it,' he said. 'We ought to be able to get in three or four sets of verses each before they stop us.'

"This suited me all right, for we were working on space, and the pay was very small ... so we slambanged away at each other for weeks and weeks, not until they stopped us, but until we ran out of material. I think that Lawson put his case better than I did, but I had the better case, so that honours (or dishonours) were fairly equal."

It is now nearly one hundred years since those sets of verses were first published in the *Bulletin* and it is fitting in this year of Australia's celebration that the best-known works of these two famous men should be published as companion volumes.

A. B. Paterson was born at Narrambla Homestead, near Orange, in central New South Wales on 17 February 1864. He was to spend his childhood firstly at his parents' property 'Buckinbah' near Yeoval and then at their station 'Illalong' in the Yass district. He attended the public school at Binalong until he was old enough to be sent to school in Sydney and he completed his education at Sydney Grammar School. At 'Illalong' Paterson spent a very happy and secure childhood, growing to know and love the bush and its people and this knowledge provided a background for much of his work.

On leaving school, Paterson studied law and was admitted as a solicitor in 1886. For the next thirteen years he practised law in Sydney but managed to find time for his many sporting activities. He was a well-known and successful amateur rider and polo player and also enjoyed tennis and golf. He was, too, making a name for himself through his verses, which appeared regularly in the *Bulletin*, usually under the nom de plume of "The Banjo".

His first collection of poetry, containing such favourites as "The Man from Snowy River" and "Clancy of The Overflow", was published by Angus and Robertson in 1895 and was an immediate success. It was in the same year that, visiting friends in Queensland, he heard a tune and wrote what was to become Australia's unofficial national anthem, "Waltzing Matilda".

In 1899, at the outbreak of the Boer War, Paterson determined to go to South Africa and offered his services to *The Sydney Morning Herald* as a war correspondent. He saw the war at first hand and the dispatches he sent back over the next twelve months were very well received. On his return he was asked to lecture on his war experiences and he travelled extensively in both New South Wales and Victoria, one of his tours taking him north to Tenterfield, where he met and fell in love with his future wife, Alice Walker, of Tenterfield Station.

It was at this time that Paterson decided to become a full-time journalist and, in 1903, the year of his marriage, he was appointed editor of *The Evening News*, a Sydney daily newspaper. Until 1908 Paterson, now settled in the city, continued as an editor and during these years his daughter Grace and son Hugh were born. Wanting to give his children a country upbringing, however, he moved the family to 'Coodra Vale', a 40,000 acre property in the foothills of the Snowy Mountains. The venture was not particularly successful and, in 1914, he was considering the possibility of wheat farming in Grenfell, when war was declared. Hoping to become a war correspondent again, he travelled to England but was unable to obtain a post so he became an ambulance driver for one of the private hospitals being set up in France. In 1915 he returned to Australia to join the newly formed Remount Unit, being commissioned as a lieutenant. He spent the remainder of the war in the Middle East, rising to the rank of major.

After the war Paterson combined his journalism with his knowledge of horses, when he was appointed editor of *The Sydney Sportsman*. He retired from full-time journalism in 1930, but continued to contribute articles to a number of publications. During the next ten years he was to write his memoirs, published as *Happy Dispatches*, verses for children, *The Animals Noah Forgot*, another novel *The Shearer's Colt*, and, for his grand-daughters, tales of his childhood at 'Illalong'.

Paterson died in Sydney on 5 February 1941, his contribution to Australian literature recognised during his lifetime. In 1938 he was appointed a Commander of the British Empire. He, himself, was very modest about his work and rarely discussed it, but in an article written for the final edition of *The Sunday Mail*, he took the opportunity to explain the origins of some of his best-loved works and ended by saying:

". . . looking back on a long life I suppose I can count myself fortunate to have seen so many of the changes and developments in a new country. The 'covered waggons' and the 'nesters' of America had their counterparts in our bullock drays and our free selectors; the main difference being that in early American days individuals shot out their quarrels with revolvers, and the States shot out their quarrels in a civil war. Luckily, Australia was spared these experiences. Swinburne wrote in his "Triumph of Time":

> "It is not much that a man can save
>   On the sands of life, in the straits of time,
> Who swims in sight of the great third wave
>   That never a swimmer shall cross or climb;
> Some waif washed up with the strays and spars
> That ebb-tide shows to the shore and the stars
> Weed from the water, grass from a grave,
>   A broken blossom, a ruined rhyme.

"Our 'ruined rhymes' are not likely to last long, but if there is any hope at all of survival it comes from the fact that such writers as Lawson and myself had the advantage of writing in a new country. In all museums throughout the world one may see plaster casts of footprints of weird animals, footprints preserved for posterity, not because the animals were particularly good of their sort, but because they had the luck to walk on the lava while it was cooling. There is just a faint hope that something of the same sort may happen to us."

Rosamund Campbell & Philippa Harvie
Sydney, 1988

Clancy of The Overflow

I had written him a letter which I had, for want of better
   Knowledge, sent to where I met him down the Lachlan, years ago,
He was shearing when I knew him, so I sent the letter to him,
   Just "on spec", addressed as follows: "Clancy, of The Overflow".

And an answer came directed in a writing unexpected,
   (And I think the same was written with a thumbnail dipped in tar)
'Twas his shearing mate who wrote it, and *verbatim* I will quote it:
   "Clancy's gone to Queensland droving, and we don't know where he are."

In my wild erratic fancy visions come to me of Clancy
   Gone a-droving "down the Cooper" where the western drovers go;
As the stock are slowly stringing, Clancy rides behind them singing,
   For the drover's life has pleasures that the townsfolk never know.

And the bush hath friends to meet him, and their kindly voices greet him
   In the murmur of the breezes and the river on its bars,
And he sees the vision splendid of the sunlit plains extended,
   And at night the wondrous glory of the everlasting stars.

I am sitting in my dingy little office, where a stingy
   Ray of sunlight struggles feebly down between the houses tall,
And the foetid air and gritty of the dusty, dirty city
   Through the open window floating, spreads its foulness over all.

And in place of lowing cattle, I can hear the fiendish rattle
   Of the tramways and the buses making hurry down the street,
And the language uninviting of the gutter children fighting,
   Comes fitfully and faintly through the ceaseless tramp of feet.

And the hurrying people daunt me, and their pallid faces haunt me
   As they shoulder one another in their rush and nervous haste,
With their eager eyes and greedy, and their stunted forms and weedy,
   For townsfolk have no time to grow, they have no time to waste.

And I somehow rather fancy that I'd like to change with Clancy,
   Like to take a turn at droving where the seasons come and go,
While he faced the round eternal of the cashbook and the journal —
   But I doubt he'd suit the office, Clancy, of "The Overflow".

Shearing at Castlereagh

The bell is set aringing, and the engine gives a toot,
There's five and thirty shearers here are shearing for the loot,
So stir yourselves, you penners-up and shove the sheep along,
The musterers are fetching them a hundred thousand strong,
And make your collie dogs speak up — what would the buyers say
In London if the wool was late this year from Castlereagh?

The man that "rung" the Tubbo shed is not the ringer here,
That stripling from the Cooma side can teach him how to shear.
They trim away the ragged locks, and rip the cutter goes,
And leaves a track of snowy fleece from brisket to the nose;
It's lovely how they peel it off with never stop nor stay,
They're racing for the ringer's place this year at Castlereagh.

The man that keeps the cutters sharp is growling in his cage,
He's always in a hurry and he's always in a rage —
"You clumsy-fisted muttonheads, you'd turn a fellow sick,
You pass yourselves as shearers? You were born to swing a pick!
Another broken cutter here, that's two you've broke today,
It's awful how such crawlers come to shear at Castlereagh."

The youngsters picking up the fleece enjoy the merry din,
They throw the classer up the fleece, he throws it to the bin;
The pressers standing by the rack are waiting for the wool,
There's room for just a couple more, the press is nearly full;
Now jump upon the lever, lads, and heave and heave away,
Another bale of golden fleece is branded "Castlereagh".

The Old Australian Ways

The London lights are far abeam
   Behind a bank of cloud,
Along the shore the gas lights gleam,
   The gale is piping loud;
And down the Channel, groping blind,
   We drive her through the haze
Towards the land we left behind —
The good old land of "never mind",
   And old Australian ways.

The narrow ways of English folk
   Are not for such as we;
They bear the long-accustomed yoke
   Of staid conservancy:
But all our roads are new and strange
   And through our blood there runs
The vagabonding love of change
That drove us westward of the range
   And westward of the suns.

The city folk go to and fro
   Behind a prison's bars,
They never feel the breezes blow
   And never see the stars;
They never hear in blossomed trees
   The music low and sweet
Of wild birds making melodies,
Nor catch the little laughing breeze
   That whispers in the wheat.

Our fathers came of roving stock
   That could not fixed abide:
And we have followed field and flock
   Since e'er we learnt to ride;
By miner's camp and shearing shed,
   In land of heat and drought,
We followed where our fortunes led,
With fortune always on ahead
   And always further out.

The wind is in the barley grass,
  The wattles are in bloom;
The breezes greet us as they pass
  With honey-sweet perfume;
The parakeets go screaming by
  With flash of golden wing,
And from the swamp the wild ducks cry
Their long-drawn note of revelry,
  Rejoicing at the spring.

So throw the weary pen aside
  And let the papers rest,
For we must saddle up and ride
  Towards the blue hill's breast;
And we must travel far and fast
  Across their rugged maze,
To find the Spring of Youth at last,
And call back from the buried past
  The old Australian ways.

When Clancy took the drover's track
  In years of long ago,
He drifted to the outer back
  Beyond the Overflow;
By rolling plain and rocky shelf,
  With stockwhip in his hand,
He reached at last, oh lucky elf,
The Town of Come-and-Help-Yourself
  In Rough-and-Ready Land.

And if it be that you would know
  The tracks he used to ride,
Then you must saddle up and go
  Beyond the Queensland side —
Beyond the reach of rule or law,
  To ride the long day through,
In Nature's homestead — filled with awe:
You then might see what Clancy saw
  And know what Clancy knew.

A Grain of Desert Sand

Beneath the blue Egyptian skies,
  With ramp and roller, guide and stay,
I saw the Pyramids arise
  And I shall see them pass away.

I watched when Alexander passed;
  I saw Napoleon's flag unfurled —
The greatest and perhaps the last
  Of men whose footsteps shook the world.

To each his hour of pride and place,
  Arab and Persian, Greek and Jew;
Mahomet trod upon my face,
  Darius spurned me with his shoe.

And yet I am not Priest or King,
  Sultan or Chief in high command.
I am that one unchanging thing,
  A grain of desert sand.

Sunrise on the Coast

Grey dawn on the sand-hills — the night wind has drifted
  All night from the rollers a scent of the sea;
With the dawn the grey fog his battalions has lifted,
  At the scent of the morning they scatter and flee.

Like mariners calling the roll of their number
  The sea fowl put out to the infinite deep.
And far overhead — sinking softly to slumber —
  Worn out by their watching, the stars fall asleep.

To eastward where resteth the dome of the skies on
    The sea line stirs softly the curtain of night;
And far from behind the enshrouded horizon
    Comes the voice of a God saying, "Let there be light."

And lo, there is light! Evanescent and tender,
    It glows ruby-red where 'twas now ashen grey;
And purple and scarlet and gold in its splendour —
    Behold, 'tis that marvel, the birth of a day!

Our Earliest Inhabitants

"Arms and the man I sing," or, in other words, I would like to try to tell something of the primitive life of the Australian Aborigines who, in my opinion, have been given what is known as a "very rough spin" by their chroniclers.

I have always taken a great interest in the Aborigines and, when I found myself living for a month or two alongside a blacks' camp in the buffalo country, I made some notes and tried to get some sort of picture of their lives.

I tried to study out, not so much what they did as why they did it. Even a blackfellow has his reasons: buffalo shooters also. Figure to yourself, then, a collection of wurlies, mostly made of reeds and boughs, just stuck down without any order or method a couple of hundred yards from the buffalo camp. Here live a branch of the Kar-ka-doo tribe, and the first thing that struck me was the fine physique of the men. Compared to inland blacks, they were giants, and well-nourished giants at that. They had been reared on a diet of wild ducks, wild geese, fish, and birds' eggs in season, while the inland natives thought themselves lucky to get possums and iguanas. Here, then, was the first lesson, that food will change a feeble people into strong men — a thing worth considering in these days of the dole. Living close to the coast, they were constantly visited by Malays after pearl shell and *bêche-de-mer*, and they showed in their countenances a strong infusion of Malay blood. This was all to the good, as a dash of outbreeding helps to give physique and intelligence. Some of the piccaninnies showed a dash of bronze in their colouring.

They were still creatures of the Stone Age, as the men carried (mostly for show) the flint-topped spears which had been their main weapons before the coming of the white man.

Looking at the men loafing about the camp, while the gins rubbed salt and arsenic into the buffalo hides and the piccaninnies played with the dogs, it was hard to believe that they had ever thought of anything beyond the necessities of getting a living: and yet these people had thought out a quite intricate system of tribal laws and customs.

Had I only enough learning to make proper use of it, I was seeing not only the beginnings of a people but the beginnings of a social system: all their laws related to food, the barter of goods, and the upbringing of children, and these laws seemed to be founded on self-preservation.

For instance, they had a law of taboo, which they called *komali*, forbidding the younger members the eating of certain food, so that their elders might have enough in times of scarcity. It might seem a short-sighted policy to starve the children and to feed the old folk, but, come what may, the tribe had to go on, and those capable of reproducing themselves had to be kept alive. Other examples of *komali* were founded on sheer superstition, such as the belief that if a pregnant woman ate the flesh of a pelican her child would have a huge mouth and that if she ate garfish the child would have a beak like Cyrano de Bergerac.

Except for the slight infusion of Malay blood, the natives were very inbred and everybody was everybody else's aunt, uncle or cousin. This worked well in one way because there was a law that, if a child's parent died, its relatives were bound to look after it. This gave the child a chance of survival and any female relative coming to the child's rescue had the right to be called "mother", though she might be a grandmother or grand-aunt.

One day there was a great stir in the blacks' camp and a boy named Mercal-lackie came over to the buffalo shooters' lines and said that he had found his mother and asked for some tobacco for her. He was told to produce his mother for inspection, and he brought over a lubra not much older than himself. It turned out that this lubra's grandmother and Mercal-lackie's grandmother were sisters, and this gave her the right to be called "mother" by the boy.

They had other laws directed to keeping the tribe going. For instance, if a married man died, his widow automatically passed to his brother, who had the power to give her to anybody he wished: the lady was not consulted. Even though she might hate her brother-in-law most bitterly, she was expected to go on bearing children to him for the good of the tribe. In short, there seemed to be a reason for everything they did, a reason not always apparent on the surface.

They had their own ideas of discipline, too. If a lot of children were playing together and they were wanted at the camp, someone would call out *"Be-are-lallah coo-way"* ("Children, come here!") and it would be the flat of the hand and the end of the yam stick for those who did not come. I have seen worse discipline in more refined civilisations. Even their religion, based as it was solely on the fear of a devil-devil of their own imagining, seemed to keep them in order well enough. At any rate, it was better than nothing, and the words of an unknown philosopher occurred to me:

> You may measure the world with a square and level
> And watch how the dead leaves fall
> But man must have some kind of a devil
> To frighten himself withal.

So much for this bird's-eye view of a primitive people. With the coming of the buffalo shooters, such tribes as were on the spot were given employment as skinners and curers of hides. They were "on the staff" and behaved themselves with appropriate arrogance towards less-favoured tribes which could only hang round and cadge. No shooter in his senses would trust even his own blacks with a rifle, but they were allowed to have tomahawks, and with these they developed a technique in bull fighting equal to the best traditions of Spain.

Mustering all the dogs in camp, they would set out until they found a buffalo and set the dogs on him. The buffalo, though very fast for awhile, especially through long grass, is a short-winded brute and before long he would bail up and charge the dogs. Then the native with the tomahawk would hide behind a tree, as close as he dared to the scene of action; and the buffalo, in his rushes at the dogs, was sure to come, sooner or later, closer to the tree. Out springs the native and hamstrings him with a blow of the tomahawk, and the animal, unable to move, is despatched with spear and the tomahawk in a manner too grisly for description.

Be it noted that they thought of all this for themselves, showing that they were not without invention, nor afraid of risk if they thought the venture worthwhile. I doubt whether a lot of white men armed with a single tomahawk would have done any better.

There is a certain satisfaction in being able to put in these few kind words on behalf of the blacks, who are generally rated as the lowest, least enterprising and most helpless of the human race. Primitive they were, no doubt, and utterly unfitted to cope with civilisation: but they had enough intelligence to invent the boomerang and the womerah, the latter a crotched stick which fitted on to the end of a spear, and with this they could drive a spear through a deal board at a distance of fifty yards. Except for the people of the poisoned arrows, few primitive men had as dangerous a weapon. Enterprise they had, too, for they would take an alligator, going out on to the lagoons in their rickety little dugouts and stabbing down into the water, putting their whole weight on the end of the spear. Sometimes the alligator thus prodded would give a leap which would jerk the spearman overboard, and before one could say "knife" the blackfellow, the alligator, and all the tribal dogs would be in the water together. Add to this the squealing of the gins and piccaninnies and the shouts of the warriors on the bank, and you had a first-class movie subject with action and sound effects. With all our civilisation, do we get any more wholesome excitement out of life?

Pioneers

They came of bold and roving stock that would not fixed abide;
There were the sons of field and flock since e'er they learned to ride;
We may not hope to see such men in these degenerate years
As those explorers of the bush — the brave old pioneers.

'Twas they who rode the trackless bush in heat and storm and drought;
'Twas they that heard the master-word that called them further out;
'Twas they that followed up the trail the mountain cattle made
And pressed across the mighty range where now their bones are laid.

But now the times are dull and slow, the brave old days are dead
When hardy bushmen started out, and forced their way ahead
By tangled scrub and forests grim towards the unknown west,
And spied the far-off promised land from off the ranges' crest.

Oh! ye, that sleep in lonely graves by far-off ridge and plain,
We drink to you in silence now as Christmas comes again,
The men who fought the wilderness through rough, unsettled years —
The founders of our nation's life, the brave old pioneers.

On Kiley's Run

The roving breezes come and go
 On Kiley's Run,
The sleepy river murmurs low,
And far away one dimly sees
Beyond the stretch of forest trees —
Beyond the foothills dusk and dun —
The ranges sleeping in the sun
 On Kiley's Run.

'Tis many years since first I came
 To Kiley's Run,
More years than I would care to name

Since I, a stripling, used to ride
For miles and miles at Kiley's side,
The while in stirring tones he told
The stories of the days of old
    On Kiley's Run.

I see the old bush homestead now
    On Kiley's Run,
Just nestled down beneath the brow
Of one small ridge above the sweep
Of river flat, where willows weep
And jasmine flowers and roses bloom,
The air was laden with perfume
    On Kiley's Run.

We lived the good old station life
    On Kiley's Run,
With little thought of care or strife.
Old Kiley seldom used to roam,
He liked to make the Run his home,
The swagman never turned away
With empty hand at close of day
    From Kiley's Run.

We kept a racehorse now and then
    On Kiley's Run,
And neighb'ring stations brought their men
To meetings where the sport was free,
And dainty ladies came to see
Their champions ride; with laugh and song
The old house rang the whole night long
    On Kiley's Run.

The station hands were friends I wot
    On Kiley's Run,
A reckless, merry-hearted lot —
All splendid riders, and they knew
The "boss" was kindness through and through.
Old Kiley always stood their friend,
And so they served him to the end
    On Kiley's Run.

But droughts and losses came apace
    To Kiley's Run,
Till ruin stared him in the face;

He toiled and toiled while lived the light,
He dreamed of overdrafts at night:
At length, because he could not pay,
His bankers took the stock away
   From Kiley's Run.

Old Kiley stood and saw them go
   From Kiley's Run.
The well-bred cattle marching slow;
His stockmen, mates for many a day,
They wrung his hand and went away.
Too old to make another start,
Old Kiley died — of broken heart,
   On Kiley's Run.

The owner lives in England now
   Of Kiley's Run.
He knows a racehorse from a cow;
But that is all he knows of stock:
His chiefest care is how to dock
Expenses, and he sends from town
To cut the shearers' wages down
   On Kiley's Run.

There are no neighbours anywhere
   Near Kiley's Run.
The hospitable homes are bare,
The gardens gone; for no pretence
Must hinder cutting down expense:
The homestead that we held so dear
Contains a half-paid overseer
   On Kiley's Run.

All life and sport and hope have died
   On Kiley's Run.
No longer there the stockmen ride;
For sour-faced boundary riders creep
On mongrel horses after sheep,
Through ranges where, at racing speed,
Old Kiley used to "wheel the lead"
   On Kiley's Run.

There runs a lane for thirty miles
   Through Kiley's Run.
On either side the herbage smiles,

But wretched trav'lling sheep must pass
Without a drink or blade of grass
Thro' that long lane of death and shame:
The weary drovers curse the name
    Of Kiley's Run.

The name itself is changed of late
    Of Kiley's Run.
They call it "Chandos Park Estate".
The lonely swagman through the dark
Must hump his swag past Chandos Park.
The name is English, don't you see,
The old name sweeter sounds to me
    Of "Kiley's Run".

I cannot guess what fate will bring
    To Kiley's Run —
For chances come and changes ring —
I scarcely think 'twill always be
Locked up to suit an absentee;
And if he lets it out in farms
His tenants soon will carry arms
    On Kiley's Run.

Home Life

Before going any further on this journey, let us consider home life after the railway came; when we were at any rate partially civilised and got mail every day instead of once a week. Speaking of life in the bush, the Australian poet Brunton Stephens has told us that "this eucalyptic cloisterdom is anything but gay", but we managed to enjoy ourselves in our own way.

We outgrew the original homestead of four big rooms and some skillion rooms were added, but, as the family continued to grow, more space was needed, and a four-roomed house was brought in from the holding of a selector who had sold out to the station. This house, not a very large one, was jacked up onto rollers by the bullock driver and a bush carpenter, who were in charge of operations. We watched it coming through the trees swaying like a ship at sea, but holding together. Arrived after its voyage, there was some very delicate work with bullocks, hauling it onto its new foundations. When it is required to move a whole house an inch and a half, a bullock team is hardly the handiest method in the world, but the driver somehow made those bullocks understand what was wanted and when he spoke to them, never raising his voice, they would just put their weight into the yokes an ounce at a time. We children gave all the credit to the two leading bullocks, Rodney and Spot, whom we considered to be as knowing as men and a lot stronger. Slowly, slowly, the building slid into position and the bullock driver's reputation was made.

Compared with the western place, "Illalong" was poor country, but a previous owner had planted a garden with all sorts of English plants and trees, cypress, holly, hawthorn, and a glorious avenue of acacias. The orchard, too, was a delight, with its figs, walnuts, mulberry trees, cherries, grapes, apples and peaches. In a good season we would fill a clothes basket with grapes or figs, and when the clothes basket was filled there seemed to be just as much fruit as ever.

Sometimes the girls were afraid to gather the figs and grapes because of the bees and hornets which came in thousands to sip the juice from the ripening fruit. The Australian hornet is a man-at-arms, with his red and black banded uniform and his sting like the dagger of a bravo. Not that he would go out of his way to attack anybody, but he was a short-tempered gentleman, and if a small hand gathering fruit happened to touch him he would consider himself insulted and would use his dagger without waiting for apologies. One of the station boys said, "If it comes to being bit by a snake or stung by a hornet, give me the snake."

Then there were the birds who insisted on their rights to the fruit: little silver-eyes nibbling away industriously with their tiny beaks; parrots biting slices out of the peaches with their pincer-like jaws; and the leatherheads whose heads and necks were bare of feathers so that they would not get their plumage in a mess while digging into the fruit. We did not exactly grudge the birds their share but it was disconcerting, while sitting in a fork swaying perilously, to see the silver-eyes and parrots gorging away at the ripest plums and peaches which always grew at the ends of the branches, just out of our reach. The leatherheads were grey birds, bare-necked as vultures and not, apparently, gifted with any brains: and yet they were the most expert nest builders of the lot, weaving long grasses and strips of stringybark into beautiful hanging nests which swung from the twigs right out on the end of the gum tree branches where nobody could climb. Not even the iguana, that terror to small birds, dared trust his weight on the frail twigs where the leatherheads hung their nests, and they built them so high from the ground that Mr Iguana was due for a very nasty fall if the branches gave way with him.

Other fruit lovers were the bower birds, who must have had the collector's instinct, for they built bowers of sticks and lined them with grasses and decorated them with pieces of glass, coloured rags and bright stones. One can imagine the pride with which one bower bird showed to another the neck of a glass bottle, in the days when the necks of glass bottles were none too numerous. However, they did not let their mania for collecting interfere with their appetites and, if they were a hundred yards away, down at the bottom of the garden, they could scent an apple being peeled in the house and would fly up and sit on the window sill, hoping to get a share of the core or the peelings. They were very friendly people, the bower birds, and were quite prepared to have a fruit lunch with anybody.

But life was not all birds and fruit and flowers. We had to work fairly hard. The girls gathered eggs from the fowls which ran wild all over the place, scores and scores of them, nesting in old barns, under the water tanks, or living the life of Riley as wild birds, never coming near the house and nesting among the masses of variegated thistles in the old sheep yard. Dodging through these thistles after nests, it was nothing unusual to see half a dozen fowls rise up like rocketing pheasants and fly for a hundred yards or so, to the accompaniment of a chorus of cackles from their mates hidden away in the thistle bed. There were no foxes, and, as for the native cats, well, the fowls bred faster than the native cats could eat them. A hundred eggs in a day was just a fair tally, and these eggs had to be put away in lime water as a reserve against the cold weather. Motherless lambs were brought to the house and installed as pets, and when anyone went up the yard he was always beset by lambs wagging their tails and getting in his road. A motherless foal was brought in, shy and frightened at first; but once he felt his feet he took charge of the place, chased the lambs and the dogs, and wound up by chasing the cook out of the kitchen. After this exploit he was judged old enough to go out into the paddocks; and one day a Hindoo hawker came in badly rattled and said that a colt foal had "sparred up at him like a prize-fighter", and what sort of horses did we keep, anyhow?

The strongest character about the place was the pet white cockatoo known as "Uncle". He had been brought in by a black boy who had picked him up when he fell out of the parental nest in the spout of a tree and, as he was only able to flutter a few yards, the boy had caught him and brought him along. "Plenty savvy, that feller," said the boy. "Plenty talk, him know a lot, all same old man." At first he was most uninteresting, for his only accomplishment was to sit on a perch swaying himself backwards and forwards, keeping up a never-ending complaint "ah-ah-ah-ah" until we wondered that he did not get a sore throat.

Uncle's life seemed to be just one long complaint until one day we heard our father calling mother from the bottom of the garden. As we knew father was out on the run, it was inexplicable. We ran into the garden thinking that perhaps he had had a fall from his horse and was making his way home; and there we found the cockatoo practising the first words he had learned. His first impersonation was such a success that he soon learned to call the dogs by their names and they, regarding him as a superior intellect, never dared to interfere with him.

Cockatoos spend a lot of their time in digging for yams, and he soon learned to dig up plants or seeds; when washing was put out on the line he would wait till everyone had gone and then he would walk along the clothes line like a man on a tightrope, pulling out the clothes pegs and letting the washing drop on the ground and one day, when he had no other mischief on hand, he was found on the roof patiently loosening, with his powerful beak, the screws which held the sheets of galvanised iron in place. Because he was so full of knowledge, we had called him Uncle Remus, and father said that he was a blessing in disguise for it kept everyone interested to know what he was doing and gave them something to talk about. At any hour of the day someone was liable to say, "What's Uncle doing?" and it generally turned out that he was in some mischief or other. Sometimes Uncle would go for a fly round the house, but if he went out into the paddocks, the wild cockatoos would have none of him and he had to make the best of his way home, shrieking for help. After these exploits he might be heard whispering softly to himself, like one whose brain has been turned by much meditation. Then he would burst into maniac shrieks of disgust which would be heard a mile away, had there been anyone to hear him.

from *Illalong Children*

The Parrot's Nest

The little green and gold parakeets flashed like jewels through the sunshine, going so fast that it took two men to watch them, one to say, "Here they come," and the other to say, "There they go"; but, like all other birds at that time of year, their minds were on rearing a family. They were such carefree little fellows that it was hard to regard them as being serious about anything.

All the time that they were going at such headlong speed, and even when they were hanging to the ends of the gum tree branches sucking honey from the blossoms, their eyes were on the various dead spouts which are common to all gum trees. To make a nest they had to climb into one of these spouts and clear away the old rotten wood and dust which had once been solid timber. This they would excavate with their beaks until they could go down the spout for a foot or so, where their young would be fairly safe. On this unpromising foundation of dust and rotten wood they would lay their white eggs, for the egg of a highly coloured bird is nearly always white.

The parakeets lacked ambition. They lived on honey until the ringbarking of the gum trees made honey scarce, then they took to eating fruit, making many enemies for themselves thereby.

Most parakeets breed well away from houses, but it so happened that one pair of parakeets with, perhaps, less sense than the others, selected a spout in a dead tree close to "Illalong" homestead for their nest. We say that perhaps they had less sense than the others but, as things turned out, they might have had more. We watched their proceedings with interest and all went well until one day Jack saw a strange sight. He saw a crow, one of the most detested birds in the bush, hanging by its claws to the spout which contained the young parakeets and tapping like a woodpecker at the entrance. The crow's object was a mystery. The spout was only large enough to admit a parakeet, and the crow had no chance of getting down it to seize the young fledglings. What, then, was the crow's idea in wasting his time tapping on the doorway of a parakeet's nest? Crows have more brains than most other birds, and they do not waste their time in tapping on dead timber.

In his own line of business, which consists solely of getting his living, the crow has no superior in the bird world; at all-round sagacity a white cockatoo would beat him easily, however. Jack stood and watched the crow tapping for a while. Nothing happened and the crow flew away without any remark, leaving a very much puzzled little boy behind him. Returning to the house, Jack found that Mr Masson, the Government surveyor, had arrived on his annual visit. Mr Masson was a good run-of-the-mob surveyor, but his special talent lay in his knowledge of birds and animals. Anything that walked, flew, climbed, dived, or burrowed was an open book to Mr Masson. Also, there were few to equal him with a shotgun. There were no motor cars in those days, and he did all his travelling in a four-horse waggonette driven by one of his staff. Should a quail rise out of the long grass by the roadside, Mr Masson could pick up his gun and bring down the quail while the waggonette was still being driven at full trot; and if anybody thinks that an easy feat, well, he is welcome to his opinion.

To him Jack confided his problem about the crow, and Mr Masson, who had been a small boy himself and was still a small boy at heart, listened with great interest. "Tapping at the door of a parrot's nest, was he? He knew that the young parrots, if they were old enough, would come to the door of the nest to get fed; and there they would find Mr Crow, and instead of being fed they would be eaten. This is an old trick of Mr Crow. I suppose the young parrots must have been asleep, so Mr Crow flew away. He will go back there tomorrow and we will see what can be done about him. I know a trick that might surprise even Mr Crow."

The next day two waggonettes started out from the station for a bush picnic. In one waggonette were Mr Masson and his staff; the other was filled with the family from the station. We had very faint hopes that anyone would be able to outwit a crow, and father said in joke, "If you shoot that crow, Mr Masson, I'll eat it!"

"If I shoot that crow," said Mr Masson, "I'm afraid I cannot let you eat it. I want to nail his body up on the trees so as to scare away other crows."

When we arrived at the tree where the parakeets had made their nest the provisions were unpacked and Mr Masson's cook made a fire to boil the billy. "Now," said Mr Masson, "you see that fire? As soon as the smoke goes up, every crow within miles will see it and will come overhead. And even those crows which are too far away to see it will see the others coming this way and will follow them. Tell one crow anything and you tell them all. They have as good a signal system as any army. But I do not expect to bring any great crowd of crows today, for at this time of year each pair keeps to its own patch of country unless they smell a dead bullock or something that makes it worth their while to fly a long way. We may only see a few crows, but they will be the ones we want."

The picnic was over, the gear was packed in the waggonettes and all the party climbed into their seats except Mr Masson. He drew his gun and cartridges from the tail of his waggonette and put fresh sticks on the fire.

"You all drive away," he said. "I am going to plant myself under that bush. Crows cannot count above five, so when they see the waggonettes go away they will think we have all gone. They will come up from one tree to another and, when they see no one about, they will fly down to see if there are any scraps left. They are so used to getting scraps from luncheon parties that they almost think they have been invited. They will get a shotgun lunch if they come down today."

So this was the trick which was to be played on Mr Crow. He was to be brought into range in the belief that there was nobody left about the camp.

We all drove out of sight of the camp, but we could still see the treetops about it. Suddenly there was a thrill of excitement when a crow dropped down from the blue sky and sat on the top of a dead tree. By and by another crow dropped down from the sky and he, too, sat on a nearby tree, and there they remained, watching and waiting. Not a sound could be heard, not a movement seen at the camp.

Then other crows could be seen, wheeling about, and the first two crows decided to come down without any delay. If they waited there would be a crowd of crows at a banquet, barely enough for two.

We watched them fly down and throw themselves backwards in the air at the sight of something they saw on the ground; then there were two shots and the two crows were almost blown to pieces in the air.

So died two detestable villains, who had taken just one chance too many; and the parakeets were free to fly headlong through the trees and gather food for their young in the almost certain hope of finding them alive on their return.

from *Illalong Children*

The Downfall of Mulligan's

The sporting men of Mulligan's were an exceedingly knowing lot: in fact, they had obtained the name amongst their neighbours of being a little bit too knowing. They had "taken down" the sporting men of the adjoining town in a variety of ways. They were always winning maiden plates with horses which were shrewdly suspected to be old and well-tried performers in disguise. When the sports of Paddy's Flat unearthed a phenomenal runner in the shape of a blackfellow called Frying-Pan Joe, the Mulligan contingent immediately took the trouble to discover a blackfellow of their own, and they made a match and won all the Paddy's Flat money with ridiculous ease; then their blackfellow turned out to be a well-known Sydney performer. They had a man who could fight, a man who could be backed to jump five feet ten, a man who could kill eight pigeons out of nine at thirty yards, a man who could make a break of fifty or so at billiards if he tried; they could all drink, and they all had that indefinite look of infinite wisdom and conscious superiority which belongs only to those who know something about horseflesh. They knew a great many things which they never learnt at a Sunday school; at cards and such things they were perfect adepts; they would go to immense trouble to work off a small swindle in a sporting line, and the general consensus of opinion was that they were a very "fly" crowd at Mulligan's, and if you went there you wanted to "keep your eyes skinned" or they'd "have" you over a threepenny bit.

There were races at Sydney one Christmas, and a chosen and select band of the Mulligan sportsmen were going down to them. They were in high feather, having just won a lot of money from a young Englishman at pigeon shooting, by the simple yet ingenious method of slipping blank cartridges into his gun when he wasn't looking, and then backing the bird; also they knew several dead certainties for the races. They intended to make a fortune out of the Sydney people before they came back, and their admirers who came to see them off only asked them as a favour to leave money enough among the Sydney crowd to make it worthwhile for another detachment to go down later on. Just as the train was departing a priest came running on to the platform, and was bundled by the porters into the carriage where our Mulligan friends were, the door was slammed to, and away they went. His Reverence was hot and perspiring, and for a few minutes he mopped himself with a handkerchief, while the silence was unbroken except by the rattle of the train.

After a while one of the Mulligan fraternity got out a pack of cards and proposed a game to while away the time. There was a young squatter in the carriage who looked as if he might be induced to lose a few pounds, and the sportsmen thought they would be neglecting their opportunities if they did not try and "get a bit to go on with" from him. He agreed to play, and just as a matter of courtesy, they asked the priest whether he would take a hand.

"What game d'ye play?" he asked, in a melodious brogue. They explained that any game was equally acceptable to them, but they thought it right to add that they generally played for money. "Shure an' it don't matter for wanst in a way," sez he — "Oi'll take a hand bedad — I'm only going about fifty miles, so I can't lose a fortune." Then they lifted a light portmanteau onto their knees to make a table, and five of them — three of the Mulligan's crowd and the two strangers — started to have a little game of poker. Things looked rosy for the Mulligan's boys and they chuckled as they thought how soon they were making a beginning, and what a magnificent yarn they would have to tell about how they rooked the priest on the way down.

Nothing very sensational resulted from the first few deals, and the priest began to ask questions of the others. "Be ye going to the races?" he enquired. They said that they were. "Ah! and I suppose ye'll be betting with these bookmakers — bettin' on the horses, will yez! They do be terrible knowing men, these bookmakers, they tell me. I wouldn't bet much if I was ye," he said, with an affable smile. "If ye go bettin' ye will be took in with these bookmakers." The boys from Mulligan's listened with a bored air and reckoned that by the time they parted the priest would have learnt that they were well able to look after themselves. They went steadily on with the game, and the priest and the young squatter won slightly; this was part of the plan to lead them on to the plunge. They neared the station where the priest was to get out. He had won something rather more than they liked, and the signal was passed round to "put the cross on" — i.e., to manipulate the hands so as to get back his winnings and let him go. Poker is a game at which a man need not risk much unless he feels inclined, and on this deal the priest chose not to risk anything and stood out; consequently when they drew up at the station he still had a few pounds of their money. He half rose and then he said: "Bedad, and I don't like going away with yer money. Oi'll go on to the next station so as ye can have revinge." Then he sat down again, and the play went on in earnest.

The man of religion seemed to have the Devil's own luck. When he was dealt a good hand he invariably backed it well, and if he had a bad one he would not risk anything. The sports grew painfully anxious as they saw him getting further and further ahead of them, prattling away and joking all the time like a big schoolboy. The squatter was the biggest loser so far as they had got, but the priest was the only winner. All the others were out of pocket. His Reverence played with great dash, and seemed to know a lot about the game; and when they arrived at the second station he was in pocket a good round sum. He rose to leave them, with many expressions of regret at having robbed them of their money, and laughingly promising full revenge next time. Just as he was opening the door of the carriage, one of the Mulligan's fraternity said in a stage whisper, "I thought that was how it would be. He's a sinkpocket, and won't give us our revenge now. If he can come this far, let him come on to Sydney and play for double the stakes." The priest heard the remark and turned quickly round. "Bedad, an' if *that's* yer talk, Oi'll go on wid yez and play ye fer double stakes from here to the other side of glory. Play on, now! Do yez think men are mice because they eat cheese? It isn't one of the Ryans would be fearing to give any man his revenge!" He snorted defiance at them, grabbed his cards and waded in. The others felt that a crisis was at hand and settled down to play in a dead silence. The priest kept on winning steadily. The gamblers saw that something decisive must be done, and the leader of the party, the "old man" — "The Daddy," as they put it — decided to make a big plunge and get all the money back on one hand. By a dexterous manipulation of the cards, which luckily was undetected, he dealt himself four kings, almost the best hand at poker. Then he began with assumed hesitation to bet on his hand; he kept raising the stake little by little until the priest exclaimed, "Sure yez are trying to bluff, so ye are!" and immediately started raising it on his part. The others had dropped out of the game and watched with painful interest the stake grow and grow. The Mulligan fraternity felt a cheerful certainty that the "old man" had made everything secure, and they looked upon themselves as mercifully delivered from a very unpleasant situation. The priest went on doggedly raising the stake in response to his antagonist's challenges until it had attained huge dimensions. Then he said, "Sure, that's high enough," and he put into the pool sufficient to entitle him to see his opponent's hand. The "old man" with great gravity laid down his four kings; the Mulligan boys let a big sigh of relief escape them; they were saved — he surely couldn't beat four kings. Then the priest laid down four aces and scooped the pool.

The sportsmen of Mulligan's never quite knew how they got out to Randwick to the races. They borrowed a bit of money in Sydney and found themselves in the saddling paddock in a half-dazed condition trying to realise what had happened to them. During the afternoon they were up at the end of the lawn near the Leger stand, and from that enclosure they could hear the babel of tongues, the small bookmakers, pea-and-thimble men, confidence men, plying their trades. In the tumult of voices they heard one which seemed familiar. After a while suspicion became certainty, and they knew that it was the voice of Father Ryan, who had cleaned them out. They walked to the fence and looked over. They could hear his voice distinctly, and this is what he was saying, "Pop it down, gents! Pop it down! If you don't put down a brick you can't pick up a castle! I'll bet no one here can find the knave of hearts out of these three cards. I'll bet half-a-sovereign no one here can find the knave!" Then the crowd parted a little, and through the opening they could see him distinctly — a three-card man — doing a great business and showing wonderful dexterity with the pasteboard.

This was the downfall of Mulligan's. There is still enough money in Sydney to make it worthwhile for another detachment of knowing sportsmen to come down from that city; but the next lot will hesitate about playing cards with strangers in the train.

The "Bottle-Oh" Man

I ain't the kind of bloke as takes to any steady job —
    I drives a bottle cart around the town.
A man what keeps his eye about need never want a bob —
    I couldn't bear to work for every brown.
There's lots of 'andy things about in everybody's yard,
    There's cocks and 'ens a-running to and fro,
And little dorgs what comes and barks — we takes 'em off their guard;
    And we puts 'em with the Empty Bottle, oh!

    So it's "Any empty bottles, any empty bottles, oh!"
    You can hear us shout for half a mile or so;
    You can see the women rushing
    To take in the Monday's washing
    When they hear the cry of "Empty Bottle, oh!"

I'm driving down by Wexford Street, and up a window goes —
    A girl puts out 'er 'ead and looks at me,
An all right tart with ginger hair and freckles on 'er nose —
    I stops the cart and walks across to see.
"There ain't no bottles 'ere," says she, "since father took the pledge."
    "No bottles 'ere?" says I. "I'd like to know
Wot right you 'ave to stick your 'ead outside the winder-ledge,
    If you 'aven't got no Empty Bottle, oh!"

I sometimes give the 'orse a spell, and then the push and me
    We takes a little trip to Chowder Bay;
Oh, ain't it nice the 'ole day long a-gazing at the sea
    And a-hiding of the tanglefoot away!
But when the booze gets 'old of us and fellers starts to "scrap",
    There's some what likes blue metal for to throw!
But as for me, I always says, for laying out a trap,
    Oh, there's nothing like an Empty Bottle, oh!"

A Mountain Station

I bought a run a while ago,
　　On country rough and ridgy,
Where wallaroos and wombats grow —
　　The Upper Murrumbidgee.
The grass is rather scant, it's true,
　　But this a fair exchange is,
The sheep can see a lovely view
　　By climbing up the ranges.

And "She-oak Flat" 's the station's name,
　　I'm not surprised at that, sirs:
The oaks were there before I came,
　　And I supplied the flat, sirs.
A man would wonder how it's done,
　　The stock so soon decreases —
They sometimes tumble off the run
　　And break themselves to pieces.

I've tried to make expenses meet,
　　But wasted all my labours,
The sheep the dingoes didn't eat
　　Were stolen by the neighbours.
They stole my pears — my native pears —
　　Those thrice-convicted felons,
And ravished from me unawares
　　My crop of paddymelons.

And sometimes under sunny skies,
　　Without an explanation,
The Murrumbidgee used to rise
　　And overflow the station.
But this was caused (as now I know)
　　When summer sunshine glowing
Had melted all Kiandra's snow
　　And set the river going.

And in the news, perhaps you read:
　　"Stock passings. Puckawidgee,
Fat cattle: Seven hundred head
　　Swept down the Murrumbidgee;
Their destination's quite obscure,

I've tried to make expenses meet,
But wasted all my labours,
The sheep the dingoes didn't eat
Were stolen by the neighbours.

A Mountain Station, p. 32

On the outer Barcoo where the churches are few,
And men of religion are scanty,
On a road never cross'd 'cept by folk that are lost,
One Michael Magee had a shanty.

A Bush Christening, p. 34

But, somehow, there's a notion,
Unless the river falls, they're sure
    To reach the Southern Ocean."

So after that I'll give it best;
    No more with Fate I'll battle.
I'll let the river take the rest,
    For those were all my cattle.
And with one comprehensive curse
    I close my brief narration,
And advertise it in my verse —
    "For Sale! A Mountain Station".

The Uplift

When the drays are bogged and sinking, then it's no use sitting thinking,
    You must put the teams together and must double-bank the pull.
When the crop is light and weedy, or the fleece is burred and seedy,
    Then the next year's crop and fleeces may repay you to the full.

        So it's lift her, Johnny, lift her,
        Put your back in it and shift her,
    While the jabber, jabber, jabber of the politicians flows.
        If your nag's too poor to travel
        Then get down and scratch the gravel
    For you'll get there if you walk it — if you don't, you'll feed the crows.

Shall we waste our time debating with a grand young country waiting
    For the plough and for the harrow and the lucerne and the maize?
For it's work alone will save us in the land that fortune gave us
    There's no crop but what we'll grow it; there's no stock but what we'll raise.

        When the team is bogged and sinking
        Then it's no use sitting thinking.
    There's a roadway up the mountain that the old black leader knows:
        So it's lift her, Johnny, lift her,
        Put your back in it and shift her,
    Take a lesson from the bullock — he goes slowly, but he goes!

A Bush Christening

On the outer Barcoo where the churches are few,
    And men of religion are scanty,
On a road never cross'd 'cept by folk that are lost,
    One Michael Magee had a shanty.

Now this Mike was the dad of a ten-year-old lad,
    Plump, healthy, and stoutly conditioned;
He was strong as the best, but poor Mike had no rest
    For the youngster had never been christened.

And his wife used to cry, "If the darlin' should die
    Saint Peter would not recognise him."
But by luck he survived till a preacher arrived,
    Who agreed straightaway to baptise him.

Now the artful young rogue, while they held their collogue,
    With his ear to the keyhole was listenin',
And he muttered in fright while his features turned white,
    "What the divil and all is this christenin'?"

He was none of your dolts, he had seen them brand colts,
    And it seemed to his small understanding,
If the man in the frock made him one of the flock,
    It must mean something very like branding.

So away with a rush he set off for the bush,
    While the tears in his eyelids they glistened —
"'Tis outrageous," says he, "to brand youngsters like me,
    I'll be dashed if I'll stop to be christened!"

Like a young native dog he ran into a log,
    And his father with language uncivil,
Never heeding the "praste" cried aloud in his haste,
    "Come out and be christened, you divil!"

But he lay there as snug as a bug in a rug,
    And his parents in vain might reprove him,
Till his reverence spoke (he was fond of a joke)
    "I've a notion," says he, "that'll move him."

"Poke a stick up the log, give the spalpeen a prog;
 Poke him aisy — don't hurt him or maim him,
'Tis not long that he'll stand, I've the water at hand,
 As he rushes out this end I'll name him.

"Here he comes, and for shame! ye've forgotten the name —
 Is it Patsy or Michael or Dinnis?"
Here the youngster ran out, and the priest gave a shout —
 Take your chance, anyhow, wid 'Maginnis'!"

As the howling young cub ran away to the scrub
 Where he knew that pursuit would be risky,
The priest, as he fled, flung a flask at his head
 That was labelled "Maginnis's Whisky!"

And Maginnis Magee has been made a J.P.,
 And the one thing he hates more than sin is
To be asked by the folk who have heard of the joke,
 How he came to be christened "Maginnis"!

A Bushman's Song

I'm travellin' down the Castlereagh, and I'm a station hand,
I'm handy with the ropin' pole, I'm handy with the brand,
And I can ride a rowdy colt, or swing the axe all day,
But there's no demand for a station hand along the Castlereagh.

So it's shift, boys, shift, for there isn't the slightest doubt
That we've got to make a shift to the stations further out
With the packhorse runnin' after, for he follows like a dog,
We must strike across the country at the old jig-jog.

This old black horse I'm riding — if you'll notice what's his brand,
He wears the crooked R, you see — none better in the land.
He takes a lot of beatin', and the other day we tried,
For a bit of a joke, with a racing bloke, for twenty pounds aside.

It was shift, boys, shift, for there wasn't the slightest doubt,
That I had to make him shift, for the money was nearly out;
But he cantered home a winner, with the other one at the flog —
He's a red-hot sort to pick up with his old jig-jog.

I asked a cove for shearin' once along the Marthaguy:
"We shear non-union, here," says he. "I call it scab," says I.
I looked along the shearin' floor before I turned to go —
There were eight or ten dashed Chinamen a-shearin' in a row.

It was shift, boys, shift, for there wasn't the slightest doubt
It was time to make a shift with the leprosy about.
So I saddled up my horses, and I whistled to my dog,
And I left his scabby station at the old jig-jog.

I went to Illawarra where my brother's got a farm,
He has to ask his landlord's leave before he lifts his arm;
The landlord owns the countryside — man, woman, dog, and cat,
They haven't the cheek to dare to speak without they touch their hat.

It was shift, boys, shift, for there wasn't the slightest doubt
Their little landlord god and I would soon have fallen out;
Was I to touch my hat to him? — was I his bloomin' dog?
So I makes for up the country at the old jig-jog.

But it's time that I was movin', I've a mighty way to go
Till I drink artesian water from a thousand feet below;
Till I meet the overlanders with the cattle comin' down,
And I'll work a while till I make a pile, then have a spree in town.

So, it's shift, boys, shift, for there isn't the slightest doubt
We've got to make a shift to the stations further out;
The packhorse runs behind us, for he follows like a dog,
And we cross a lot of country at the old jig-jog.

Saltbush Bill

Now this is the law of the Overland that all in the west obey,
A man must cover with travelling sheep a six-mile stage a day;
But this is the law which the drovers make, right easily understood,
They travel their stage where the grass is bad, but they camp where the grass
    is good;
They camp, and they ravage the squatter's grass till never a blade remains,
Then they drift away as the white clouds drift on the edge of the saltbush
    plains,
From camp to camp and from run to run they battle it hand to hand,
For a blade of grass and the right to pass on the track of the Overland.

For this is the law of the Great Stock Routes, 'tis written in white and black —
The man that goes with a travelling mob must keep to a half-mile track;
And the drovers keep to a half-mile track on the runs where the grass is dead,
But they spread their sheep on a well-grassed run till they go with a two-mile
    spread.
So the squatters hurry the drovers on from dawn till the fall of night,
And the squatters' dogs and the drovers' dogs get mixed in a deadly fight;
Yet the squatters' men though they hunt the mob, are willing the peace to
    keep,
For the drovers learn how to use their hands when they go with the travelling
    sheep;
But this is the tale of a jackaroo that came from a foreign strand,
And the fight that he fought with Saltbush Bill, the King of the Overland.

Now Saltbush Bill was a drover tough, as ever the country knew,
He had fought his way on the Great Stock Routes from the sea to the Big
    Barcoo;
He could tell when he came to a friendly run that gave him a chance to
    spread,
And he knew where the hungry owners were that hurried his sheep ahead;
He was drifting down in the Eighty drought with a mob that could scarcely
    creep,
(When the kangaroos by the thousands starve, it is rough on the travelling
    sheep).
And he camped one night at the crossing place on the edge of the Wilga run,
"We must manage a feed for them here," he said, "or the half of the mob are
    done!"
So he spread them out when they left the camp wherever they liked to go,
Till he grew aware of a Jackaroo with a station hand in tow,

And they set to work on the straggling sheep, and with many a stockwhip
    crack
They forced them in where the grass was dead in the space of the half-mile
    track;
So William prayed that the hand of fate might suddenly strike him blue
But he'd get some grass for his starving sheep in the teeth of that Jackaroo.
So he turned and he cursed the Jackaroo, he cursed him alive or dead,
From the soles of his great unwieldy feet to the crown of his ugly head,
With an extra curse on the moke he rode and the cur at his heels that ran,
Till the Jackaroo from his horse got down and he went for the drover man;
With the station hand for his picker-up, though the sheep ran loose the while,
They battled it out on the saltbush plain in the regular prize ring style.

Now, the new chum fought for his honour's sake and the pride of the English
    race,
But the drover fought for his daily bread with a smile on his bearded face;
So he shifted ground and he sparred for wind and he made it a lengthy mill,
And from time to time as his scouts came in they whispered to Saltbush Bill —
"We have spread the sheep with a two-mile spread, and the grass it is
    something grand,
You must stick to him, Bill, for another round for the pride of the Overland."

The new chum made it a rushing fight, though never a blow got home,
Till the sun rode high in the cloudless sky and glared on the brick-red loam,
Till the sheep drew in to the shelter trees and settled them down to rest,
Then the drover said he would fight no more and he gave his opponent best.
So the new chum rode to the homestead straight and he told them a story
    grand
Of the desperate fight that he fought that day with the King of the Overland.
And the tale went home to the public schools of the pluck of the English swell,
How the drover fought for his very life, but blood in the end must tell.
But the travelling sheep and the Wilga sheep were boxed on the Old Man
    Plain.
'Twas a full week's work ere they drafted out and hunted them off again,
With a week's good grass in their wretched hides, with a curse and a
    stockwhip crack,
They hunted them off on the road once more to starve on the half-mile track.
And Saltbush Bill, on the Overland, will many a time recite
How the best day's work that ever he did was the day that he lost the fight.

The Cook's Dog

CHAPTER V

And now can we sing the epic of the shearing shed, the throbbing of the oil engine, the whirr of the shearing machines, the barking of dogs and the clatter and scuffling of frightened sheep. The shed itself is about the size of a small cathedral, built of heavy, roughly dressed timber, with a galvanised iron roof, supported on massive timber uprights. The floor of the shed is raised on heavy piles to the height of about four feet above the ground. At one end of the shed are a set of drafting and forcing yards, into which a mass of sheep — about a couple of thousand — are hustled. From this, they are forced up a ramp to the raised floor of the shed. Inside the shed the resemblance to a cathedral is intensified by the rows of towering pillars that support the roof, and the dim religious light in the corners and under the sloping side roofs, where the congregation is represented by some hundreds of stubborn terrified sheep, packed into a solid woolly mass. The Latin proverb *"facilisest descensus averni"* is translated in Australia as, "The road to hell is sheep": anyone who has had to hustle thousands of passive-resistant sheep into a shed and to pack them into the catching pens will admit that is the only possible translation. The shearing floor runs down the centre of the cathedral, smooth as a dancing floor, polished by the friction of sheeps' bodies, and slippery as glass, from the grease in the wool. A heavy beam of timber runs along each side of the shearing floor about eight feet above it, and to this are clamped a row of brackets about eight feet apart. From each bracket there comes down a flexible jointed affair like a snake — a core of twisted catgut inside a leather covering. At the end of each snake is the shearing machine.

The shearing machine is a contraption consisting of a steel comb and cutter with screws to tighten or loosen the friction. The engine is set going, the wheels and the brackets whirr: each man lets his machine run a few seconds to test the tension: then he throws the gear off, and the whizzing machine hangs silent, while he strides into the catching pen alongside his stand and carries out a sheep, kicking and struggling. Dumping the animal on its rump, he reaches up and throws the gear on again, opens up the fleece, and in an instant all down the double line of machines, tense men are peeling off the wool.

Bent almost double, the shearers send the machine whizzing round the animals, and as each is shorn it is slid down a chute out into the counting pens. Boys rush up and down the board picking up fleeces.

At the wool table, the classer and his mate fix up the fleeces, discarding dirty, inferior, and broken stuff, and throwing each fleece into its proper bin.

The pressers, as soon as enough fleeces are ready, jam their press full, jump on the levers, stitch the bale up, brand it, weigh it, and roll it away. Everybody works at high speed.

Sweat drips from the shearers. There is shouting of men and waving of bags and barking of dogs as fresh sheep are forced into the catching pens. The expert toils like a beaver, sharpening and adjusting combs and cutters on a whizzing emery wheel, slackening up the bearings of the driving machinery, fixing up hand pieces and lubricating his engine. A sort of fever of energy seems to be in everyone's blood.

The recognised cracks shear for dear life, watching each other out of the corners of their eyes, to see how each man's tally is mounting up. The wool peels off the sheep in great snowy waves and the pickers-up bump into each other as they run backwards and forwards with armfuls of fleece or grab for the brooms to sweep up pieces and locks from the floor.

The shearing shed at Wombat Hill, like most others of its time, was built in the shape of a capital T, the crosspiece of the T being a large empty expanse of floor used for storing the bales and for pressing, branding and weighing operators. The tail of the T was the shearing floor, with the catching pens standing in the wool room.

The whole shed had their eyes on the recognised cracks — Macauley, the two Graces, and Handkerchief Roberts. No one took any notice of the learner, Smith, who seemed to be taking things very easily. He walked leisurely to his pen after each sheep, lit his pipe and puffed contentedly, or strolled over to the bucket of inky black tea that stood stewing at the end of the shearing floor, and took his time about having a drink. No hurry nor nerve strain about Mr Smith!

Duncan was mercifully out of the shed, working in the yards, and the shed was in charge of the expert. A boundary rider's boy was dodging about the shed as an interested spectator, now and again giving a hand to pen up sheep, adding his shrill voice to the tumult or helping to fill a bale.

After a while he took a stroll round outside the shed and came back to the expert in a state of considerable excitement. The expert was feverishly grinding a cutter for a waiting shearer, and over the noise of the engine and the buzzing of the grindstone he could hardly make out what the boy said. At last he gathered that the youngster was saying that number three pen was full.

"Full! What of? Speak up, you goat!"

"It's full of sheep," shrilled the boy.

"Full of sheep! How did they get in there?"

"He's shore 'em, that learner! You'll have to count 'em out or they'll smother."

The expert reflected bitterly that there was always something unusual happening at Duncan's shed, and, handing over the cutter, he ran round the shed to see what the boy was talking about. Sure enough, the learner's pen was full, almost to suffocating point, of beautifully shorn sheep, while nobody else's pen was even uncomfortably crowded.

He counted the sheep out into a bigger yard, noted their number in a pocket book, and ran back into the shed to see whether, for some humorous reason, somebody had been putting extra sheep down the learner's shute.

As he got up, the learner had just let a sheep go down the shute. He looked hard at the expert and the small boy as they came and stood by his stand but said not a word. A look of grim humour crossed his face and, when he went to his pen for the next sheep, he took a little time selecting it. He carried it out, sat it down carefully, tucked its head methodically under the crook of his arm, threw on the power, and for the first time in his life the expert saw a really first-class shearer at work.

He held the machine loosely, almost carelessly, in his grip, and passed it round the body of the sheep with long sweeping movements, and the fleece just rippled off it in one unbroken blanket of wool. A few lightning touches here and there, apparently haphazardly, and the legs and head were trimmed, and a sheep shorn to the very skin was shot down the chute. It all looked so simple and easy it reminded the expert of the only time he ever saw a first-class professional play billiards. Not a word did the shearer utter but got another sheep and started in the same effortless, unhurried way to peel its fleece off.

His hat was on his head all the time and while he was shearing the next sheep the hat shifted a bit and threatened to fall off. He never paused in his shearing, but looked at the small boy and gave an upward jerk of his head. The small boy, whose wits were not of the brightest, took no notice. Again, a jerk of the head and again no result. Then the great man spoke, and fixing his eye on the small boy, he said sharply, "Lid!" The small boy grasped the situation and the hat and hung the latter on a nail.

"I've got you now," said the expert. "Ain't you Silent Smith that shore the big tally at Nocoleche — two hundred and twenty or something? Ain't you him?"

The silent one nodded, grinned, and went off for another sheep.

Silent Smith! Silent Smith! The news flew round the shed and out into the yards. Imagine Norman Brookes or Gerald Patterson being discovered *incognito* as a competitor in a small suburban lawn tennis tournament. Imagine John Roberts, in his prime, getting in on an easy mark into a billiard handicap promoted by a local publican. No wonder that the picking-up boys all wanted a simultaneous drink of tea, and that the yard hands all found work to do inside the shed, and the shearers, as each man finished his sheep, strolled over to have a look at the celebrity at work. Even the expert, who ought to have known better, stood gaping. That is how things were when Duncan suddenly made his appearance in the shed.

Duncan had been having a verbal round or two with the cook, and was even more cantankerous than usual. The cook had presented a list of stuff that he wanted bought, and, as Duncan was quite sure he had never eaten any of these things himself, he could not see what shearers and shed hands wanted with them. When he arrived at the shed to find all hands gaping at one shearer, he boiled over. "What's doing here?" he screamed. "What's doing here? I'll sack every man in the shed, so I will!"

Handkerchief Roberts walked over to his pen, unhooked the handpiece of his machine, and handed it to Duncan with a courtly bow. "Here you are," he said, "here's my machine, you can put somebody else on my pen. I've got my reputation to consider! What'll they say up in Cunnamulla and Longreach when they hear that Handkerchief Roberts was outclassed by a learner? Every time I'd look at meself in the glass I'd say: 'There's a man that thought he could shear!' If I shore here a full day I'd lose me self-respect for ever."

"Your self-respect, you flash character," said Duncan. "Get out of my shed!"

Here he caught sight of a sheep going down Cassidy's shute with all the wool left on the legs, giving the animal the appearance of a naked man walking in white topboots. He rushed at the offender. "I'll raddle that sheep," he yelled, "you don't leave half the wool on the sheep with me, Cassidy, I'll raddle that sheep!"

Cassidy promptly unhooked his machine and laid it down on the edge of his pen.

"Me and you'll part, then, Duncan," he said. "You want a barber, not a shearer. You want a lather pot and a razor used on them sheep. I'm off."

Duncan watched two of his best shearers walk out of the shed. He had a curious incapacity for handling men, his method always being to quarrel and bounce his way along. His mind was as prickly as a hedgehog and at the bottom of his character was a streak of obstinacy a foot wide. Uneducated, ignorant and self-made, he looked on life as one long combat with enemies, and he had no idea of conciliation or diplomacy. He knew well enough that both Cassidy and Handkerchief Roberts were leaving because they would have no trouble in getting pens at other sheds, while he might have a good deal of trouble in filling their places: but the very idea of admitting that he wanted them to stop was so repugnant to him that he would rather let them go than exercise his undoubted right to make them carry out their agreements. As for this learner — well, he felt that he had been made a laughing stock of, and that the story would go all over Australia. How Silent Smith had passed himself off on him as a learner. But humour was a sealed book to him, so he paced up and down the shearing shed floor watching the men at their work and wondering what would be the next trouble.

It came soon enough. A great barking of dogs and bleating of sheep announced the arrival of a flock from one of the back paddocks, and the musterer came in to make his report. "We're fifty sheep short," he said. "Somebody has left the Big Hill's gate open and they must have got into the mountain. The tracks is all washed out by the rain. Someone'll have to go after 'em. I got to do the Limestone paddick tomorrer."

"I'll go myself," said Duncan. "I know the mountain better than any of you."

"You'll want to take a dorg, then. If they've got up in the rocks you'll never get round them on a horse. You'll want a good dorg, too. Y'haven't got a dorg, have yer?"

Just at this moment the cook came up with a couple of buckets of tea and some brownies — a sort of bread made with brown sugar. Dumping his burden down, he entered cheerfully, and unasked, into the conversation. "I'll lend yer a dorg," he said, "a real good dorg! One I bred meself. You take him and give him a trial and if you take a fancy to him you can have him for a fiver. Wouldn't sell him, only a dorg's no use to me while I'm cookin'."

"Perhaps he won't follow me?" said Duncan.

"Oh yes, he will," said the cook, "he's like that. So long as he knows he's goin' after sheep, he'll follow anybody. You take him. A run'll do him good, and, if you like him, we'll say a fiver."

There was nothing else for it. Every other serviceable dog on the place was at work somewhere, either in the yards or mustering, and in mountain country a dog is worth three men. When Duncan came back to the homestead that night and told Ellen that he was going out at daylight after lost sheep in the mountain, she begged to be allowed to go. Miss Tabitha was not proficient on a horse and decided to stay at home and hunt Paddy along a bit, and so ended the first day's shearing.

CHAPTER VI

Next day, Ellen and her uncle set out for the Big Hill paddock. Duncan carried a tin quart pot strapped to his saddle for making tea, some slices of bread, and fried chops. Their horses were a couple of little, wiry old grass-fed ponies that jogged along contentedly at about five miles an hour. They halted at the shed to pick up the cook's dog. He was a little red dog that at a distance might easily be mistaken for a fox. As soon as he saw the horses he followed happily enough, glad to be off the chain.

They rode along in silence, Duncan thinking of the various troubles that beset graziers at shearing time, and Ellen recalling memories of her trip out, and wondering what was going to be the outcome of it all. They rode through aisles of gum trees, over big clearings where the trees had been killed by ringbarking, following up spurs and across windswept plateaux till at last they came to a gate in a six-wire fence. Here Duncan dismounted and walked about searching the ground for tracks.

"This is my outer boundary," he said. "Cronin thinks the sheep got out at this gate and they may have poked on up into the mountain. Sheep are like anything else — they like to wander about a bit in the spring. Now the trouble is, there's a mob of wild sheep up in this mountain, and if this lot have got with the wild ones I don't know what we'll do. Those wild sheep have been here for three years and nobody can get them out 'cos it's too rough for a horse, and if you put a dog round them they scatter and all run different ways. They've beat all these flash fellows about here and their dogs. It's very seldom anybody ever sees 'em. They're as wild as hawks."

They rode on over country increasingly difficult, working their way up into the mountain. Sometimes they came out on a spur and could see the craggy, barren summit of the mountain a thousand feet or more above them. Then they plunged into gullies, along sidelines, over tussocks of rough grass, and up steep slopes, the ponies clattering on the loose stones. At times a patch of country, too barren to produce trees, gave them a bit of open going: at others they threaded their way through saplings so thick that their knees grazed them as they passed. Sometimes Ellen shut her eyes and clung to the saddle for dear life as her pony picked his way round rocks with a sheer drop of a hundred feet into the valley below her. The dog trotted behind them. Duncan's eyes ceaselessly swept the ground looking for tracks.

Suddenly, he pulled his pony up and pointed to the ground. "Look," he said, "there has been a small mob along here quite lately. It might be those we want or it might be the wild sheep. We'll run these tracks a bit and see what they are."

For a mile or so they followed the tracks, which had been made since the rain and were clear enough in the gullies and on soft ground. On the stony hillsides and plateaux, old Duncan followed them by some sort of instinct, and the dog, too, began to take an interest in the proceedings, running on in front with his nose to the ground and guiding them confidently over country too stony to show any tracks at all.

Presently, some fresh droppings showed that they were close on the sheep, and then they came out of thick timber on to the edge of a big cleared plateau, where some whirlwind had years ago thrown down all the trees, leaving only the rotting trunks and branches. Halfway across this plateau, a mob of about forty sheep were walking steadily, their heads pointed to the mountain. Now and again they stopped for a moment to nibble at a patch of grass, but they were obviously uneasy and were making for the mountain with as little delay as possible. They were not like any sheep that Ellen had ever seen, for their fleeces almost touched the ground. A sheep that is shorn every year will, as a rule, cast its wool off if not shorn at the usual time, but sheep let run wild and never shorn will often grow two and sometimes three years' wool without casting it. These sheep were wild, fantastic-looking creatures, with their fleeces flapping about them as they walked.

Old Duncan's eyes lit up as he watched them. Miser and all as he was, the spirit of a sportsman was not quite dead in him. "The wild sheep, the wild sheep," he whispered. "I'd dearly like to get 'em. We'll put the dog round 'em and see how he shapes. No doubt they'll beat him, but we'll have a try at them, anyways." He turned to the dog, which was staring at the sheep, never in his life having seen sheep quite like those before. Duncan gave a low whistle and a wave of his hand. "Get away back," he said.

As he spoke, the sheep caught sight of them, and, with a whistle of astonishment, the whole mob set off at a scrambling rush for the mountain. The dog stretched out after them like a greyhound; now hidden among the fallen timber, now flashing into sight in a bit of open ground. He gained on the sheep at a great pace: as he drew close to them he wheeled away and raced on, making a wide detour so as to get ahead of them. Ellen and her uncle followed up as fast as the ponies could scramble over the rocks and fallen timber. "Good dog, that," said the old man, "look how wide he works. Come on."

Going like an arrow, the dog soon outpaced the sheep and showed directly in their path, about a hundred yards or more ahead of them. The sheep stopped and stared at him. Ellen and her uncle pulled their ponies up and watched in silence. Inch by inch, the dog drew down toward the sheep, his ears pricked and his eyes fixed on the mob. The sheep huddled together, uncertain what to do, and one or two made short dashes out of the mob as if intending to leave it altogether. Then, as the dog halted, they came back to their mates.

"They'll break if he pushes 'em too close," said old Duncan. "That's always their game. They'll be all over the mountain in ones and twos in a minute."

The dog made no move to get closer to the sheep. He seemed to be thinking things over. Then he suddenly turned and trotted away up the hill. The sheep, with heads up, stared at him till he was out of sight. Then, timidly, they followed after him, still making for their original point. Duncan and Ellen hustled their horses over the rise and over a stony gully, and came up against a sharp spur of the mountain: all above them was mountainside with rocks and stumps, so steep that a horse could not walk up it. Far above them the wild sheep were steadily making their way upwards.

"Look at the dog," said Ellen, "what is he doing? He is away in front of the sheep and he is not trying to bring them this way at all. He's running away, and the sheep are running after him!"

Duncan jumped down and tied his pony to a mountain oak sapling. "Get down," he said, "that dog is either an awful fool, or the best dog that ever came to these parts. I believe he knows what he is doing. We'll go after him on foot and see how things shape. All the years I've been with sheep and dogs I never saw a dog have sense like that. Give me your pony till I tie him up."

While he was tying the pony up, the dog and sheep worked out of sight. They followed after them on foot, scrambling up the precipitous face of the mountain. Behind them they could see for miles and miles over the flat country, could see the river bordered by its fringe of oaks and the toylike homestead that they had left that morning. In front of them was just rugged scrub and rocks. They climbed and panted and slipped and stumbled, making their way slowly till they got to the top of the steep spur, but instead of finding any open country they ran up against another stiff climb, just as bad as the last. The sheep and dog had vanished altogether; gone clean out of sight, and the intense eerie stillness of the Australian bush seemed to settle down and mock them.

They looked at each other for a while silently, straining their ears to catch any sound of the vanished game, but no sound came: all the vast mountainside seemed in a trance.

"What will we do now, uncle?" said Ellen. "Can we go after them?"

Old Duncan seemed to have quite relapsed into the dogged hopeless state of mind that was natural to him. For a while, in the ardour of the hunt, he had seemed quite changed, but in the face of defeat he was very much the old Duncan.

"We could if we had wings," he said. "No other way. We'd better get back to the horses and wait till the dog comes. He might be an hour. He'll fool about with those sheep till they break and run all over the place, and then he'll bail one up and wait there for us to come. When he gets tired of that he'll come back to where he left the horses."

"And if we've gone?"

"Then he might come back to the shed, or he might go home to wherever he lives. He's only been a day at the shed and he might sooner go home. And then that thievin' rascal of a cook would say I had lost the dog, and want me to pay for him."

Truly things looked bad. They had not got the wild sheep, they had not found the station sheep, and they had lost a five-pound dog. Ellen had meant, while out on this expedition, to try to get a little closer to her uncle and establish some sort of friendly relations with him, but this disaster had sent all such schemes to the winds.

Tired and dispirited, with torn clothes and scratched boots, they shuffled painfully over the loose rocks and dodged among tree trunks and scrub back towards the horses.

Suddenly, a faint rattle of a far-off stone falling turned them both round in their tracks. There, on a distant spur of the hill far above them were the sheep, still together but now trotting steadily down hill towards them. As they came jumping from rock to rock, their fleeces swung out at each jump like ballet dancers' skirts. The old ram leading the way was evidently uneasy and kept looking behind him: and there, about two hundred yards behind them, gliding from cover to cover, patiently working first to one flank of the mob and then to the other, guiding them down off the hill and to the slopes below, was the cook's dog.

"Look, look," screeched the old man, "he's got 'em! He's got 'em! They've got sick of running uphill and now they'll try to slip away down one of the spurs. He must have gone ahead of them, till they got tired and then turned them. Saw ye ever the like o' that? Now, listen! They'll come here and try to get off on this spur, and across to the other hill. You run up to that black stump there, and when they come out on to the open, just show yourself. Don't wave your arms or frighten them. They might break back and scatter all over the place. Just show yourself and then they'll turn down the main spur and I'll be waiting on the other side of the gully to block them off there. When they see me they'll go full rush down the main pad because it's the easiest way, and we must just trust the dog to go after them and keep them together till we can catch up with the horses. If he doesn't get too close to them, he'll hold them easy enough: and surely he wouldn't make a mess of such a simple thing as that after doing a bit of work like this. Hurry, Ellen, hurry, and just show yourself. That's all."

He was off like a rabbit, hopping from one fallen log to another, down the steep side of the spur and up the other slope, laboriously making his way by holding on to the tree trunks and saplings till he had established himself on the other side of the ridge. While the old man was scrambling one way, Ellen, wild with excitement, was making her way in the other direction to the black stump. She felt an awful sense of responsibility. In her mind's eye she saw herself coming up too late, or showing herself too soon, and sending the sheep scurrying all over the mountainside.

Breathless, she arrived at the stump, just as the leader of the mob showed out on the open. Feeling like Napoleon on the rocks at St Helena, she stepped out from behind the stump and stood confronting the sheep.

With a loud whistle through his nostrils, the old leader wheeled and made a rush over to the other spur, followed by his flock. Just as they faced the steep incline old Duncan stepped out from behind a tree, and in another instant with a cataract of woolly fleeces, bounding bodies and clattering feet, the mob swept down the main gully, headed for the easy country below, the dog following them.

The sheep came past Ellen at an easy canter, the dog, his eyes fixed ahead of him and all attention, concentrated on his work. Ellen called out to him, "Good dog, good dog," but he paid no attention at all. A great maestro playing a difficult piece does not even hear the ill-timed applause of the stalls. In another instant dog and sheep had swept down out of sight.

It was a case of rush for the horses then, scrambling over boulders and tripping over fallen branches. When they got to the horses, these philosophers were still chewing oak leaves, and there was mounting in hot haste. As soon as they got to their saddles, Ellen was terrified at seeing her uncle — hat in hand and white hair flying in the breeze — set his pony at a hand gallop down the awful stony ravine up which they had toiled so laboriously an hour before.

There did not seem to be a foothold for a goat. The little water-worn pad made by wild sheep and wallabies took right-angled turns round knife-edged rocks, was lost on precipitous stony sidelines and was found again in narrow passes between trees. The old man just yelled back one sentence of encouragement, "Let his head alone and he'll get down all right." And off he went.

Frightened, bumping, wildly excited, Ellen followed him, her pony with the bit loose in its mouth turning, slipping, and jumping, with every second a violent fall apparently inevitable. Stumps flashed past; on steep sidelines the moss-covered rock seemed almost to graze her knees, but the descent was made at last and there, in a patch of fairly open country, they came on the sheep huddled together and puffing wildly, all gathered into a compact mob, while a hundred yards off, watching with a look of concentrated wisdom, lay the cook's dog.

Campin' Round Coonamble

Campin' round Coonamble,
   Keepin' up the strike,
Through the black soil country
   Plugging on the "bike";
Half a thousand shearers,
   What had we to gain
Campin' round Coonamble,
   Campin' in the rain?

Twenty bob a hundred
   Shearing with machines!
Good enough in these times
   We know what it means —
Sinking tanks and fencing,
   Shearing's better pay
Twenty bob a hundred,
   Twenty bob a day!

Every little farmer
   Up Monaro side
Sends the boys a-shearing,
   Hoping to provide
Something for the homestead;
   All his hopes are vain,
While we're round Coonamble,
   Campin' in the rain.

Up at old man Tobin's,
   First pen on the right,
Don't I know his wethers,
   Know 'em all by sight!
Many a year I shore 'em
   Like to shear again,
Better game than campin',
   Campin' in the rain.

What's the use of talking
   Five-and-twenty bob,
While there's hundreds hungry
   Looking for a job?
Darling Harbour casuals,

What's the use of talking
    Five-and-twenty bob,
While there's hundreds hungry
    Looking for a job?

Campin' Round Coonamble, p. 48

The hard, resentful look which you may notice on the faces of all bushmen comes from a long course of dealing with the merino sheep.

The Merino Sheep, p. 52

Hollow in the cheek,
Cadging from the Government
Two days' work a week.

When with peal of trumpets,
    And with beat of drums,
Labour's great millennium
    Actually comes;
When each white Australian,
    Master of his craft,
Keeps a foreign servant
    Just to do the graft;

When the price of shearing
    Goes to fifty bob,
And there's no man hungry
    Looking for a job;
Then, if they oppress us,
    Then we'll go again
Campin' round Coonamble,
    Campin' in the rain.

The Merino Sheep

The prosperity of Australia is absolutely based on a beast — the merino sheep. If all the sheep in the country were to die, the big banks would collapse like card houses, the squatting securities, which are their backbone, being gone. Business would perish, and the money we owe to England would be as hopelessly lost to that nation as if we were a South American state. The sheep, and the sheep alone, keeps us going. On the back of this beneficent creature we all live. Knowing this, people have got the impression that the merino sheep is a gentle, bleating animal that gets its living without trouble to anybody, and comes up every year to be shorn with a pleased smile upon its amiable face. It is my purpose here, as one having experience, to exhibit the merino sheep in its true light, so that the public may know what kind of brute they are depending on.

And first let us give him what little credit is his due. No one can accuse him of being a ferocious animal. No one could ever say that a sheep attacked him without provocation, though there is an old bush story of a man who was discovered in the act of killing a neighbour's wether. "Hullo," said the neighbour. "What's this? Killing my sheep! What have you got to say for yourself?" "Yes," said the man, with an air of virtuous indignation. "I *am* killing your sheep. I'll kill *any* man's sheep that bites *me!*" But as a rule the merino refrains from using his teeth on people, and goes to work in another way.

The truth is that the merino sheep is a dangerous monomaniac, and his one idea is to ruin the man who owns him. With this object in view, he will display a talent for getting into trouble and a genius for dying that are almost incredible. If a mob of sheep see a bushfire closing round them, do they run away out of danger? Not at all; they rush round and round in a ring till the fire burns them up. If they are in a river bed, with a howling flood coming down, they will stubbornly refuse to cross three inches of water to save themselves. Dogs and men may bark and shriek, but the sheep won't move. They will wait there till the flood comes and drowns them all, and then their corpses go down the river on their backs with their feet in the air. A mob of sheep will crawl along a road slowly enough to exasperate a snail, but let a lamb get away from the mob in a bit of rough country, and a racehorse can't head him back again. If sheep are put into a big paddock with water in three corners of it, they will resolutely crowd into the fourth corner and die of thirst. When sheep are being counted out at a gate, if a scrap of bark be left on the ground in the gateway, they will refuse to step over it until dogs and men have sweated and toiled and sworn and "heeled 'em up", and "spoke to 'em", and fairly jammed them at it. Then the first one will gather courage, rush at the fancied obstacle, spring over it about six feet in the air and dart away. The next does exactly the same, but jumps a bit higher. Then comes a rush of them following one another in wild bounds like antelopes, until one "over-jumps himself" and alights on his head, a performance which nothing but a sheep could compass.

This frightens those still in the yard, and they stop running out, and the dogging and shrieking and hustling and tearing have to be gone through all over again. This on a red-hot day, mind you, with clouds of blinding dust about, with the yolk of wool irritating your eyes, and with, perhaps, three or four thousand sheep to put through. The delay throws out the man who is counting, and he forgets whether he left off at 45 or 95. The dogs, meanwhile, take the first chance to slip over the fence and hide in the shade somewhere. Then there are loud whistlings and oaths, and calls for Rover and Bluey, and at last a dirt-begrimed man jumps over the fence, unearths a dog and hauls him back to work by the ear. The dog sets to barking and heeling 'em up again, and pretends that he thoroughly enjoys it, but he is looking out all the time for another chance to "clear". And *this* time he won't be discovered in a hurry.

To return to our muttons. There is a well-authenticated story of a shipload of sheep being lost once, because an old ram jumped overboard into the ocean, and all the rest followed him. No doubt they did, and were proud to do it. A sheep won't go through an open gate on his own responsibility, but he would gladly and proudly follow another sheep through the red-hot portals of Hades: and it makes no difference whether the leader goes voluntarily or is hauled struggling and kicking and fighting every inch of the way. For pure, sodden stupidity there is no animal like the merino sheep. A lamb will follow a bullock dray drawn by sixteen bullocks and driven by a profane "colonial" with a whip, under the impression that this aggregate monstrosity is his mother. A ewe never knows her own lamb by sight, and apparently has no sense of colour. She can recognise her own lamb's voice half a mile off among a thousand other voices apparently exactly similar, but when she gets within five yards of her lamb she starts to smell all the lambs in reach, including the black ones, though her own may be a white lamb. The fiendish resemblance which one sheep bears to another is a great advantage to them in their struggles with their owners. It makes them more difficult to draft out of a strange flock, and much harder to tell when any are missing.

Concerning this resemblance between sheep, there is a story told of a fat old Murrumbidgee squatter who gave a big price for a famous ram called, say, Sir Oliver. He took a friend out one day to inspect Sir Oliver, and overhauled that animal with a most impressive air of sheep wisdom. "Look here," he said, "at the fineness of the wool. See the serrations in each thread of it. See the density of it. Look at the way his legs and belly are clothed — he's wool all over, that sheep. Grand animal, grand animal!" Then they went and had a drink, and the old squatter said, "Now, I'll show you the difference between a champion ram and a second-rater." So he caught a ram and pointed out his defects. "See here — not half the serrations that other sheep had. No density of fleece to speak of. Bare-bellied as a pig, compared with

Sir Oliver. Not that this isn't a fair sheep, but he'd be dear at one-tenth Sir Oliver's price. By the way, Johnson" (to his overseer) "what ram *is* this?" "That, sir," replied the astounded functionary, "that's Sir Oliver, sir!" And so it was.

There is another kind of sheep in Australia, as great a curse in his own way as the merino — namely, the cross-bred or half-merino-half-Leicester animal. The cross-bred will get through, under or over any fence you like to put in front of him. He is never satisfied on his owner's run, but always thinks other people's runs must be better, so he sets off to explore. He will strike a course, say, south-east, and so long as the fit takes him he will keep going south-east through all obstacles, rivers, fences, growing crops — anything. The merino relies on passive resistance for his success; the cross-bred carries the war into the enemy's camp, and becomes a living curse to his owner day and night. Once there was a man who was induced in a weak moment to buy twenty cross-bred rams, and from that hour the hand of fate was upon him. They got into all the paddocks they shouldn't have been in. They scattered themselves all over the run promiscuously. They got into the cultivation paddock and the vegetable garden at their own sweet will. And then they took to roving. In a body they visited the neighbouring stations, and played havoc with the sheep all over the district. The wretched owner was constantly getting fiery letters from his neighbours: "Your . . . rams are here. Come and take them away at once", and he would have to go off nine or ten miles to drive them home. Any man who has tried to drive rams on a hot day knows what purgatory is. He was threatened with actions for trespass for scores of pounds damages every week. He tried shutting them up in the sheep yard. They got out and went back to the garden. Then he gaoled them in the calf pen. Out again and into a growing crop. Then he set a boy to watch them, but the boy went to sleep, and they were four miles away across country before he got on to their tracks. At length, when they happened accidentally to be at home on their owner's run, there came a huge flood. His sheep, mostly merinos, had plenty of time to get on to high ground and save their lives, but, of course, they didn't, and they were almost all drowned. The owner sat on a rise above the waste of waters and watched the dead animals go by. He was a ruined man. His hopes in life were gone. But he said, "Thank God, those rams are drowned, anyhow." Just as he spoke there was a splashing in the water, and the twenty rams solemnly swam ashore and ranged themselves in front of him. They were the only survivors of thousands of sheep. He broke down utterly, and was taken to an asylum for insane paupers. The cross-breds had fulfilled their destiny.

The cross-bred drives his owner out of his mind, but the merino ruins his man with greater celerity. Nothing on earth will kill cross-breds, while nothing will keep merinos alive. If they are put on dry saltbush country they die of drought. If they are put on damp, well-watered country they die of worms, fluke, and foot rot. They die in the wet seasons and they die in the dry ones. The hard, resentful look which you may notice on the faces of all bushmen comes from a long course of dealing with the merino sheep. It is the merino sheep which dominates the bush, and which gives to Australian literature its melancholy tinge, and its despairing pathos. The poems about dying boundary riders and lonely graves under mournful she-oaks are the direct outcome of the author's too close association with that soul-destroying animal, the merino sheep. A man who could write anything cheerful after a day in the drafting yards would be a freak of nature.

It's Grand

It's grand to be a squatter
  And sit upon a post,
And watch your little ewes and lambs
  A-giving up the ghost.

It's grand to be a "cockie"
  With wife and kids to keep,
And find an all-wise Providence
  Has mustered all your sheep.

It's grand to be a western man,
  With shovel in your hand,
To dig your little homestead out
  From underneath the sand.

It's grand to be a shearer,
  Along the Darling side,
And pluck the wool from stinking sheep
  That some days since have died.

It's grand to be a rabbit
  And breed till all is blue,
And then to die in heaps because
  There's nothing left to chew.

It's grand to be a Minister
  And travel like a swell,
And tell the central district folk
  To go to — Inverell.

It's grand to be a Socialist
　　And lead the bold array
That marches to prosperity
　　At seven bob a day.

It's grand to be an unemployed
　　And lie in the Domain,
And wake up every second day
　　And go to sleep again.

It's grand to borrow English tin
　　To pay for wharves and Rocks,
And then to find it isn't in
　　The little money-box.

It's grand to be a democrat
　　And toady to the mob,
For fear that if you told the truth
　　They'd hunt you from your job.

It's grand to be a lot of things
　　In this fair southern land,
But if the Lord would send us rain,
　　That would, indeed, be grand!

A Singer of the Bush

There is waving of grass in the breeze
　　And a song in the air,
And a murmur of myriad bees
　　That toil everywhere.
There is scent in the blossom and bough,
　　And the breath of the spring
Is as soft as a kiss on a brow —
　　And springtime I sing.

There is drought on the land, and the stock
   Tumble down in their tracks
Or follow — a tottering flock —
   The scrub-cutter's axe.
While ever a creature survives
   The axes shall swing;
We are fighting with fate for their lives —
   And the combat I sing.

The Swagman's Rest

We buried old Bob where the bloodwoods wave
   At the foot of the Eaglehawk;
We fashioned a cross on the old man's grave,
   For fear that his ghost might walk;
We carved his name on a bloodwood tree,
   With the date of his sad decease,
And in place of "Died from effects of spree",
   We wrote, "May he rest in peace".

For Bob was known on the Overland,
   A regular old bush wag,
Tramping along in the dust and sand,
   Humping his well worn swag.
He would camp for days in the river bed,
   And loiter and "fish for whales".
"I'm into the swagman's yard", he said,
   "And I never shall find the rails."

But he found the rails on that summer night
   For a better place — or worse,
As we watched by turns in the flickering light
   With an old black gin for nurse.
The breeze came in with the scent of pine,
   The river sounded clear,
When a change came on, and we saw the sign
   That told us the end was near.

But he spoke in a cultured voice and low —
    "I fancy they've 'sent the route';
I once was an army man, you know,
    Though now I'm a drunken brute;
But bury me out where the bloodwoods wave,
    And if ever you're fairly stuck,
Just take and shovel me out of the grave,
    And, maybe, I'll bring you luck.

"For I've always heard —" here his voice fell weak,
    His strength was well-nigh sped,
He gasped and struggled and tried to speak,
    Then fell in a moment — dead.
Thus ended a wasted life and hard,
    Of energies misapplied —
Old Bob was out of the "swagman's yard"
    And over the Great Divide.

The drought came down on the field and flock,
    And never a raindrop fell,
Though the tortured moans of the starving stock
    Might soften a fiend from hell.
And we thought of the hint that the swagman gave
    When he went to the Great Unseen —
We shovelled the skeleton out of the grave
    To see what his hint might mean.

We dug where the cross and the graveposts were,
    We shovelled away the mould,
When sudden a vein of quartz lay bare
    All gleaming with yellow gold.
'Twas a reef with never a fault nor baulk
    That ran from the range's crest,
And the richest mine on the Eaglehawk
    Is known as "The Swagman's Rest".

The Daylight is Dying

The daylight is dying
  Away in the west,
The wild birds are flying
  In silence to rest;
In leafage and frondage
  Where shadows are deep,
They pass to its bondage —
  The kingdom of sleep.
And watched in their sleeping
  By stars in the height,
They rest in your keeping,
  Oh, wonderful night.

When night doth her glories
  Of starshine unfold,
'Tis then that the stories
  Of bushland are told.
Unnumbered I hold them
  In memories bright,
But who could unfold them,
  Or read them aright?
Beyond all denials
  The stars in their glories
The breeze in the myalls
  Are part of these stories.
The waving of grasses,
  The song of the river
That sings as it passes
  For ever and ever,
The hobble chains rattle,
  The calling of birds,
The lowing of cattle
  Must blend with the words.
Without these, indeed, you
  Would find it ere long,
As though I should read you
  The words of a song
That lamely would linger
  When lacking the rune,
The voice of the singer,
  The lilt of the tune.

But, as one half-hearing
   An old-time refrain,
With memory clearing,
   Recalls it again,
These tales, roughly wrought of
   The bush and its ways,
May call back a thought of
   The wandering days,
And, blending with each
   In the mem'ries that throng,
There haply shall reach
   You some echo of song.

Looking Backward

Possibly the most popular part of Kipling's reminiscences in his book *Something of Myself* was his account of how he got his material. Adam Lindsay Gordon, too, gave a sort of poetical summary of his inspirations when he wrote:

They came in all guises, some vivid
   To clasp and to keep;
Some sudden and swift, as the livid
   Blue thunderflames leap.
This came with the first breath of clover
With memories renewed to the rover:
That flashed when the black horse turned over
   Before the long sleep.

Lacking the ability to write anything like either of those masters, I had to imitate the gentleman who was sentenced to ten years' hard labour and told the judge that he would never live to do it: whereupon His Honour very kindly told him, "Do as much of it as you can."

I had to write what I could.

"Clancy of the Overflow", now. This ballad had its being from a lawyer's letter which I had to write to a gentleman in the bush who had not paid his debts. I got an answer from a friend of his who wrote the exact words:

Clancy's gone to Queensland droving
And we don't know where he are.

So there it was — the idea, the suggestion of the drover's life, the metre, the exact words for a couple of lines of verse, all delivered by Her Majesty's mail at a cost of a postage stamp.

As Cardinal Newman once wrote an *Apologia pro vitam suam* I may disarm criticism by explaining that I never aimed very high; in fact, I never "aimed" anywhere, but just wrote of the little things I knew about.

"Pardon, the Son of Reprieve" was an early effort, founded on a family story. My father's cousin (known as "Blenty" because he wore spectacles, and "blenty" is, I believe, the Scotch for a man who wears spectacles) — my father's cousin, anyway, owned a bush racehorse called Pardon in the days when they ran mile races in three heats. Pardon was left in a stable at a bush pub on a very rigid diet, awaiting his race on the morrow, but being gifted with brains and resource Mr Pardon managed to knock down the rails of his stall and get at a bale of lucerne. Tradition goes that by the time daylight came he had eaten most of it; but, discounting this somewhat, we may assume that he had eaten as much as he could hold and he seemed in no shape for racing. In these circumstances his victory was, to say the least of it, creditable, and earned the tribute of a set of verses.

Now for something as to accuracy.

Kipling in his reminiscences describes how he took the risk of putting a well in the interior of a mediaeval castle, arguing to himself that they must have had a well, otherwise they would perish of thirst when besieged. Passionately addicted to accuracy, Kipling spent years of apprehension, fearing that somebody would come along and prove that there could not have been any such well in any such castle. Kipling was like that — he would rather be illiterate than inaccurate; and we may understand his joy when excavations proved that there really was a well in this very castle, whereupon Kipling chortled and jubilated. In my verses "The Travelling Post Office" I took the risk of describing how a letter was sent to "care of Conroy's sheep" rather than to any post office. I argued that they must sometimes send letters that way, because the destination of travelling sheep is sometimes changed and a letter might lie unclaimed at a post office. Years afterwards I was travelling down the Diamantina on a coach. Across the waste of plain there came a lonely horseman to intercept us, and as he rode up he said, "Have you got any letters on board for J. Riley, care of the Carrandotta cattle?" and, sure enough, the driver had one. I felt inclined to ask Mr Riley to give me the envelope, but I feared it might provoke an unpleasant incident such as occurred on the same trip when a bronzed and bearded bushman about seven feet high nearly wrung my hand off, saying that he had ridden thirty miles that day to shake hands with the man who wrote "When Your Pants Begin to Go". Lawson wrote that, but I didn't undeceive the giant, not knowing how he might take it.

"On Kiley's Run" was the story of a station, or rather a lot of stations rolled into one. I am old enough to have seen the transition from cattle to sheep, and to have seen a station of eighty thousand acres all taken up in six-hundred-and-forty-acre blocks with their attendant conditional leases. Some of these blocks were taken up by *bona fide* settlers, and others by dummies acting in the interests of the station owners. At the age of seventeen I held one of these dummy blocks myself, and duly transferred it when the time came. The *bona fide* settlers were referred to in speeches as the "sturdy yeomanry, the country's pride"; but in course of time almost all these *bona fide* settlers sold their blocks to the station owners and moved on to fresh fields and pastures new, leaving things exactly as they were when they started — except that the station had become a vast freehold instead of a vast leasehold. Paddocking came in instead of shepherding, the few remaining mobs of wild horses were run down and impounded and boundary riders who could not afford to indulge in flashness took the places of the cattle hands. Thus passed the principal picturesque feature of Australian station life.

"The Man from Snowy River" was written to describe the cleaning up of the wild horses in our own district, which was rough enough for most people, but not nearly as rough as they had it on the Snowy. To make any sort of job of it I had to create a character, to imagine a man who would ride better than anybody else, and where would he come from except from the Snowy? And what sort of horse would he ride except a half-thoroughbred mountain pony? Kipling felt in his bones that there must have been a well in his mediaeval fortress, and I felt equally convinced that there must have been a man from the Snowy River. I was right. They have turned up from all the mountain districts — men who did exactly the same ride and could give you chapter and verse for every hill they descended and every creek they crossed. It was no small satisfaction to find that there really had been a Man from Snowy River — more than one of them.

Such was the material and such the work, rough and unpolished like its subject; and looking back on a long life I suppose I can count myself fortunate to have seen so many of the changes and developments in a new country. The "covered waggons" and the "nesters" of America had their counterparts in our bullock drays and our free selectors; the main difference being that in early American days individuals shot out their quarrels with revolvers, and the States shot out their quarrels in a civil war. Luckily, Australia was spared these experiences. Swinburne wrote in his "Triumph of Time":

> It is not much that a man can save
>   On the sands of life, in the straits of time,
> Who swims in sight of the great third wave
>   That never a swimmer shall cross or climb;
> Some waif washed up with the strays and spars
> That ebb-tide shows to the shore and the stars
> Weed from the water, grass from a grave.
>   A broken blossom, a ruined rhyme.

Our "ruined rhymes" are not likely to last long, but if there is any hope at all of survival it comes from the fact that such writers as Lawson and myself had the advantage of writing in a new country. In all museums throughout the world one may see plaster casts of the footprints of weird animals, footprints preserved for posterity, not because the animals were particularly good of their sort, but because they had the luck to walk on the lava while it was cooling. There is just a faint hope that something of the same sort may happen to us.

The Man from Snowy River

There was movement at the station, for the word had passed around
That the colt from old Regret had got away,
And had joined the wild bush horses — he was worth a thousand pound,
So all the cracks had gathered to the fray.
All the tried and noted riders from the stations near and far
Had mustered at the homestead overnight,
For the bushmen love hard riding where the wild bush horses are,
And the stock horse snuffs the battle with delight.

There was Harrison, who made his pile when Pardon won the cup,
The old man with his hair as white as snow;
But few could ride beside him when his blood was fairly up —
He would go wherever horse and man could go.
And Clancy of The Overflow came down to lend a hand,
No better horseman ever held the reins;
For never horse could throw him while the saddle girths would stand,
He learnt to ride while droving on the plains.

And one was there, a stripling on a small and weedy beast,
He was something like a racehorse undersized,
With a touch of Timor pony — three parts thoroughbred at least —
And such as are by mountain horsemen prized.
He was hard and tough and wiry — just the sort that won't say die —
There was courage in his quick impatient tread;
And he bore the badge of gameness in his bright and fiery eye,
And the proud and lofty carriage of his head.

But still so slight and weedy, one would doubt his power to stay,
And the old man said, "That horse will never do
For a long and tiring gallop — lad, you'd better stop away,
Those hills are far too rough for such as you."

So he waited sad and wistful — only Clancy stood his friend —
"I think we ought to let him come," he said;
"I warrant he'll be with us when he's wanted at the end,
For both his horse and he are mountain bred.

"He hails from Snowy River, up by Kosciusko's side,
Where the hills are twice as steep and twice as rough,
Where a horse's hoofs strike firelight from the flint stones every stride,
The man that holds his own is good enough.
And the Snowy River riders on the mountains make their home,
Where the river runs those giant hills between;
I have seen full many horsemen since I first commenced to roam,
But nowhere yet such horsemen have I seen."

So he went — they found the horses by the big mimosa clump —
They raced away towards the mountain's brow,
And the old man gave his orders, "Boys, go at them from the jump,
No use to try for fancy riding now.
And, Clancy, you must wheel them, try and wheel them to the right.
Ride boldly, lad, and never fear the spills,
For never yet was rider that could keep the mob in sight,
If once they gain the shelter of those hills."

So Clancy rode to wheel them — he was racing on the wing
Where the best and boldest riders take their place,
And he raced his stockhorse past them, and he made the ranges ring
With the stockwhip, as he met them face to face.
Then they halted for a moment, while he swung the dreaded lash,
But they saw their well-loved mountain full in view,
And they charged beneath the stockwhip with a sharp and sudden dash,
And off into the mountain scrub they flew.

Then fast the horsemen followed, where the gorges deep and black
Resounded to the thunder of their tread,
And the stockwhips woke the echoes, and they fiercely answered back
From cliffs and crags that beetled overhead.
And upward, ever upward, the wild horses held their way,
Where mountain ash and kurrajong grew wide;
And the old man muttered fiercely, "We may bid the mob good day,
No man can hold them down the other side."

When they reached the mountain's summit, even Clancy took a pull,
It well might make the boldest hold their breath,
The wild hop scrub grew thickly, and the hidden ground was full
Of wombat holes, and any slip was death.

But the man from Snowy River let the pony have his head,
And he swung his stockwhip round and gave a cheer,
And he raced him down the mountain like a torrent down its bed,
While the others stood and watched in very fear.

He sent the flint stones flying, but the pony kept his feet,
He cleared the fallen timber in his stride,
And the man from Snowy River never shifted in his seat —
It was grand to see that mountain horseman ride.
Through the stringybarks and saplings, on the rough and broken ground,
Down the hillside at a racing pace he went;
And he never drew the bridle till he landed safe and sound,
At the bottom of that terrible descent.

He was right among the horses as they climbed the further hill,
And the watchers on the mountain standing mute,
Saw him ply the stockwhip fiercely, he was right among them still,
As he raced across the clearing in pursuit.
Then they lost him for a moment, where two mountain gullies met
In the ranges, but a final glimpse reveals
On a dim and distant hillside the wild horses racing yet,
With the man from Snowy River at their heels.

And he ran them single-handed till their sides were white with foam.
He followed like a bloodhound on their track,
Till they halted cowed and beaten, then he turned their heads for home,
And alone and unassisted brought them back.
But his hardy mountain pony he could scarcely raise a trot,
He was blood from hip to shoulder from the spur;
But his pluck was still undaunted, and his courage fiery hot,
For never yet was mountain horse a cur.

And down by Kosciusko, where the pine-clad ridges raise
Their torn and rugged battlements on high,
Where the air is clear as crystal, and the white stars fairly blaze
At midnight in the cold and frosty sky,
And where around The Overflow the reed beds sweep and sway
To the breezes, and the rolling plains are wide,
The man from Snowy River is a household word today,
And the stockmen tell the story of his ride.

The Cast-Iron Canvasser

The firm of Sloper and Dodge, book publishers and printers, was in great distress. These two enterprising individuals had worked up an enormous business in time payment books, which they sold all over Australia by means of canvassers. They had put a lot of money into the business — all they had, in fact. And now, just as everything was in thorough working order, the public had revolted against them. Their canvassers were ill-treated and molested by the country folk in all sorts of strange bush ways. One man was made drunk, and then a two-horse harrow was run over him; another was decoyed out into the desolate ranges on pretence of being shown a gold mine, and then his guide galloped away and left him to freeze all night in the bush. In mining localities, on the appearance of a canvasser, the inhabitants were called together by beating a camp oven lid with a pick, and the canvasser was given ten minutes to leave the town alive. If he disregarded the hint he would as likely as not fall accidentally down a disused shaft. The people of one district applied to their member of Parliament to have canvassers brought under the Noxious Animals Act and demanded that a reward should be offered for their scalps. Reports were constantly published in the country press about strange, gigantic birds that appeared at remote free selections, and frightened the inhabitants to death — these were Sloper and Dodge's sober and reliable agents, wearing the neat, close-fitting suits of tar and feathers with which their enthusiastic yokel admirers had presented them. In fact, it was too hot altogether for the canvassers, and they came in from north and west and south, crippled and disheartened, and handed in their resignations. To make matters worse, Sloper and Dodge had just got out a map of Australasia on a great scale, and if they couldn't sell it, ruin stared them in the face; and how could they sell it without canvassers!

The two members of the firm sat in their private office. Sloper was a long, sanctimonious individual, very religious and very bald — "beastly, awfully bald". Dodge was a little, fat American, with bristly black hair and beard, and quick, beady eyes. He was eternally smoking a reeking black pipe, and swallowing the smoke, and then puffing it out through his nose in great whiffs, like a locomotive on a steep grade. Anybody walking into one of those whiffs incautiously was likely to get paralysed, the tobacco was so strong.

As the firm waited, Dodge puffed nervously at his pipe and filled the office with noxious fumes. The two partners were in a very anxious and expectant condition.

Just as things were at their very blackest, an event had happened which promised to relieve all their difficulties. An inventor, a genius, had come forward, who offered to supply the firm with a patent cast-iron canvasser, a figure which he said when wound up would walk about, talk by means of a phonograph, collect orders, and stand any amount of ill usage and wear and tear. If this could indeed be done, then they were saved. They had made an appointment with the genius to inspect his figure, but he was half an hour late, and the partners were steeped in gloom.

Just as they despaired of his appearing at all, a cab rattled up to the door, and Sloper and Dodge rushed unanimously to the window. A young man, very badly dressed, stepped out of the cab, holding over his shoulder what looked like the upper half of a man's body. In his disengaged hand he held a pair of human legs with boots and trousers on. Thus equipped he turned to the cabman to ask his fare, but the man with a yell of terror whipped up his horse, and disappeared at a hand gallop, and a woman who happened to be going by went howling down the street, saying that "Jack the Ripper" had come to town. The man bolted in at the door, and toiled up the dark stairs, tramping heavily under his hideous load, the legs and feet which he dragged after him making an unearthly clatter. He came in and put his burden down on the sofa.

"There you are, gents," he said. "There's your canvasser."

Sloper and Dodge recoiled in horror. The upper part of the man had a waxy face, dull, fishy eyes, and dark hair; he lounged on the sofa like a corpse at ease, while his legs and feet stood by, leaning stiffly against the wall. The partners looked at him for a while in silence, and felt like two men haunted by a cast-iron ghost.

"Fix him together, for God's sake," said Dodge. "Don't leave him like that — he looks awful."

The genius grinned, and soon fixed the legs on.

"Now he looks better," said Dodge, poking about the figure. "Looks as much like life as most — ah, would you, you brute!" he exclaimed, springing back in alarm, for the figure had made a violent La Blanche swing at him.

"That's all right," said the genius, "that's a notion of my own. It's no good having his face knocked about, you know — lot of trouble to make that face. His head and body are all full of concealed springs, and if anybody hits him in the countenance, or in the pit of the stomach — favourite place to hit canvassers, the pit of the stomach — it sets a strong spring in motion, and he fetches his right hand round with a swipe that'll knock them into the middle of next week. It's an awful hit. Griffo couldn't dodge it, and Slavin couldn't stand against it. No fear of any man hitting *him* twice. And he's dog-proof too. His legs are padded with tar and oakum, and if a dog bites a bit out of him, it will take that dog the rest of his life to pick his teeth clean. Never bite anybody again, that dog won't. And he'll talk, talk, talk, like a pious conference gone mad; his phonograph can be charged for 100,000 times, and all you've got to do is to speak into it what you want him to say, and he'll say it. He'll go on saying it till he talks his man silly, or gets an order. He has an order form in his hand, and as soon as anyone signs it and gives it back to him, that sets another spring in motion, and he puts the order in his pocket, turns round, and walks away. Grand idea isn't he? Lor' bless you, I fairly love him."

Evidently he did, for as he spoke the genius grinned affectionately at his monster.

"What about stairs?" said Dodge.

"No stairs in the bush," said the inventor blowing a speck of dust off his apparition; "all ground floor houses. Anyhow, if there were stairs we could carry him up and let him fall down afterwards, or get flung down like any other canvasser."

"Ha! Let's see him walk," said Dodge.

The figure walked all right, stiff and erect.

"Now let's hear him yabber," was the next order.

Immediately the genius touched a spring, and a queer, tin-whistly voice issued from the creature's lips, and he began to sing, "Little Annie Rooney".

"Good!" said Dodge, "he'll do. We'll give you your price. Leave him here tonight, and come in tomorrow, and we'll start you off to some place in the back country with him. Have a cigar."

And Mr Dodge, much elated, sucked at his pipe, and blew out through his nose a cloud of nearly solid smoke, which hung and floated about the door, and into which the genius walked as he sidled off. It fairly staggered him, and they could hear him sneezing and choking all the way downstairs. Then they locked up the office, and made for home, leaving the figure in readiness for his travels on the ensuing day.

Ninemile was a quiet little place, sleepy beyond description. When the mosquitoes in that town settled on anyone, they usually went to sleep, and forgot to bite him. The climate was so hot that the very grasshoppers used to crawl into the hotel parlours out of the sun. There they would climb up the window curtains and go to sleep, and if anybody disturbed them they would fly into his eye with a great whizz, and drive the eye clean out at the back of his head. There was no likelihood of a public riot at Ninemile. The only thing that could rouse the inhabitants out of their lethargy was the prospect of a drink at somebody else's expense. And for those reasons it was decided to start the canvasser in this forgotten region; and then move him on to more populous and active localities if he proved a success. They sent up the genius, and a companion who knew the district well. The genius was to manage the automaton, and the other was to lay out the campaign, choose the victims, and collect the money, if they got any, geniuses being notoriously unreliable and loose in their cash. They got through a good deal of whisky on the way up, and when they arrived at Ninemile, they were in a cheerful mood, and disposed to take risks.

"Who'll we begin on?" said the genius.

"Oh, d—— it," said the other, "let's start on Macpherson."

Macpherson was the big bug of the place. He was a gigantic Scotchman, six feet four in his socks, freckled all over with freckles as big as half-crowns. His eyebrows would have made decent-sized moustaches even for a cavalryman, and his moustaches looked like horns. He was a fighter, from the ground up, and, moreover, he had a desperate "down" on canvassers generally and on Sloper and Dodge's canvassers in particular. This eminent firm had once published a book called *Remarkable Colonials*, and Macpherson had written out his own biography for it. He was intensely proud of his pedigree, and his grand relations, and in his narrative made out that he was descended from the original Pherson or Fhairshon who swam round Noah's Ark with his title deeds in his teeth. He showed how his people had fought under Alexander the Great and Timour, and had come over to England some centuries before the Conqueror. He also proved that he was related in a general way to one emperor, fifteen kings, twenty-five dukes, and earls and lords and viscounts innumerable. He dilated on the splendour of the family estates in Scotland, and the vast wealth of his relatives and progenitors. And then, after all, Sloper and Dodge managed to mix him up with some other fellow, some low-bred Irish ruffian who drove a corporation cart! Macpherson's biography gave it forth to the astonished town that he was born in Dublin of poor but honest parents, that his father when a youth had lived by selling matches, until one day he chanced to pick up a cigar end, and, emboldened by the possession of so much capital, had got married, and the product was Macpherson.

It was a terrible outrage. Macpherson at once became president for the whole of the western districts of the *Remarkable Colonials* Defence League, the same being a fierce and homicidal association got up to resist, legally and otherwise, paying for the books. Also, he has sworn by all he held sacred that every canvasser who came to harry him in future should die, and he had put up a notice on his office door, "Canvassers come in here at their own risk". He had a dog which he called a dog of the "hold 'em" breed, and this dog could tell a canvasser by his walk, and would go for him on sight. The reader will understand, therefore, that when the genius and his mate proposed to start on Macpherson, they were laying out a capacious contract for the cast-iron canvasser, and were taking a step which could only have been inspired by a morbid craving for excitement, aided by the influence of backblock whisky.

The genius wound the figure up in the back parlour of the pub. There were a frightful lot of screws to tighten before the thing would work, but at last he said it was ready, and they shambled off down the street, the figure marching stiffly between them. It had a book stuck under its arm and an order form in its hand. When they arrived opposite Macpherson's office (he was a land agent and had a ground-floor room) the genius started the phonograph working, pointed the figure straight at Macpherson's door and set it going, and then the two conspirators waited like Guy Fawkes in his cellar.

The figure marched across the road and in at the open door, talking to itself loudly in a hoarse, unnatural voice.

Macpherson was writing at his table and looked up.

The figure walked bang through a small collection of flower-pots, sent a chair flying, tramped heavily in the spittoon, and then brought up against the table with a loud crash and stood still. It was talking all the time.

"I have here," it said, "a most valuable work, a map and geography of Australia, which I desire to submit to your notice. The large and increasing demand of bush residents for time payment works has induced the publishers of this —"

"My God!" said Macpherson, "it's a canvasser. Here, Tom Sayers, Tom Sayers!" and he whistled and called for the dog. "Now," he said, "will you go out of this office quietly, or will you be thrown out? It's for yourself to decide, but you've only got while a duck wags his tail to decide in. Which'll it be?"

— "works of modern ages," said the canvasser. "Every person subscribing to this invaluable work will receive, in addition, a flat-iron, a railway pass for a year, and a pocket compass. If you will please sign this order —"

Just here Tom Sayers, the bulldog, came tearing through the office, and, without waiting for orders, hitched straight onto the calf of the canvasser's leg. To Macpherson's intense amazement the piece came clear away, and Tom Sayers rolled about the floor with his mouth full of some sticky substance which seemed to surprise him badly.

The long Scotchman paused awhile before this mystery, but at last he fancied he had got the solution. "Got a cork leg, have you?" said he. — "Well, let's see if your ribs are cork, too," and he struck the canvasser a terrific blow on the fifth button of the waistcoat.

Quicker than the lightning's flash came that terrific right-handed cross-counter. It was so quick that Macpherson never even knew what happened to him. He remembered striking his blow, and afterwards all was a blank. As a matter of fact, the canvasser's right hand, which had been adjusted by the genius for a high blow, landed just on the butt of Macpherson's ear and dropped him like a fowl. The gasping and terrified bulldog fled from the scene, and the canvasser stood over his fallen foe and droned on about the virtues of his publication, stating that he had come there merely as a friend, and to give the inhabitants of Ninemile a chance to buy a book which had already earned the approval of Dan O'Connor and the Earl of Jersey.

The genius and his mate watched this extraordinary drama through the window. They had kept up their courage with whisky and other stimulants, and now looked upon the whole affair as a wildly hilarious joke.

"By Gad! he's done him," said the genius as Macpherson went down, "done him in one hit. If he don't pay as a canvasser I'll take him to town and back him to fight Joe Goddard. Look out for yourself; don't you handle him!" he continued as the other approached the figure. "Leave him to me. As like as not, if you get fooling about him, he'll give you a smack in the snout that'll paralyse you."

So saying, he guided the automaton out of the office and into the street, and walked straight into — a policeman.

By a common impulse the genius and his mate at once ran rapidly away in different directions, and left the figure alone with the officer.

He was a fully ordained sergeant, by name Aloysius O'Grady; a squat, rosy little Irishman. He hated violent arrests and all that sort of thing, and had a faculty of persuading drunks and disorderlies and other fractious persons to "go quietly along with him", that was little short of marvellous. Excitable revellers, who were being carried along by their mates, struggling violently, would break away from their companions, and prance gaily along to the lock-up with the sergeant, whom, as likely as not, they would try to kiss on the way. Obstinate drunks who would do nothing but lie on the ground and kick their feet in the air, would get up like birds, serpent-charmed, and go with him to durance vile. As soon as he saw the canvasser, and noted his fixed, unearthly stare, and listened to his hoarse, unnatural voice, he knew what was the matter — it was a man in the horrors, a common enough spectacle at Ninemile. The sergeant resolved to decoy him into the lock-up, and accosted him in a friendly and free-and-easy way.

"Good day t'ye," he said.

"— Most magnificent volume ever published, jewelled in fourteen holes, working on a ruby roller, and in a glass case," said the book canvasser. "The likenesses of the historical personages are so natural that the book must not be left open on the table, or the mosquitoes will ruin it by stinging the faces of the portraits."

It then dawned on the sergeant that he was dealing with a book canvasser.

"Ah, sure," he said, "what's the use of tryin' to sell books at all, at all, folks does be peltin' them out into the street, and the nanny-goats lives on them these times. I sent the childher out to pick 'em up, and we have 'em at my place now — barrowloads of 'em. Come along wid me now, and I'll make you nice and comfortable for the night," and he laid his hand on the outstretched palm of the figure.

It was a fatal mistake. By so doing he set in motion the machinery which operated the figure's left arm, and it moved that limb in towards its body, and hugged the sergeant to its breast, with a vice-like grip. Then it started in a faltering, and uneven, but dogged way to walk towards the steep bank of the river, carrying the sergeant along with it.

"Immortal Saints!" gasped the sergeant, "he's squazin' the livin' breath out of me. Lave go now loike a dacent sowl, lave go. And oh, for the love of God, don't be shpakin' into my ear that way"; for the figure's mouth was pressed tight against the sergeant's ear, and its awful voice went through and through the little man's head, as it held forth about the volume. The sergeant struggled violently, and by so doing set some more springs in motion, and the figure's right arm made terrific swipes in the air. A following of boys and loafers had collected by this time. "Bly me, how he does lash out!" was the admiring remark they made. But they didn't altogether like interfering, notwithstanding the sergeant's frantic appeals, and things would have gone hard with him had his subordinate Constable Dooley not appeared on the scene.

Dooley, better known to the town boys as the "Wombat", from his sleepy disposition, was a man of great strength. He had originally been quartered at Redfern, Sydney, and had fought many bitter battles with the Bondi Push, the Black Red Push, and the Surry Hills Push. After this the duty at Ninemile was child's play, and he never ran in less than two drunks at a time; it was beneath his dignity to be seen capturing a solitary inebriate. If they wouldn't come any other way, he would take them by the ankles and drag them after him. The townsfolk would have cheerfully backed him to arrest John L. Sullivan if necessary; and when he saw the sergeant in the grasp of an inebriate he bore down on the fray full of fight.

"I'll soon make him lave ye go, sergeant," he said, and he tried to catch hold of the figure's right arm, to put on the "police twist". Unfortunately at that exact moment the sergeant's struggles touched one of the springs in the creature's breast with more than usual force. With the suddenness and severity of a horse kick, it lashed out with its right hand, catching the redoubtable Dooley a regular thud on the jaw, and sending him to grass, as if he had been shot. For a few minutes he "lay as only dead men lie". Then he got up bit by bit, and wandered off home to the police barracks, and mentioned casually to his wife that John L. Sullivan had come to town, and had taken the sergeant away to drown him. After which, having given orders that if anybody called that visitor was to be told he had gone out of town fifteen miles to serve a summons on a man for not registering a dog, he locked himself into a cell for the rest of the day.

Meanwhile, the canvasser, still holding the sergeant tightly clutched to its breast, was marching straight towards the river. Something had disorganised the voice arrangements, and it was now positively shrieking at the sergeant's ear, and, as it yelled, the little man yelled louder, "I don't want yer accursed book. Lave go of me, I say!" He beat with his fists on its face, and kicked at its shins without the slightest avail. A short, staggering rush, a wild shriek from the officer, and the two of them toppled over the steep bank and went souse into the bottomless depths of the Ninemile Creek.

That was the end of the whole matter. The genius and his mate returned to town hurriedly, and lay low, expecting to be indicted for murder. Constable Dooley drew up a report for the Chief of Police, which contained so many strange and unlikely statements that the department concluded the sergeant must have got drunk and drowned himself, and that Dooley saw him do it, but was too drunk to pull him out. Anyone unacquainted with Ninemile would have expected that a report of the occurrence would have reached the Sydney papers. As a matter of fact the storekeeper did think about writing a report, but decided that it was too much trouble. There was some idea of asking the Government to fish the two bodies out of the river, but about that time an agitation was started in Ninemile to have the Federal capital located there, and the other thing was forgotten. The genius drank himself to death; the "Wombat" became Sub-Inspector of Police; and a vague tradition about "a bloke who came up here in the horrors, and drownded poor old O'Grady", is the only memory that remains of that wonderful creation, the cast-iron canvasser.

As for the canvasser himself there is a rusted mass far down in the waters of the creek, and in its arms it holds a skeleton dressed in the rags of what was once a police uniform. And on calm nights the passers-by sometimes imagine they can hear, rising out of the green and solemn depths, a husky, slushy voice, like that of an iron man with mud and weeds and dishcloths in his throat, and that voice is still urging the skeleton to buy a book in monthly parts. But the canvasser's utterance is becoming weak and used up in these days, and it is only when the waters are low and the air is profoundly still that he can be heard at all.

An Idyll of Dandaloo

On western plains, where shade is not,
 'Neath summer skies of cloudless blue,
Where all is dry and all is hot,
 There stands the town of Dandaloo —
A township where life's total sum
Is sleep, diversified with rum.

Its grass-grown streets with dust are deep,
 'Twere vain endeavour to express
The dreamless silence of its sleep,
 Its wide, expansive drunkenness.
The yearly races mostly drew
A lively crowd to Dandaloo.

There came a sportsman from the east,
 The eastern land where sportsmen blow,
And brought with him a speedy beast —
 A speedy beast as horses go.
He came afar in hope to "do"
The little town of Dandaloo.

Now this was weak of him, I wot —
 Exceeding weak, it seemed to me —
For we in Dandaloo were not
 The Jugginses we seemed to be;
In fact, we rather thought we knew
Our book by heart in Dandaloo.

We held a meeting at the bar,
    And met the question fair and square —
"We've stumped the country near and far
    To raise the cash for races here;
We've got a hundred pounds or two —
Not half so bad for Dandaloo.

"And now, it seems, we have to be
    Cleaned out by this here Sydney bloke,
With his imported horse; and he
    Will scoop the pool and leave us broke.
Shall we sit still, and make no fuss
While this chap climbs all over us?"

The races came to Dandaloo,
    And all the cornstalks from the west,
On ev'ry kind of moke and screw,
    Came forth in all their glory drest.
The stranger's horse, as hard as nails,
Look'd fit to run for New South Wales.

He won the race by half a length —
    Quite half a length, it seemed to me —
But Dandaloo, with all its strength,
    Roared out, "Dead heat!" most fervently;
And, after hesitation meet,
The judge's verdict was "Dead heat!"

And many men there were could tell
    What gave the verdict extra force:
The stewards, and the judge as well —
    They all had backed the second horse.
For things like this they sometimes do
In larger towns than Dandaloo.

They ran it off; the stranger won,
    Hands down, by near a hundred yards.
He smiled to think his troubles done;
    But Dandaloo held all the cards.
They went to scale and — cruel fate! —
His jockey turned out underweight.

Perhaps they'd tampered with the scale!
    I cannot tell. I only know
It weighed him *out* all right. I fail
    To paint that Sydney sportsman's woe.
He said the stewards were a crew
Of low-lived thieves in Dandaloo.

He lifted up his voice, irate,
  And swore till all the air was blue;
So then we rose to vindicate
  The dignity of Dandaloo.
"Look here," said we, "you must not poke
Such oaths at us poor country folk."

We rode him softly on a rail,
  We shied at him, in careless glee,
Some large tomatoes, rank and stale,
  And eggs of great antiquity —
Their wild, unholy fragrance flew
About the town of Dandaloo.

He left the town at break of day,
  He led his racehorse through the streets,
And now he tells the tale, they say,
  To every racing man he meets.
And Sydney sportsmen all eschew
The atmosphere of Dandaloo.

Brumby's Run

The Aboriginal term for a wild horse is "brumby". At a recent trial in Sydney
a Supreme Court Judge, hearing of "brumby horses", asked, "Who is
Brumby, and where is his run?"

It lies beyond the western pines
  Towards the sinking sun,
And not a survey mark defines
  The bounds of "Brumby's run".

On odds and ends of mountain land
  On tracks of range and rock,
Where no one else can make a stand,
  Old Brumby rears his stock —

A wild, unhandled lot they are
  Of every shape and breed,
They venture out 'neath moon and star
  Along the flats to feed.

But when the dawn makes pink the sky
  And steals along the plain,
The Brumby horses turn and fly
  Towards the hills again.

The traveller by the mountain track
  May hear their hoofbeats pass,
And catch a glimpse of brown and black,
  Dim shadows on the grass.

The eager stock horse pricks his ears
  And lifts his head on high
In wild excitement when he hears
  The Brumby mob go by.

Old Brumby asks no price or fee
  O'er all his wide domains:
The man who yards his stock is free
  To keep them for his pains.

So, off to scour the mountainside
  With eager eyes aglow,

To strongholds where the wild mobs hide
   The gully-rakers go.

A rush of horses through the trees,
   A red shirt making play;
A sound of stockwhips on the breeze,
   They vanish far away!

Ah, me! before our day is done
   We long with bitter pain
To ride once more on Brumby's run
   And yard his mob again.

Wild Horses

I have lately been talking on human beings; now I am asked to talk about animals, wild cattle and wild horses, and, if I get time, something about wild dogs. I suppose the first question that occurs to you is, "How did there come to be wild horses and wild cattle in Australia?" Neither horses nor cattle are natives here, and one would think that after bringing them all the way from England they would be too valuable to be let go. Well, this was the way of it.

There is now living in one of the suburbs of Sydney a man eighty-five years of age, and seventy years ago he and three brothers went out from Maitland district and took up a million square miles of country in Queensland. They took cattle out there and they had to shoot a lot of blacks before they would let the cattle alone, but I can tell you something about that another time. Well then, these men went out there; they took out a big mob of horses and of course they would have to drop a few horses here and there on the road. Horses that got away or were dropped, while the explorers and first settlers were going out, formed the nucleus of a wild mob. Then, later on, when the outlying stations had horse paddocks, there was another cause of wild horses. A few horses would get away owing to a fence being burnt or broken down and that would mean another wild mob. When the young colts in this mob grew up, the old stallion would hunt them out of the mob and the young ones would go away with a few mares and start another mob: and soon they were all over the country.

Even as late as fifty years ago when the country was pretty well settled, wild horses still kept cropping up. The little bush townships used to be laid out with commons of, say, four square miles, and the inhabitants of these little bush towns used to run their horses on the common. They had to have horses, for there were no motor cars, and any true bushman would scorn to be seen dead on one of the old-fashioned high-wheeled bicycles that were used in those days. They used to reckon that riding a bicycle was wheeling your stomach at the expense of your legs, with a good chance of getting killed thrown in. So they all had to have horses. Now, these horses would stay on the common as long as it suited them, but if the grass got short or if they felt like a change, which horses very often do, they would wander away up into the hills. There were no fences to speak of and they could go just where they liked. Sometimes a mare with a big, half-grown colt foal at foot would stray away with the others and they would poke away into a blind gully up in the hills and, before they were found again, the colt would have grown into a stallion and would have established himself as lord of a harem and an infernal nuisance to the whole district. Of course, the owners always meant to go out and get those horses before they got too wild, but you know how it is; they say that Spain is the land of *mañana* — tomorrow — but the bush was the land of the day after tomorrow, and the owners found it easier to pinch a horse from a travelling mob or plant a horse belonging to a drunken traveller rather than go out and chance their necks in the bush after a half-wild mob.

So the stallion would establish himself up in the hills with a few mares and, when the spring came on, he would come down to the common and drive off any mares that were there and add them to his harem. Incidentally, he might murder any gelding that tried to go with the mares, for a stallion is a very good imitation of a pirate king when he gets the chance to run things his own way; and that was the origin of the mobs of wild horses.

Sometimes, riding through the bush, you would catch sight of a mob of them and then off they'd go full split, their hoofs sounding like a cavalry charge, manes and tails flying, the stallion driving the mares and foals in front of him and looking over his shoulder at you as much as to say that for two pins he'd come back and take a fall out of you. (*Mr Halbert, could we get sound effects of a mob galloping, whips cracking, etc?*)

Sometimes there would be casual mobs of dry mares and geldings without any stallion and, as these had no foals to delay them, they would set the best riders in Australia a task to get them out of that rough country where they had no weight on their backs and knew every foot of the going. In some rough country stations in the early days, the wild horses got to be as big a plague as the wallabies and rabbits were in later times, and they used to put up trap yards with wings running out into the bush and the riders would start a mob going and would try to go with it fast enough to keep on the wings of the mob and crack the whips and swing the mob into the trap yard. Then they would shoot them just like vermin. It seems a terrible thing to us nowadays to think of shooting horses wholesale — just as bad as it seems to an Englishman to shoot a fox: but it had to be done, for if they didn't get rid of the horses, the horses would get rid of them.

The horse shooting days were pretty well done when I came into the business, and we used to run them in with the mistaken idea of breaking them in and making some money out of them. Half a dozen of us would go out and we'd ride half a dozen good horses blind getting the mob in. Then the crack riders among us would pick out a horse each and start to break it in. By the time that it had kicked every dog in the place, or those that it had missed it had kicked others twice for, by the time that it had broken every bridle and rolled in every saddle on the place and by the time that every rider had been run against at least one tree in every paddock, then it was saleable at about thirty bob if anyone could be found fool enough to buy it. You see, they were mostly old, and breaking in old horses, especially when they have been wild, is like teaching an old cannibal to be a vegetarian.

I remember riding into Yass with a mate who was on one of the wild horses and we were going along quite well until all of a sudden, without the slightest warning, the wild horse sprang sideways off the track into the stringybark scrub and set off full split as hard as he could go. It's a wonder he didn't knock his rider's brains out. It turned out there was a man coming up on the other side of a hill where we were riding, and we couldn't hear him, and we couldn't see him, but the wild horse had heard him and smelt him and he was off and away as hard as he could split.

I've heard of men getting good horses out of brumby mobs, but the only good ones ever I saw were up on Mount Kosciusko. I went up to the summit with the Mitchells who afterwards owned Trafalgar. I made this trip years before there were any buildings or any roads on Kosciusko: and when we got to the summit we changed on to brumby horses they had with them. You see, all about the summit there are quagmires, patches of rotten ground that look quite sound till you get on them, and then a horse will bog down to his ears. The flat country horses would walk into these places and get smothered, but you couldn't get a Kosciusko brumby on to one of them with a block and tackle. They knew them by instinct.

I have never seen wild horses at liberty long enough to see whether they deteriorate or alter in type very much. Cattle certainly will. Cattle that have been out in these scrubs for a few generations run down into little wild, sharp-horned things with great big bat ears. I suppose they are always listening for trouble. I did catch a glimpse once of some of the wild Port Essington ponies up in the far north of Australia. They had been there then about fifty years, and they were little rabbits of things, but I think that originally they were just the little ponies brought down from the Malay Archipelago when they brought down the buffalo, so they may not have altered so much in size.

Anyhow, I think they are there still if any of you want to go after them and have a look at them, but you want to take a lot of quinine for the malaria and a good cheesecloth mosquito net, for you never saw anything like the Port Essington mosquitoes.

What's that? I don't care where you've been, or what you've seen, I say you have never seen mosquitoes till you have been in the Territory. You've got to have a cheesecloth mosquito net because the ordinary net is no good up there. Why isn't it any good? Because when they settle on it, it tears with their weight and once they get inside the net, there's nothing but a skeleton left in the bed by the time your friends get to you.

In the army horse depot in Egypt we had fifty thousand horses through our hands, and of course there were some very queer sorts, though you would hardly expect to find wild horses in an army remount camp. Well, I struck one pony in an American shipment that was snow-white the front half of him and coal-black the last half of him. Well, I thought I would ride this joker myself because the army were always growling at us remount officers for keeping the best horses for ourselves, and I wanted to see what they'd say about this circus proposition. He was a well-shaped pony with good paces, but a nasty, sour, suspicious brute. He'd kick the eye out of a needle and one day he grabbed me by the shoulder with his teeth and bit a big piece out of a British warm overcoat and it takes an adze or a chisel to make any impression on a British Warm. An American fellow that came over with the shipment told me that this was an Indian pony broken in by Indians; when a horse is broken in by a black-fellow or a Chinaman or an Indian, he never takes to a white man, except with his teeth.

Well, sure enough, a young officer came along one day to draw some horses and he said, "What about issuing me that horse you're riding?" So I said, "This horse would be no use to you; he's a bad character," and, of course, the more I ran the horse down, the more he wanted him. That's the worst of having anything to do with horses; nobody will ever believe a word you say. So at last I said, "All right, take him, he's got to go out to somebody, but I warn you you're looking for trouble."

So he had him led away with the others and the next thing I heard was that this horse had emptied him off somewhere near the front line and had run away with his saddle and equipment and had joined the Turks. I suppose the horse liked the smell of the Turks better than the white men — he felt more at home. He was reverting to his native instincts.

Wild cattle are only found in very dense scrub country. If they come out into open country anybody can get them, but where country is really thick a few head of station cattle may poke away into the scrub and, if they have water and feed there, they take a lot of getting out after a generation or two. Up in the Territory there were jungles pretty well full of wild cattle that had gone in there when Fisher's stations were abandoned. You couldn't follow them a yard in the jungles and the only way to get them was this. There were a couple of men there with a mob of quiet cattle and they would let these cattle feed outside the jungles in the moonlight. Then the scrub cattle would scent them and you'd hear the scrub bulls bellowing a challenge: "boo-oo-oo, boo-oo-oo," and after a while the scrub mob would come out and mix with the quiet cattle. Then the men would dash in on their horses between the mob and the jungle and they'd crack whips, and fire revolvers and shout, and try to rush the mob away from the jungle out into the open. Mostly a scrub bull or two would try to break back and then it was "bang, bang" and they would try to drop him with the revolvers before the mob followed him. It was a rough game, galloping about there in the moonlight over all sorts of broken country and cutting loose with revolvers at full gallop. They might shoot each other. Any cattle they got that way they used to sell to some Chinese miners for beef. It was a funny way for men to get a living, and as for roughness — it was the real thing, all right.

Up on Jardine's station on York Peninsula, I saw pretty wild cattle too, let me tell you. The Jardines had the pick of all Queensland in their day and yet they took up this frightful rough scrubby tract of coast country and when I was up there if you went out to muster cattle, all you would see was just their tails going like mad through the scrub. When they wanted station beef, they would send a couple of men with a rifle and packhorse and one of those men would ride alongside a beast and shoot him at full gallop like the Indians used to shoot buffalo. Then they would butcher the beast where he fell and bring the meat in on the packhorse to the head station. Some of the Jardines' aristocratic connections in England would have got a shock if they had seen their descendants running down their food like savages in the scrub, but it was a rough place then and I'll bet it's a rough place still. Not much chance of it altering.

There are not many places in Australia now where there are wild cattle or wild horses, but if any of you that are listening to me has a mob of scrub cattle or brumby horses on his place, I would advise him to let them alone and make a tourist attraction out of them. There's a man at Pennant Hills, near Sydney, making quite a lot of money by showing a couple of dozen native bears, just native bears sitting in saplings and eating gum leaves. A mob of wild horses going across country at full speed is a great sight and it ought to draw a lot better than native bears; more life about it, anyhow.

The Geebung Polo Club

It was somewhere up the country, in a land of rock and scrub,
That they formed an institution called the Geebung Polo Club.
They were long and wiry natives from the rugged mountainside,
And the horse was never saddled that the Geebungs couldn't ride;
But their style of playing polo was irregular and rash —
They had mighty little science, but a mighty lot of dash:
And they played on mountain ponies that were muscular and strong,
Though their coats were quite unpolished, and their manes and tails were
   long.
And they used to train those ponies wheeling cattle in the scrub:
They were demons, were the members of the Geebung Polo Club.

It was somewhere down the country, in a city's smoke and steam,
That a polo club existed, called the Cuff and Collar Team.
As a social institution 'twas a marvellous success,
For the members were distinguished by exclusiveness and dress.
They had natty little ponies that were nice, and smooth, and sleek,
For their cultivated owners only rode 'em once a week.
So they started up the country in pursuit of sport and fame,
For they meant to show the Geebungs how they ought to play the game;
And they took their valets with them — just to give their boots a rub
Ere they started operations on the Geebung Polo Club.

Now my readers can imagine how the contest ebbed and flowed,
When the Geebung boys got going it was time to clear the road;
And the game was so terrific that ere half the time was gone
A spectator's leg was broken — just from merely looking on.
For they waddied one another till the plain was strewn with dead,
While the score was kept so even that they neither got ahead.
And the Cuff and Collar captain, when he tumbled off to die,
Was the last surviving player — so the game was called a tie.

Then the captain of the Geebungs raised him slowly from the ground,
Though his wounds were mostly mortal, yet he fiercely gazed around;
There was no one to oppose him — all the rest were in a trance,
So he scrambled on his pony for his last expiring chance,
For he meant to make an effort to get victory to his side;
So he struck at goal — and missed it — then he tumbled off and died.

By the old Campaspe River, where the breezes shake the grass,
There's a row of little gravestones that the stockmen never pass,

For they bear a crude inscription saying, "Stranger, drop a tear,
For the Cuff and Collar players and the Geebung boys lie here."
And on misty moonlit evenings, while the dingoes howl around,
You can see their shadows flitting down that phantom polo ground;
You can hear the loud collisions as the flying players meet,
And the rattle of the mallets, and the rush of ponies' feet,
Till the terrified spectator rides like blazes to the pub —
He's been haunted by the spectres of the Geebung Polo Club.

The Open Steeplechase

I had ridden over hurdles up the country once or twice,
By the side of Snowy River with a horse they called "The Ace".
And we brought him down to Sydney, and our rider, Jimmy Rice,
Got a fall and broke his shoulder, so they nabbed me in a trice —
Me, that never wore the colours, for the Open Steeplechase.

"Make the running," said the trainer, "it's your only chance whatever,
Make it hot from start to finish, for the old black horse can stay,
And just think of how they'll take it, when they hear on Snowy River
That the country boy was plucky, and the country horse was clever.
You must ride for old Monaro and the mountain boys today."

"Are you ready?" said the starter, as we held the horses back,
All ablazing with impatience, with excitement all aglow;
Before us like a ribbon stretched the steeplechasing track,
And the sunrays glistened brightly on the chestnut and the black
As the starter's words came slowly, "Are — you — ready? Go!"

Well, I scarcely knew we'd started, I was stupid-like with wonder
Till the field closed up beside me and a jump appeared ahead.
And we flew it like a hurdle, not a baulk and not a blunder,
As we charged it all together, and it fairly whistled under,
And then some were pulled behind me and a few shot out and led.

So we ran for half the distance, and I'm making no pretences
When I tell you I was feeling very nervous-like and queer,
For those jockeys rode like demons; you would think they'd lost their senses

If you saw them rush their horses at those rasping five foot fences —
And in place of making running I was falling to the rear.

Till a chap came racing past me on a horse they called "The Quiver",
And said he, "My country joker, are you going to give it best?
Are you frightened of the fences? Does their stoutness make you shiver?
Have they come to breeding cowards by the side of Snowy River?
Are there riders on Monaro? —" but I never heard the rest.

For I drove The Ace and sent him just as fast as he could pace it,
At the big black line of timber stretching fair across the track,
And he shot beside The Quiver. "Now," said I, "my boy, we'll race it.
You can come with Snowy River if you're only game to face it;
Let us mend the pace a little and we'll see who cries a crack."

So we raced away together, and we left the others standing,
And the people cheered and shouted as we settled down to ride,
And we clung beside The Quiver. At his taking off and landing
I could see his scarlet nostril and his mighty ribs expanding,
And The Ace stretched out in earnest and we held him stride for stride.

But the pace was so terrific that they soon ran out their tether —
They were rolling in their gallop, they were fairly blown and beat —
But they both were game as pebbles — neither one would show the feather.
And we rushed them at the fences, and they cleared them both together,
Nearly every time they clouted but they somehow kept their feet.

Then the last jump rose before us, and they faced it game as ever —
We were both at spur and whipcord, fetching blood at every bound —
And above the people's cheering and the cries of "Ace" and "Quiver",
I could hear the trainer shouting, "One more run for Snowy River".
Then we struck the jump together and came smashing to the ground.

Well, The Quiver ran to blazes, but The Ace stood still and waited,
Stood and waited like a statue while I scrambled on his back.
There was no one next or near me for the field was fairly slated,
So I cantered home a winner with my shoulder dislocated,
While the man that rode The Quiver followed limping down the track.

And he shook my hand and told me that in all his days he never
Met a man who rode more gamely, and our last set to was prime,
And we wired them on Monaro how we chanced to beat The Quiver.
And they sent us back an answer, "Good old sort from Snowy River;
Send us word each race you start in and we'll back you every time."

Do They Know?

Do they know? At the turn to the straight
   Where the favourites fail,
And every atom of weight
   Is telling its tale;
As some grim old stayer hard-pressed
   Runs true to his breed,
And with head just in front of the rest
   Fights on in the lead;
When the jockeys are out with the whips,
   With a furlong to go;
And the backers grow white to the lips —
   Do you think *they* don't know?

Do they know? As they come back to weigh
   In a whirlwind of cheers,
Though the spurs have left marks of the fray,
   Though the sweat on the ears
Gathers cold, and they sob with distress
   As they roll up the track,
They know just as well their success
   As the man on their back.
As they walk through a dense human lane,
   That sways to and fro,
And cheers them again and again,
   Do you think *they* don't know?

A Dream of the Melbourne Cup

A LONG WAY AFTER GORDON

Bring me a quart of colonial beer
And some doughy damper to make good cheer,
    I must make a heavy dinner;
Heavily dine and heavily sup
Of indigestible things full-up,
Next month they run the Melbourne Cup,
    And I have to dream the winner.

Stoke it in, boys! the half-cooked ham,
The rich ragout and the charming cham,
    I've got to mix my liquor;
Give me a gander's gaunt hind leg,
Hard and tough as a wooden peg,
And I'll grease it down with a hard-boiled egg,
    'Twill make me dream the quicker.

Now I am full of fearful feed,
Now I may dream a race indeed,
    In my restless troubled slumber;
While the nightmares race through my heated brain
And their devil riders spur amain,
The tip for the Cup will reward my pain,
    And I'll spot the winning number.

Thousands and thousands and thousands more,
Like sands on the white Pacific shore,
    The crowding people cluster;
For evermore it's the story old,
While races are bought and backers are sold,
Drawn by the greed of the gain of gold,
    In their thousands still they muster.

And the bookies' cries grow fierce and hot,
"I'll lay the Cup! The double, if not!"
    "Five monkeys, Little John, sir!"
"Here's fives bar one, I lay, I lay!"
And so they shout through the live-long day,
And stick to the game that is sure to pay,
    While fools put money on, sir!

And now in my dream I seem to go
And bet with a "book" that I seem to know —
  A Hebrew moneylender;
A million to five is the price I get —
Not bad! but before I book the bet
The horse's name I clean forget,
  His number and even gender.

Now for the start, and here they come,
And the hoof-strokes roar like a mighty drum
  Beat by a hand unsteady;
They come like a rushing, roaring flood,
Hurrah for the speed of the Chester blood!
For Acme is making the pace so good
  There are some of 'em done already.

But round the back she begins to tire,
And a mighty shout goes up: "Crossfire!" ·
  The magpie jacket's leading;
And Crossfire challenges fierce and bold,
And the lead she'll have and the lead she'll hold,
But at length gives way to the black and gold,
  Which away to the front is speeding.

Carry them on and keep it up —
A flying race is the Melbourne Cup,
  You must race and stay to win it;
And old Commotion, Victoria's pride,
Now takes the lead with his raking stride,
And a mighty roar goes far and wide —
  "There's only Commotion in it!"

But one draws out from the beaten ruck,
And up on the rails by a piece of luck
  He comes in a style that's clever;
"It's Trident! Trident! Hurrah for Hales!
Go at 'em now while their courage fails;"
"Trident! Trident! for New South Wales!"
  "The blue and white for ever!"

Under the whip! With the ears flat back,
Under the whip! Though the sinews crack,
  No sign of the base white feather;
Stick to it now for your breeding's sake,
Stick to it now though your hearts should break,

While the yells and roars make the grandstand shake,
   They come down the straight together.

Trident slowly forges ahead,
The fierce whips cut and the spurs are red,
   The pace is undiminished;
Now for the Panics that never fail!
But many a backer's face grows pale
As old Commotion swings his tail
   And swerves — and the Cup is finished.

And now in my dream it all comes back:
I bet my coin on the Sydney crack,
   A million I've won, no question!
Give me my money, you hook-nosed hog!
Give me my money, bookmaking dog!
But he disappears in a kind of fog,
   And I wake with "the indigestion".

The Oracle

AT THE RACES

No tram ever goes to Randwick races without him; he is always fat, hairy, and assertive; he is generally one of a party, and he takes the centre of the stage all the time — pays the fares, adjusts the change, chaffs the conductor, crushes the thin, apologetic stranger next him into a pulp, and talks to the whole compartment freely, as if they had asked for his opinion.

He knows all the trainers and owners, apparently — rather, he takes care to give the impression that he does. He slowly and pompously hauls out his race book, and one of his satellites opens the ball by saying, in a deferential way, "What do you like for the 'urdles, Charley?"

The Oracle looks at the book, and breathes heavily; no one else ventures to speak. "Well," he says, at last, "of course there's only one in it — if he's wanted. But that's it — will they spin him? I don't think they will. They's only a lot o' cuddies any'ow."

No one likes to expose his own ignorance by asking which horse he refers to as being able to win; and he goes on to deal out some more wisdom in a loud voice:

"Billy K —— told me" (he probably hardly knows Billy K —— by sight). "Billy K —— told me that that bay 'orse ran the best mile an' a half ever done on Randwick yesterday; but I don't give him a chance, for all that; that's the worst of these trainers. They don't know when their horses are well — half of 'em."

Then a voice comes from behind him. It is the voice of the Thin Man, who is crushed out of sight by the bulk of the Oracle.

"I think," says the Thin Man, "that that horse of Flannery's ought to run well in the Handicap."

The Oracle can't stand this sort of thing at all. He gives a snort, and wheels his bulk half-round, and looks at the speaker. Then he turns back to the compartment full of people, and says, "No 'ope."

The Thin Man makes a last effort. "Well, they backed him last night, anyhow."

"Who backed 'im?" says the Oracle.

"In Tattersall's," says the Thin Man.

"I'm sure," says the Oracle; and the Thin Man collapses.

On arrival at the course, the Oracle is in great form. Attended by his string of satellites, he plods from stall to stall, staring at the horses. The horses' names are printed in big letters on the stalls, but the Oracle doesn't let that stop his display of knowledge.

"'Ere's Blue Fire," he says, stopping at that animal's stall, and swinging his race book. "Good old Blue Fire!" he goes on loudly as a little court of people collect, "Jimmy B____" (mentioning a popular jockey) "told me he couldn't have lost on Saturday week if he had only been ridden different. I had a good stake on him, too, that day. Lor', the races that has been chucked away on this horse. They will not ride him right."

Then a trainer, who is standing by, civilly interposes. "This isn't Blue Fire," he says. "Blue Fire's out walking about. This is a two-year-old filly that's in the stall —"

"Well, I can see that, can't I?" says the Oracle, crushingly. "You don't suppose I thought Blue Fire was a mare, did you?" and he moves off hurriedly, scenting danger.

"I don't know what you thought," mutters the trainer to himself, as the Oracle retires. "Seems to me doubtful whether you have the necessary apparatus for thinking —". But the Oracle goes on his way with undiminished splendour.

"Now, look here, you chaps," he says to his followers at last. "You wait here. I want to go and see a few of the talent, and it don't do to have a crowd with you. There's Jimmy M____ over there now" (pointing to a leading trainer). "I'll get hold of him in a minute. He couldn't tell me anything with so many about. Just you wait here."

Let us now behold the Oracle in search of information. He has at various times unofficially met several trainers — has ridden with them in trams, and has exchanged remarks with them about the weather; but somehow in the saddling paddock they don't seem anxious to give away the good things that their patrons have paid for the preparation of, and he is not by way of getting any tips. He crushes into a crowd that has gathered round the favourite's stall, and overhears one hard-faced racing man say to another, "What do you like?" and the other answers, "Well, either this or Royal Scot. I think I'll put a bit on Royal Scot." This is enough for the Oracle. He doesn't know either of the men from Adam, or either of the horses from the great original pachyderm, but the information will do to go on with. He rejoins his followers, and looks very mysterious. "Well, did you hear anything?" they say.

The Oracle talks low and confidentially.

"The crowd that have got the favourite tell me they're not afraid of anything but Royal Scot," he says. "I think we'd better put a bit on both."

"What did the Royal Scot crowd say?" asks an admirer deferentially.

"Oh, they're going to try and win. I saw the stable commissioner, and he told me they were going to put a hundred on him. Of course, you needn't say I told you, 'cause I promised him I wouldn't tell." And the satellites beam with admiration of the Oracle, and think what a privilege it is to go to the races with such a knowing man.

They contribute their mites to a general fund, some putting in a pound, others half a sovereign, and the Oracle takes it into the ring to invest, half on the favourite, and half on Royal Scot. He finds that the favourite is at two to one and Royal Scot at threes, eight to one being given against anything else. As he ploughs through the ring, a whisperer (one of those broken-down followers of the turf who get their living in various mysterious ways, but partly by giving "tips" to backers) pulls his sleeve.

"What are you backing?" he says. "Favourite and Royal Scot," says the Oracle.

"Put a pound on Bendemeer," says the tipster. "It's a certainty. Meet me here if it comes off, and I'll tell you something for the next race. Don't miss it now. Get on quick!"

The Oracle is humble enough before the hanger-on of the turf, and as a bookmaker roars "Ten to one Bendemeer", the Oracle suddenly fishes out a sovereign of his own — and he hasn't money to spare for all his knowingness — and puts it on Bendemeer. His friends' money he puts on the favourite and Royal Scot, as arranged. Then they all go round to watch the race.

The horses are at the post; a distant cluster of crowded animals, with little dots of colour on their backs. Green, blue, yellow, purple, French grey, and old gold; they change about in a bewildering manner, and though the Oracle has a (cheap) pair of glasses, he can't make out where Bendemeer has got to. Royal Scot and the favourite he has lost interest in, and he secretly hopes that they will be left at the post or break their necks; but he does not confide his sentiments to his companions. They're off! The long line of colours across the track becomes a shapeless clump, and then draws out into a long string. "What's that in the front?" yells someone by the rails. "Oh, that thing of Hart's," says someone else. But the Oracle hears them not; he is looking in the mass of colour for a purple cap and grey jacket, with black armbands. He cannot see it anywhere, and the confused and confusing mass swings round the turn into the straight.

Then there is a babel of voices, and suddenly a shout of "Bendemeer! Bendemeer!" and the Oracle, without knowing which is Bendemeer, takes up the cry feverishly. "Bendemeer! Bendemeer!" he yells, waggling his glasses about, trying to see where the animal is.

"Where's Royal Scot, Charley? Where's Royal Scot?" screams one of his friends, in agony. " 'Ow's he doin'?"

"No 'ope!" says the Oracle, with fiendish glee. "Bendemeer! Bendemeer!"

The horses are at the Leger stand now, whips are out, and three horses seem to be nearly abreast — in fact, to the Oracle there seem to be a dozen nearly abreast. Then a big chestnut seems to stick his head in front of the others, and a small man at the Oracle's side emits a deafening series of yells right by the Oracle's ear: "Go on, Jimmy! Rub it into him! Belt him! It's a cake-walk! A cake-walk!" and the big chestnut, in a dogged sort of way, seems to stick his body clear of his opponents, and passes the post a winner by a length. The Oracle doesn't know what has won, but fumbles with his book. The number on the saddlecloth catches his eye. No. 7; and he looks hurriedly down the page. No. 7 — Royal Scot. Second is No. 24 — Bendemeer. Favourite nowhere.

Hardly has he realised it, before his friends are cheering and clapping him on the back. "By George, Charley, it takes you to pick 'em." "Come and 'ave a wet?" "You 'ad a quid in, didn't you, Charley?" The Oracle feels very sick at having missed the winner, but he dies game. "Yes, rather; I had a quid on," he says. "And" (here he nerves himself to smile) "I had a saver on the second, too."

His comrades gasp with astonishment. "D'ye'r that, eh? Charley backed first and second. That's pickin' 'em, if you like." They have a wet, and pour fulsome adulation on the Oracle when he collects their money.

After the Oracle has collected the winnings for his friends he meets the Whisperer again.

"It didn't win?" he says to the Whisperer in inquiring tones.

"Didn't win!" says the Whisperer who has determined to brazen the matter out. "How could he win? Did you see the way he was ridden? That horse was stiffened just after I seen you, and he never tried a yard. Did you see the way he was pulled and hauled about at the turn? It'd make a man sick. What was the stipendiary stewards doing, I wonder?"

This fills the Oracle with a new idea. All that he remembers of the race at the turn was a jumble of colours, a kaleidoscope of horses, and of riders hanging out on the horses' necks. But it wouldn't do for the Oracle to admit that he didn't see everything, and didn't know everything; so he plunges in boldly.

"O' course, I saw it," he says. "A blind man could see it. They ought to rub him out."

"Course they ought," says the Whisperer. "But look here, put two quid on Tell-tale; you'll get it all back!"

The Oracle does put on "two quid", and doesn't get it all back. Neither does he see any more of this race than he did of the last one; in fact, he cheers wildly when the wrong horse is coming in; but when the public begins to hoot, he hoots as loudly as anybody — louder if anything — and all the way home in the tram he lays down the law about stiff running, and wants to know what the stipendiaries are doing. If you go into any barber's shop, you can hear him at it, and he flourishes in suburban railway carriages; but he has a tremendous local reputation, having picked the first and second in the handicap, and it would be a bold man who would venture to question the Oracle's knowledge of racing and of all matters relating to it.

An Evening in Dandaloo

It was while we held our races —
Hurdles, sprints and steeplechases —
    Up in Dandaloo,
That a crowd of Sydney stealers,
Jockeys, pugilists and spielers
Brought some horses, real heelers,
    Came and put us through.

Beat our nags and won our money,
Made the game by no means funny,
    Made us rather blue;
When the racing was concluded,
Of our hard-earned coin denuded
Dandaloonies sat and brooded
    There in Dandaloo.

Night came down on Johnson's shanty
Where the grog was no means scanty,
    And a tumult grew
Till some wild, excited person
Galloped down the township cursing,
"Sydney push have mobbed Macpherson,
    Roll up, Dandaloo!"

Great St Denis! what commotion!
Like the rush of stormy ocean
    Fiery horsemen flew.
Dust and smoke and din and rattle,
Down the street they spurred their cattle
To the war-cry of the battle,
    "Wade in, Dandaloo!"

So the boys might have their fight out,
Johnson blew the bar-room light out,
    Then, in haste, withdrew.
And in darkness and in doubting
Raged the conflict and the shouting,
"Give the Sydney push a clouting,
    Go it, Dandaloo!"

Jack Macpherson seized a bucket,
Every head he saw, he struck it —
   Struck in earnest, too;
And a man from Lower Wattle,
Whom a shearer tried to throttle,
Hit out freely with a bottle,
   There in Dandaloo.

Skin and hair were flying thickly,
When a light was fetched, and quickly
   Brought a fact to view —
On the scene of the diversion
Every single, solid person
Came along to help Macpherson —
   All were Dandaloo!

When the list of slain was tabled,
Some were drunk and some disabled,
   Still we found it true.
In the darkness and the smother
We'd been belting one another;
Jack Macpherson bashed his brother
   There in Dandaloo.

So we drank, and all departed —
How the "mobbing" yarn was started
   No one ever knew —
And the stockmen tell the story
Of that conflict fierce and gory,
How we fought for love and glory
   Up in Dandaloo.

It's a proverb now, or near it —
At the races you can hear it,
   At the dog fights, too;
Every shrieking, dancing drover
As the canines topple over,
Yells applause to Grip or Rover,
   "Give him 'Dandaloo'!"

And the teamster slowly toiling
Through the deep black country soiling
   Wheels and axles, too,

Lays the whip on Spot and Banker,
Rouses Tarboy with a flanker —
"Redman! Ginger! Heave there! Yank her!
  Wade in, Dandaloo!"

Been There Before

There came a stranger to Walgett town,
  To Walgett town when the sun was low,
And he carried a thirst that was worth a crown,
  Yet how to quench it he did not know;
But he thought he might take those yokels down,
The guileless yokels of Walgett town.

They made him a bet in a private bar,
  In a private bar when the talk was high,
And they bet him some pounds no matter how far
  He could pelt a stone, yet he could not shy
A stone right over the river so brown,
The Darling River at Walgett town.

He knew that the river from bank to bank
  Was fifty yards, and he smiled a smile
As he trundled down, but his hopes they sank
  For there wasn't a stone within fifty mile;
For the saltbush plain and the open down
Produce no quarries in Walgett town.

The yokels laughed at his hopes o'erthrown,
  And he stood awhile like a man in a dream;
Then out of his pockets he fetched a stone,
  And pelted it over the silent stream —
He had been there before: he had wandered down
On a previous visit to Walgett town.

The Road to Gundagai

The mountain road goes up and down,
From Gundagai to Tumut town.

And branching off there runs a track,
Across the foothills grim and black,

Across the plains and ranges grey
To Sydney city far away.

It came by chance one day that I
From Tumut rode to Gundagai.

And reached about the evening tide
The crossing where the roads divide;

And, waiting at the crossing place,
I saw a maiden fair of face,

With eyes of deepest violet blue,
And cheeks to match the rose in hue —

The fairest maids Australia knows
Are bred among the mountain snows.

Then, fearing I might go astray,
I asked if she could show the way.

Her voice might well a man bewitch —
Its tones so supple, deep, and rich.

"The tracks are clear," she made reply,
"And this goes down to Sydney town,
And that one goes to Gundagai."

Then slowly, looking coyly back,
She went along the Sydney track.

And I for one was well content
To go the road the lady went;

But round the turn a swain she met —
The kiss she gave him haunts me yet!

I turned and travelled with a sigh
The lonely road to Gundagai.

The Man from Ironbark

It was the man from Ironbark who struck the Sydney town,
He wandered over street and park, he wandered up and down.
He loitered here, he loitered there, till he was like to drop,
Until at last in sheer despair he sought a barber's shop.
"'Ere! shave my beard and whiskers off, I'll be a man of mark,
I'll go and do the Sydney toff up home in Ironbark."

The barber man was small and flash, as barbers mostly are,
He wore a strike-your-fancy sash, he smoked a huge cigar;
He was a humorist of note and keen at repartee,
He laid the odds and kept a "tote", whatever that may be,
And when he saw our friend arrive, he whispered, "Here's a lark!
Just watch me catch him all alive, this man from Ironbark."

There were some gilded youths that sat along the barber's wall.
Their eyes were dull, their heads were flat, they had no brains at all;
To them the barber passed the wink, his dexter eyelid shut,
"I'll make this bloomin' yokel think his bloomin' throat is cut."
And as he soaped and rubbed it in he made a rude remark:
"I s'pose the flats is pretty green up there in Ironbark."

A grunt was all reply he got; he shaved the bushman's chin,
Then made the water boiling hot and dipped the razor in.
He raised his hand, his brow grew black, he paused awhile to gloat,
Then slashed the red-hot razor-back across his victim's throat;
Upon the newly-shaven skin it made a livid mark —
No doubt it fairly took him in — the man from Ironbark.

He fetched a wild up-country yell might wake the dead to hear,
And though his throat, he knew full well, was cut from ear to ear,

He struggled gamely to his feet, and faced the murd'rous foe:
"You've done for me! you dog, I'm beat! one hit before I go!
I only wish I had a knife, you blessed murdering shark!
But you'll remember all your life the man from Ironbark."

He lifted up his hairy paw, with one tremendous clout
He landed on the barber's jaw, and knocked the barber out.
He set to work with nail and tooth, he made the place a wreck;
He grabbed the nearest gilded youth, and tried to break his neck.
And all the while his throat he held to save his vital spark,
And "Murder! Bloody murder!" yelled the man from Ironbark.

A peeler man who heard the din came in to see the show;
He tried to run the bushman in, but he refused to go.
And when at last the barber spoke, and said "'Twas all in fun —
'Twas just a little harmless joke, a trifle overdone."
"A joke!" he cried, "By George, that's fine; a lively sort of lark;
I'd like to catch that murdering swine some night in Ironbark."

And now while round the shearing floor the list'ning shearers gape,
He tells the story o'er and o'er, and brags of his escape.
"Them barber chaps what keeps a tote, By George, I've had enough,
One tried to cut my bloomin' throat, but thank the Lord it's tough."
And whether he's believed or no, there's one thing to remark,
That flowing beards are all the go way up in Ironbark.

Three Elephant Power

A MOTOR STORY

"Them things," said Alfred the chauffeur, tapping the speed indicator with his finger, "them things are all right for the police. But, Lord, you can fix 'em up if you want to. Did you ever hear about Henery, that used to drive for old John Bull — Henery and the ellyphunt?"

Alfred was chauffeur to a friend of mine, a friend who owned a very powerful car, and Alfred was part of the car. He was an Australian youth. It is strange that in Australia the motor has already produced the motor type. Weirdly intelligent, of poor physique, Alfred might have been any age from fifteen to eighty. His education had been somewhat hurried, but there was no doubt as to his mechanical ability. He took to a car like a young duck to water. He talked motor, and thought motor, and would have accepted with — well, I won't say enthusiasm, for Alfred's motto was *Nil admirari* — but without hesitation, an offer to drive in the greatest race in the world. He could drive really well, too, and as for belief in himself, after six months' apprenticeship in a garage, he was prepared to vivisect a six-cylinder engine with the confidence of a diplomaed Bachelor of Engineering.

Barring a tendency to flash driving and a delight in "persecuting" slow cars by driving just in front of them and letting them come up and enjoy his dust, and then shooting away again, he was a very respectable member of society. When his "boss" was in the car he cloaked the natural ferocity of his instincts; but this day, with only myself as passenger on board, and a clear run of 120 miles up to the station before him, he let her loose, confident that if any trouble occurred I would be held morally responsible.

As we fled past a somnolent bush public house, Alfred, whistling softly, leant forward and turned on a little more oil.

"You never heard about Henery and the ellyphunt?" he said. "It was dead funny. Henery was a bushwacker, but clean mad on motorin'. He was wood and water joey at some squatter's place you know, and he seen a motor car go past one day, the first that ever they had in the districk. 'That's my game,' says Henery; 'no more wood and water joey for me.' So he comes to town and gets a job off Miles that had that garage at the back of Allison's. And an old cove that they call John Bull — I don't know his right name, he was a fat old cove — he used to come there to hire cars, and Henery used to drive him. And this old John Bull he had lots of stuff, so at last he reckons he's going to get a car for himself, and he promises Henery a job to drive it. A queer cove this Henery was — half mad, I think — but the best hand with a car ever I see."

While he had been talking we topped a hill and opened up a new stretch of blue-grey granite like road. Down at the foot of the hill before us was a teamster's waggon in camp: the horses in their harness munching at their nose bags, while the teamster and a mate were boiling a billy a little off to the side of the road. There was a turn in the road just below the waggon which looked a bit sharp, so of course Alfred bore down on it like a whirlwind. The big stupid team horses huddled together and pushed each other awkwardly as we passed. A dog that had been sleeping in the shade of the waggon sprang out from beneath it right in front of the car, and was exterminated without ever knowing what struck him. There was just room to clear the tail of the waggon to negotiate the turn, and as Alfred, with the calm decision of a Napoleon, swung round the bend, he found that the old teamster's hack, fast asleep, was tied to the tail of the waggon, and nothing but a most lightning-like twist of the steering wheel prevented our scooping the old animal up, and taking him on board as a passenger. As it was, we got a lot of his tail as a trophy caught on the brass of the lamp. The old steed, thus rudely awakened, lashed out good and hard, but by the time he kicked we were gone and he missed the car by a quarter of a mile. During this strenuous episode, Alfred never relaxed his professional stolidity, and when we were clear he went on with his story in the tone of a man who found life wanting in animation.

"Well, at fust, the old man would only buy one of these little eight-horse rubby dubbys that used to go strugglin' up the 'ills with the death rattle in its throat, and all the people in buggies passin' it. And o' course that didn't suit Henery. He used to get that spiked when a car passed him he'd nearly go mad. And one day he nearly got the sack for dodging his car about up a steep 'ill in front of one o' them big twenty-four Darracqs, full of 'owlin' toffs, and wouldn't let 'em get a chance to go past till they got to the top of the 'ill. But at last he persuaded old John Bull to let him go to England and buy a car for him. He was to do a year in the shops, and pick up all the wrinkles and get a car for the old man. Bit better than wood and water joeying, wasn't it?"

Our progress here was barred by our rounding a corner right onto a flock of sheep, that at once packed together into a solid mass in front of us, blocking the whole road from fence to fence. "Silly cows o' things, ain't they?" said Alfred, putting on his emergency brake, and skidding up till the car softly came to rest against the cushion-like mass — a much quicker stop than any horse-drawn vehicle could have made in the time. A few sheep were crushed somewhat, but it is well known that a sheep is practically indestructible by violence. Whatever Alfred's faults were, he could certainly drive.

"Well," he went on, lighting a cigarette, unheeding the growls of the drovers, who were trying to get the sheep to pass the car, "well, as I was sayin', Henery went to England, and he got a car. Do you know wot he got?"

"No, I don't."

" 'E got a ninety," said Alfred, giving time for the words to soak in.

"A ninety! What do you mean?"

" 'E got a ninety — a ninety-horse power racin' engine that was made for some American millionaire, and wasn't as fast as wot some other millionaire had, so he sold it for the price of the iron, and Henery got it, and had a body built for it, and he come out here, and tells us all it's a twenty mongrel — you know, one of them cars that's made part in one place and part in another, the body here and the engine there, and the radiator another place. There's lots of cheap cars made like that. So Henery he says that this is a twenty mongrel — only a four-cylinder engine — and nobody drops to what she is till Henery goes out one Sunday and waits for the big Napier that Scotty used to drive — it belonged to the same bloke that owned that big racehorse what won all the races. So Henery and Scotty they have a fair go round the park while both their bosses is at church, and Henery beat him out o' sight — fair lost him — and so Henery was reckoned the boss of the road. No one would take him on after that."

A nasty creek crossing here required all Alfred's attention. A little girl, carrying a billy can of water, stood by the stepping stones, and smiled shyly as we passed, and Alfred waved her a salute quite as though he were an ordinary human being. I felt comforted. He had his moments of relaxation, evidently, and his affections the same as other people.

"And what happened to Henery and the ninety-horse machine?" I said. "Where does the elephant come in? For a chauffeur, you're a long time coming to the elephant."

Alfred smiled pityingly.

"Ain't I tellin' yer?" he said. "You wouldn't understand if I didn't tell yer how he got the car and all that. So here's Henery," he went on, "with old John Bull goin' about in the fastest car in Australia, and old John, he's a quiet old geezer, that wouldn't drive faster than the regulations for anything, and he's that short-sighted he can't see to the side of the road. So what does Henery do, but he fixes the speed indicator — puts a new face on it, so that when the car is doing thirty, the indicator only shows fifteen, and twenty for forty and so on. So out they'd go and if Henery knew there was a big car in front of him, he'd let out to forty-five, and the pace would very near blow the whiskers off old John, and every now and again he'd look at the indicator, and it'd be showin' twenty-two and a half, and he'd say, 'Better be careful, Henery, you're slightly exceedin' the speed limit; twenty miles an hour, you know, Henery, should be fast enough for anybody, and you're doing over twenty-two.' And one day, Henery told me he was tryin' to catch up a big car that just came out from France, and it had a half-hour start of him, and he was just fairly flyin', an' there was a lot of cars on the road, and he flies past 'em so fast the old man says, 'It's very strange, Henery,' he says, 'that all the cars that are out to-day are comin' this way,' he says. You see he was passin' 'em so fast he thought they were all comin' towards him. And Henery sees a mate of his coming, so he lets out a notch or two, and the two cars flew by each other like chain lightnin'. They were each doin' about forty, and the old man, he says, 'There's a driver must be travellin' a hundred miles an hour,' he says, 'I never see a car go by so fast in my life,' he says. 'If I could find out who he is, I'd report him,' he says. 'Did you know the car, Henery?' But of course Henery, he doesn't know, so on they goes. And when they caught the French car — the owner of it thinks he has the fastest car in Australia — and Henery and the old man are seen coming, he tells his driver to let her out a little, but Henery gives the ninety-horse the full of the lever, and whips up alongside in one jump. And then he keeps there just half a length ahead of him, tormentin' him, like. And the owner of the French car he yowls out to old John Bull, 'You're goin' a nice pace for an old 'un,' he says. Old John has a blink down at the indicator. 'We're doing twenty-five,' he yells out. 'Twenty-five grandmothers,' says the bloke; but Henery put on his accelerator and left him. It wouldn't do to let the old man get wise to it, you know.''

We topped a big hill, and Alfred cut off the engine and let the car swoop as swiftly and as noiselessly as an eagle down to the flat country below.

"You're a long while coming to the elephant, Alfred," I said.

"Well, now, I'll tell you about the ellyphunt," said Alfred, letting his clutch in again, and taking up the story to the accompaniment of the rhythmic throb of the engine. "One day Henery and the old man were going a long trip over the mountain, and down the Kangaroo Valley road that's all cut out of the side of the 'ill. And after they's gone a mile or two, Henery sees a track in the road — the track of the biggest car he ever saw or heard of. An' the more he looks at it, the more he reckons he must ketch that car and see what's she made of. So he slows down passin' two yokels on the road, and he says, 'Did you see a big car along 'ere?' 'Yes, we did,' they says. 'How big is she?' says Henery. 'Biggest car ever we see,' says the yokels, and they laughed that silly way these yokels always does.

" 'How many horsepower do you think she was?' says Henery.

" 'Horse power,' they says; 'elephant power you mean! she was three elephant power!' they says; and they goes, 'Haw, haw' and Henery drops his clutch in, and off he goes after that car.''

Alfred lit another cigarette as a preliminary to the climax.

"So they run for miles, and all the time there's the track ahead of 'em, and Henery keeps lettin' her out, thinkin' that he'll never ketch that car. They went through a town so fast, the old man he says, 'What house was that we just passed?' he says. So at last they come to the top of the big 'ill, and there's the tracks of the big car goin' straight down ahead of 'em. D'you know that road? It's all cut out of the side of the mountain, and there's places where if she was to side-slip you'd go down 'undreds of thousands of feet. And there's sharp turns, too, but the surface is good, so Henery he lets her out, and down they go, whizzin' round the turns and skatin' out near the edge, and the old cove sittin' there enjoyin' it, never knowin' the danger. And comin' to one turn Henery gives a toot on the 'orn, and then he heard somethin' go 'Toot, toot' right away down the mountain. 'Bout a mile ahead it seemed to be, and Henery reckoned he'd go another four miles before he'd ketch it, so he chances them turns more than ever. And she was pretty hot, too; but he kept her at it, and he hadn't gone a full mile till he come round a turn about forty miles an hour, and before he could stop he run right into it, and wot do you think it was?"

I hadn't the faintest idea.

"A circus. One of them travellin' circuses, goin' down the coast, and one of the ellyphunts had sore feet, so they put him in a big waggon and another ellyphunt pulled in front and one pushed behind. Three ellyphunt power it was, right enough. That was the waggon that made the big track. Well, it was all done so sudden. Before Henery could stop, he runs the radiator — very near boiling she was — up against the ellyphunt's tail, and prints the pattern of the latest honeycomb radiator on the ellyphunt as clear as if you done it with a stencil plate. And the ellyphunt, he lets a roar out of him like one of them bulls bellerin', and he puts out his nose and ketches Henery round the neck, and yanks him out of the car, and chucks him right clean over the cliff, 'bout a thousand feet. But he never done nothin' to the old bloke."

"Good gracious!"

"Well, it finished Henery, killed him stone dead, of course, and the old man he was terrible cut up over losin' such a steady, trustworthy man. Never get another like him, he says."

We were nearly at our journey's end, and we turned through a gate into the home paddocks. Some young stock, both horses and cattle, came frisking and cantering after the car, and the rough bush track took all Alfred's attention. We crossed a creek, the water swishing from the wheels, and began the long pull up to the homestead. Over the clamour of the little-used second speed, Alfred concluded his narrative.

"The old bloke advertised," he said, "for another driver, a steady reliable man to drive a twenty-horse power, four-cylinder touring car. An' every driver in Sydney put in for it. Nothing like a fast car to fetch 'em, you know. And Scotty got it. Him that used to drive the Napier I was tellin' you about."

"And what did the old man say when he found he'd been running a racing car?"

"He don't know now. Scotty never told 'im. Why should he? He's drivin' about the country now, the boss of the roads, but he won't chance her near a circus. Thinks he might bump the same ellyphunt. And they reckon that ellyphunt, when he's in the circus, every time he smells a car passin' in the road, he goes near mad with fright. If he ever sees that car again, do you think he'd know it?"

Not being used to the capacities of elephants, I could not offer an opinion.

Bush Justice

The town of Kiley's Crossing was not exactly a happy hunting ground for lawyers. The surrounding country was rugged and mountainous, the soil was poor, and the inhabitants of the district had plenty of ways of getting rid of their money without spending it in court.

Thus it came that for many years old Considine was the sole representative of his profession in the town. Like most country attorneys, he had forgotten what little law he ever knew, and, as his brand of law dated back to the very early days, he recognised that it would be a hopeless struggle to try and catch up with all the modern improvements. He just plodded along the best way that he could with the aid of a library consisting of a copy of the Crown Lands Acts, the *Miner's Handbook* and an aged mouse-eaten volume called *Ram on Facts* that he had picked up cheap at a sale on one of his visits to Sydney. He was an honourable old fellow, and people trusted him implicitly, and if he did now and then overlook a defect in the title to a piece of land — well, no one ever discovered it, as on the next dealing the title always came back to him again, and was, of course, duly investigated and accepted. But it was in court that he shone particularly. He always appeared before the police magistrate who visited Kiley's once a month. This magistrate had originally been a country storekeeper, and had been given this judicial position as a reward for political services. He knew less law than old Considine, but he was a fine, big, fat man, with a lot of dignity, and the simple country folk considered him a perfect champion of a magistrate. The fact was that he and old Considine knew every man, woman, and child in the district; they knew who could be relied on to tell the truth and whose ways were crooked and devious, and between them they dispensed a very fair brand of rough justice. If anyone came forward with an unjust claim, old Considine had one great case that he was supposed to have discovered in *Ram on Facts*, and which was dragged in to settle all sorts of points. This, as quoted by old Considine, was "the great case of Dunn v. Dockerty — the 'orse outside the 'ouse". What the 'orse did to the 'ouse or *vice versa* no one ever knew; doubts have been freely expressed whether there ever was such a case at all, and certainly, if it covered all the ground that old Considine stretched it over, it was a wonderful decision.

However, genuine or not, whenever a swindle seemed likely to succeed, old Considine would rise to his feet and urbanely inform the bench that under the "well-known case of Dunn v. Dockerty — case that Your Worship of course knows — case of the 'orse outside the 'ouse", this claim must fail; and fail it accordingly did, to the promotion of justice and honesty. This satisfactory state of things had gone on for years, and might be going on yet only for the arrival at Kiley's of a young lawyer from Sydney, a terrible fellow, full of legal lore; he slept with digests and law reports; he openly ridiculed old Considine's opinions; he promoted discord and quarrels, with the result that on the first court day after his arrival, there was quite a little crop of cases, with a lawyer on each side — an unprecedented thing in the annals of Kiley's Crossing. In olden days one side or the other had gone to old Considine, and if he found that the man who came to him was in the wrong, he made him settle the case. If he was in the right, he promised to secure him the verdict, which he always did, with the assistance of *Ram on Facts* and "the 'orse outside the 'ouse". Now, however, all was changed. The new man struggled into court with an armful of books that simply struck terror to the heart of the P.M. as he took his seat on the bench. All the idle men of the district came into court to see how the old man would hold his own with the new arrival. It should be explained that the bush people look on a law case as a mere trial of wits between the lawyers and the witnesses and the bench; and the lawyer who can insult his opponent most in a given time is always the best in their eyes. They never take much notice of who wins the case, as that is supposed to rest on the decision of that foul fiend the law, whose vagaries no man may control nor understand. So, when the young lawyer got up and said he appeared for the plaintiff in the first case, and old Considine appeared for the defendant, there was a pleased sigh in court, and the audience sat back contentedly on their hard benches to view the forensic battle.

The case was simple enough. A calf belonging to the widow O'Brien had strayed into Mrs Rafferty's back yard and eaten a lot of washing off the line. There was ample proof. The calf had been seen by several people to run out of the yard with a half-swallowed shirt hanging out of its mouth. There was absolutely no defence, and in the old days the case would have been settled by payment of a few shillings, but here the young lawyer claimed damages for trespass to realty, damages for trover and conversion of personalty, damages for detinue, and a lot of other terrible things that no one had ever heard of. He had law books to back it all up, too. He opened the case in style, stating his authorities and defying his learned friend to contradict him, while the old P.M. shuffled uneasily on the bench, and the reputation of old Considine in Kiley's Crossing hung trembling in the balance.

When the old man rose to speak he played a bold stroke. He said, patronisingly, that his youthful friend had, no doubt, stated the law correctly, but he seemed to have overlooked one little thing. When he was more experienced he would no doubt be more wary. (Sensation in court.) He relied upon a plea that his young friend had no doubt overlooked — that was that plea of "cause to show". "I rely upon that plea," he said, "and of course Your Worship knows the effect of that plea." Then he sat down amid the ill-suppressed admiration of the audience.

The young lawyer, confronted with this extraordinary manoeuvre, simply raged furiously. He asserted (which is quite true) that there is no such plea known to the law of this or any other country as an absolute defence to claim for a calf eating washing off a line, or to any other claim for that matter. He was proceeding to expound the law relating to trespass when the older man interrupted him.

"My learned friend says that he never heard of such a defence," he said, pityingly. "I think that I need hardly remind Your Worship that that very plea was successfully raised as a defence in the well known case of Dunn v. Dockerty, the case of the 'orse outside the 'ouse." "Yes," said the bench, anxious to display his legal knowledge, "that case — er — is reported in *Ram on Facts*, isn't it?" "Well, it is mentioned there, Your Worship," said the old man, "and I don't think that even my young friend's assurance will lead him so far as to question so old and well-affirmed a decision!" But his young friend's assurance did lead him that far, in fact, a good deal further. He quoted decisions by the score on every conceivable point, but after at least half an hour of spirited talk, the bench pityingly informed him that he had not quoted any cases bearing on the plea of "cause to show", and found a verdict for the defendant. The young man gave notice of appeal and of prohibitions and so forth, but his prestige was gone in Kiley's.

The audience filed out of court, freely expressing the opinion that he was a "regular fool of a bloke; old Considine stood him on his head proper with that plea of 'cause to show', and so help me goodness, he'd never even heard of it!"

Saltbush Bill's Second Fight

The news came down on the Castlereagh, and went to the world at large,
That twenty thousand travelling sheep, with Saltbush Bill in charge,
Were drifting down from a dried-out run to ravage the Castlereagh;
And the squatters swore when they heard the news, and wished they were
   well away:
For the name and the fame of Saltbush Bill were over the countryside
For the wonderful way that he fed his sheep, and the dodges and tricks he
   tried.
He would lose his way on a Main Stock Route, and stray to the squatters'
   grass;
He would come to a run with the boss away, and swear he had leave to pass;
And back of all and behind it all, as well the squatters knew,
If he had to fight, he would fight all day, so long as his sheep got through:
But this is the story of Stingy Smith, the owner of Hard Times Hill,
And the way that he chanced on a fighting man to reckon with Saltbush Bill.

'Twas Stingy Smith on his stockyard sat, and prayed for an early spring,
When he stared at sight of a clean-shaved tramp, who walked with jaunty
    swing;
For a clean-shaved tramp with a jaunty walk a-swinging along the track
Is as rare a thing as a feathered frog on the desolate roads outback.
So the tramp he made for the travellers' hut, and asked could he camp the
    night;
But Stingy Smith had a bright idea, and he said to him, "Can you fight?"
"Why, what's the game?" said the clean-shaved tramp, as he looked at him
    up and down —
"If you want a battle, get off that fence, and I'll kill you for half-a-crown!
But, Boss, you'd better not fight with me, it wouldn't be fair nor right;
I'm Stiffener Joe, from the Rocks Brigade, and I killed a man in a fight:
I served two years for it, fair and square, and now I'm a trampin' back,
To look for a peaceful quiet life away on the outside track —"
"Oh, it's not myself, but a drover chap," said Stingy Smith with glee;
"A bullying fellow, called Saltbush Bill — and you are the man for me.
He's on the road with his hungry sheep, and he's certain to raise a row,
For he's bullied the whole of the Castlereagh till he's got them under cow —
Just pick a quarrel and raise a fight, and leather him good and hard,
And I'll take good care that his wretched sheep don't wander a half a yard.
It's a five-pound job if you belt him well — do anything short of kill,
For there isn't a beak on the Castlereagh will fine you for Saltbush Bill."

"I'll take the job," said the fighting man, "and hot as this cove appears,
He'll stand no chance with a bloke like me, what's lived on the game for years;
For he's maybe learnt in a boxing school, and sparred for a round or so,
But I've fought all hands in a ten foot ring each night in a travelling show;
They earnt a pound if they stayed three rounds, and they tried for it every
    night —
In a ten foot ring! Oh, that's the game that teaches a bloke to fight,
For they'd rush and clinch, it was Dublin Rules, and we drew no colour line;
And they all tried hard for to earn the pound, but they got no pound of mine:
If I saw no chance in the opening round I'd slog at their wind, and wait
Till an opening came — and it *always* came — and I settled 'em, sure as fate;
Left on the ribs and right on the jaw — and, when the chance comes, *make
    sure*!
And it's there a professional bloke like me gets home on an amateur:

"For it's my experience every day, and I make no doubt it's yours,
That a third-class pro is an over-match for the best of the amateurs —"
"Oh, take your swag to the travellers' hut," said Smith, "for you waste your
    breath;
You've a first-class chance, if you lose the fight, of talking your man to death.
I'll tell the cook you're to have your grub, and see that you eat your fill,

And come to the scratch all fit and well to leather this Saltbush Bill."

'Twas Saltbush Bill, and his travelling sheep were wending their weary way
On the Main Stock Route, through the Hard Times Run, on their six-mile
   stage a day;
And he strayed a mile from the Main Stock Route, and started to feed along,
And, when Stingy Smith came up, Bill said that the Route was surveyed
   wrong;
And he tried to prove that the sheep had rushed and strayed from their camp
   at night,
But the fighting man he kicked Bill's dog, and of course that meant a fight:

So they sparred and fought, and they shifted ground and never a sound was
   heard
But the thudding fists on their brawny ribs, and the seconds' muttered word,
Till the fighting man shot home his left on the ribs with a mighty clout,
And his right flashed up with a half-arm blow — and Saltbush Bill "went
   out".
He fell face down, and towards the blow; and their hearts with fear were
   filled,
For he lay as still as a fallen tree, and they thought that he must be killed.
So Stingy Smith and the fighting man, they lifted him from the ground,
And sent to home for a brandy flask, and they slowly fetched him round;
But his head was bad, and his jaw was hurt — in fact, he could scarcely
   speak —
So they let him spell till he got his wits, and he camped on the run a week,
While the travelling sheep went here and there, wherever they liked to stray,
Till Saltbush Bill was fit once more for the track to the Castlereagh.

Then Stingy Smith he wrote a note, and gave to the fighting man:
'Twas writ to the boss of the neighbouring run, and thus the missive ran:
"The man with this is a fighting man, one Stiffener Joe by name;
He came near murdering Saltbush Bill, and I found it a costly game:
But it's worth your while to employ the chap, for there isn't the slightest
   doubt
You'll have no trouble from Saltbush Bill while this man hangs about —"
But an answer came by the next week's mail, with news that might well appal:
"The man you sent with a note is not a fighting man at all!
He has shaved his beard, and has cut his hair, but I spotted him at a look;
He is Tom Devine, who has worked for years for Saltbush Bill as cook.
Bill coached him up in the fighting yarn, and taught him the tale by rote,
And they shammed to fight, and they got your grass and divided your five-
   pound note.
'Twas a clean take-in, and you'll find it wise — 'twill save you a lot of pelf —
When next you're hiring a fighting man, just fight him a round yourself."

And the teamsters out on the Castlereagh, when they meet with a week of
    rain,
And the waggon sinks to its axle-tree, deep down in the black soil plain,
When the bullocks wade in a sea of mud, and strain at the load of wool,
And the cattle dogs at the bullocks' heels are biting to make them pull,
When the offside driver flays the team, and curses them while he flogs,
And the air is thick with the language used, and the clamour of men and
    dogs —
The teamsters say, as they pause to rest and moisten each hairy throat,
They wish they could swear like Stingy Smith when he read that neighbour's
    note.

In Defence of the Bush

So you're back from up the country, Mister Lawson, where you went,
And you're cursing all the business in a bitter discontent;
Well, we grieve to disappoint you, and it makes us sad to hear
That it wasn't cool and shady — and there wasn't plenty beer,
And the loony bullock snorted when you first came into view;
Well, you know it's not so often that he sees a swell like you;
And the roads were hot and dusty, and the plains were burnt and brown,
And no doubt you're better suited drinking lemon squash in town.

Yet, perchance, if you should journey down the very track you went
In a month or two at furthest you would wonder what it meant,
Where the sunbaked earth was gasping like a creature in its pain
You would find the grasses waving like a field of summer grain,
And the miles of thirsty gutters blocked with sand and choked with mud,
You would find them mighty rivers with a turbid, sweeping flood;
For the rain and drought and sunshine make no changes in the street,
In the sullen line of buildings and the ceaseless tramp of feet;
But the bush hath moods and changes, as the seasons rise and fall,
And the men who know the bush land — they are loyal through it all.

But you found the bush was dismal and a land of no delight,
Did you chance to hear a chorus in the shearers' huts at night?
Did they "rise up, William Riley" by the camp-fire's cheery blaze?

Did they rise him as we rose him in the good old droving days?
And the women of the homesteads and the men you chanced to meet —
Were their faces sour and saddened like the "faces in the street",
And the "shy selector children" — were they better now or worse
Than the little city urchins who would greet you with a curse?
Is not such a life much better than the squalid street and square
Where the fallen women flaunt it in the fierce electric glare,
Where the semptress plies her sewing till her eyes are sore and red
In a filthy, dirty attic toiling on for daily bread?
Did you hear no sweeter voices in the music of the bush
Than the roar of trams and buses, and the war whoop of "the push"?
Did the magpies rouse your slumbers with their carol sweet and strange?
Did you hear the silver chiming of the bellbirds on the range?
But, perchance, the wild birds' music by your senses was despised,
For you say you'll stay in townships till the bush is civilised.
Would you make it a tea garden and on Sundays have a band
Where the "blokes" might take their "donahs", with a "public" close at hand?
You had better stick to Sydney and make merry with the "push",
For the bush will never suit you, and you'll never suit the bush.

An Answer to Various Bards

Well, I've waited mighty patient while they all came rolling in,
Mister Lawson, Mister Dyson, and the others of their kin,
With their dreadful, dismal stories of the overlander's camp,
How his fire is always smoky, and his boots are always damp;
And they paint it so terrific it would fill one's soul with gloom,
But you know they're fond of writing about "corpses" and "the tomb".
So, before they curse the bushland they should let their fancy range,
And take something for their livers, and be cheerful for a change.

Now, for instance, Mister Lawson — well, of course, we almost cried
At the sorrowful description how his "little 'Arvie" died.
And we wept in silent sorrow when "His Father's Mate" was slain;
Then he went and killed the father, and we had to weep again.
Ben Duggan and Jack Denver, too, he caused them to expire,
And he went and cooked the gander of Jack Dunn, of Nevertire;
And he spoke in terms prophetic of a revolution's beat,

When the world should hear the clamour of those people in the street;
But the shearer chaps who start it — why, he rounds on them in blame,
And he calls 'em "agitators" who are living on the game.
So, no doubt, the bush is wretched if you judge it by the groan
Of the sad and soulful poet with a graveyard of his own.

But I "over-write" the bushmen! Well, I own without a doubt
That I always see a hero in the "man from furthest out".
I could never contemplate him through an atmosphere of gloom,
And a bushman never struck me as a subject for "the tomb".
If it ain't all "golden sunshine" where the "wattle branches wave",
Well, it ain't all damp and dismal, and it ain't all "lonely grave".
And, of course, there's no denying that the bushman's life is rough,
But a man can easy stand it if he's built of sterling stuff;
Tho' it's seldom that the drover gets a bed of eiderdown,
Yet the man who's born a bushman, he gets mighty sick of town,
For he's jotting down the figures, and he's adding up the bills
While his heart is simply aching for a sight of southern hills.
Then he hears a wool team passing with a rumble and a lurch,
And although the work is pressing yet it brings him off his perch.
For it stirs him like a message from his station friends afar
And he seems to sniff the ranges in the scent of wool and tar;
And it takes him back in fancy, half in laughter, half in tears,
To a sound of other voices and a thought of other years,
When the woolshed rang with bustle from the dawning of the day,
And the shear blades were a-clicking to the cry of "wool away!"
When his face was somewhat browner and his frame was firmer set,
And he feels his flabby muscles with a feeling of regret.
Then the wool team slowly passes and his eyes go sadly back
To the dusty little table and the papers in the rack,
And his thoughts go to the terrace where his sickly children squall,
And he thinks there's something healthy in the bush life after all.

But we'll go no more a-droving in the wind or in the sun,
For our fathers' hearts have failed us and the droving days are done.
There's a nasty dash of danger where the long-horned bullock wheels,
And we like to live in comfort and to get our reg'lar meals.
And to hang about the townships suits us better, you'll agree,
For a job at washing bottles is the job for such as we.
Let us herd into the cities, let us crush and crowd and push
Till we lose the love of roving and we learn to hate the bush;
And we'll turn our aspirations to a city life and beer,
And we'll sneak across to England — it's a nicer place than here;
For there's not much risk of hardship where all comforts are in store,
And the theatres are plenty and the pubs are more and more.

But that ends it, Mister Lawson, and it's time to say good-bye,
We must agree to differ in all friendship, you and I;
And our personal opinions — well, they're scarcely worth a rush,
For there's some that like the city and there's some that like the bush;
And there's no one quite contented, as I've always heard it said,
Except one favoured person, and *he* turned out to be dead.
So we'll work our own salvation with the stoutest hearts we may,
And if fortune only favours we will take the road some day,
And go droving down the river 'neath the sunshine and the stars,
And then we'll come to Sydney and vermilionise the bars.

Singers Among Savages

I have to try to tell you in ten minutes what it took me fifty years to find out — that is, something about poetry.

Now poetry is not always appreciated and even that great writer Lord Macaulay said, "No person can be a poet or enjoy poetry without a certain unsoundness of mind." He was what you might call a "poet scorner".

But people have been writing and reading poetry for thousands of years, and surely they cannot all have been of unsound mind. There must be some reason for the grip that poetry has on the human race, and, as I have been a good deal among savage peoples, I have tried to trace its beginnings. It is possible that poetry is an inherited instinct and not a modern development at all. Even the lower animals seem to have this instinct, for birds sing, dogs get together and howl (which I suppose is their way of singing) and certain varieties of frogs run a very definite chorus. You will hear one old fellow booming out the solo while the rest take up the refrain. In my opinion these were the primeval beginnings of poetry, but I won't ask you to go back as far as the frogs: let us start with the earliest days of the human race.

When our ancestors wore no clothes, when their wardrobe consisted of a coat of paint and a nose ring, before they could even talk properly, they had poetry and the poetry came about in this way.

They had tribal dances, they used to paddle about in canoes, and sometimes they had to roll a big log or shift a big stone. They needed something to mark the time like the "left right, left right" of a drill sergeant. They wanted to make all their dance steps together, or to dip their paddles together, or to pull on the log together. Also they wanted something to put some heart into the performers: so they improvised a kind of chant, which afterwards became poetry. I verified this when I was out among what are possibly the most primitive people in the world — the wild blacks of the Northern Territory of Australia. They had a kind of chant to mark the time for their corroborees. One chant went something like this: *"Chin-a-ma-li chin-a-ma-li chin-a-ma-li ma lon a me chin-a-ma-li chin-a-ma-li"*. It does not sound very much with one man giving it, but if you could have heard it with the gins slapping their thighs and beating sticks together in time with the chant, while the warriors pranced about shaking their spears, you would have felt like picking up a spear and taking part in the performance yourself.

It was the same with the South Sea Island crews in the pearling fleets off Thursday Island. About twenty or thirty of them would come aboard the schooner and dance for hours to a kind of chant: *"Heema hala, heema hala"*, while they went through a dance like a sort of quadrille.

They were all fine big men and they would boom out this chant and their feet would slap down on the deck in perfect time — they would have brought the house down on any stage in the world. These chants were like the sailors' shanties that they used when pulling on a rope before the days of steam windlasses.

The words meant nothing; you know the business:

> Hi ho, blow the man down
> Blow the man down from the Liverpool town
> Give a man time and we'll blow a man down:

but any old sailor will tell you what a good shanty man was worth to a crew. These chants meant nothing in particular, but they marked the time, they stirred up the performers and they were the beginnings of poetry.

The next step was when the tribes began to get a fair command of language. When the warriors of the tribe were returning from a victory over their enemies, some fellow with a loud voice and a good opinion of himself would begin to shout the glad tidings, using the same kind of rhythmical chant, but putting his descriptions into words. He was the world's first poet and as he probably accompanied his chant with some sort of dance and some imitation of the blows struck in the fight, he was also the world's first operatic performer. When he struck his spear and his shield together, he produced the world's first sound effects for the wireless. If the tribe did not like his poetry, they silenced him with a waddy and another man got his job.

These recitals of events that actually happened were what you might call poetry of fact: then came poetry of fiction. The tribal poet, finding that there was nothing doing about the camp, would imagine himself pursued by three polar bears, and that he turned round and killed the lot. Then he would make up a poem about it.

The tribe would know that this poem was all lies, and that this man never faced a bear in his life, but if he gave a good description, if he could make his hearers say to one another, "That's exactly how I felt when that last bear was after me", if he could do that, then his poem would last, and when it was being recited years afterwards some old greybeard of the tribe would get up and say, "I was the man that killed those bears".

That is the greatest compliment a writer can have; to know that he has written a thing so truly that people not only believe that it happened but that it happened to themselves. I have had the same compliment paid me, in my own small way, by having men write in and say that they were the original of the Man from Snowy River. I expect, when I am dead, the place will be full of survivors of the charge of Snowy River — like the survivors of the charge of Balaclava.

After the poems of fact and fiction came the poems of fancy; poems about emotions: poems about moonlight and beautiful women: poems about life, and love and liquor: and if they had the touch of genius, if they could make their hearers say, "That's just how I felt when I was in love or when I was in liquor", then those poems would live. Poetry is older than civilisation, possibly older than speech, and it will make men laugh or love or weep or fight better than any acting or any speech making.

Of course, this only applies to real poetry, not to the verse that most of us write. There is a great difference between poetry and verse, and when a man speaks of real poetry he should always take his hat off. It is very rare and very wonderful. One might almost think that true poetry is the work of some disembodied spirit who has a message to deliver to mankind. Having selected the medium for the message, the spirit shouts in his ear night and day, "Write, write, write", and thus great poems are written. Sometimes the spirit selects as the medium of his message a man of the most unlikely description. Two of the greatest of English poets — Byron and Swinburne — were human degenerates, but they wrote wonderful poetry.

Now as to modern verse writing. There is nothing new under the sun and modern writers work on the same lines as the old tribal singers.

Rudyard Kipling, whom I know very well, is a true tribal poet with modern improvements. He picks up a phrase or an incident and turns it into a verse, always using the right words and not too many of them. I first met him in the South African war, where he happened to ride into Lichtenberg alongside an Australian trooper who said that the scent of the wattles reminded him of home. From this Kipling made a very beautiful set of verses:

> The scent of the wattle round Lichtenberg
> Riding in in the rain.

I asked Henry Lawson how he got his ideas and he said, "I can catch ideas anywhere, but I can't always make 'em go in harness. Simple stuff is the best. One day I picked up a pair of pants and found they had a hole in the stern and I wrote, 'You've got to face your troubles when your pants begin to go'. That hit them where they lived, for most of them had to face their troubles in life."

I got the idea for my own verses "Clancy of the Overflow" through writing a business letter to a man named Clancy and getting the reply, "We don't know where he are." I made that into a verse, as I thought that most of us had a bit of a craving for the free life, the air and the sunshine, and to be done with the boss and the balance sheet.

There is plenty of stuff to be picked up in Australia, new stuff that people will like — the only difficulty is to write it properly.

When you ask yourself what is the most permanent work that a man can do in the world, the answer is poetry. When the Ayrshire ploughman Robert Burns first started to write, he was told that he was mad and that he should stick to ploughing: but the work of Robert Burns will outlast the strongest castle in Scotland. The Greek poet Homer had to beg his bread, but his work has outlasted the whole of the old Greek civilisation: and they have had to send men to repair Westminster Abbey, but they will never have to repair the work of Shakespeare. Poetry lasts longer even than sculpture, for when the savages overrun a civilisation the first thing they do is break up the statues with an axe: but they cannot do this to a poem.

Rudyard Kipling

Without haste, without rest — The world's hardest worker —
A man of many houses — "You must get things right" — A
genius with no redeeming vices — Kipling and the butcher —
"You must buy Empire lamb" — "It's their guts they think
about."

One expects a great literary genius to be in some way a sort of freak: drink, women, temperament, idleness, irregularity of habits — nearly all the great writers of the past have had one or other of these drawbacks, and some of them have had them all. Byron's life consisted mostly of purple patches; and Swinburne was not the hero of the song about the good young man that died. So, when I went to stay with Kipling in England, I was prepared for literally anything. Would he drink? Would he be one of those men who had half a dozen wives with a complementary number of concubines? Would he sit up all night telling me how good he was, or would he recite his own poetry with appropriate gestures?

None of these things happened. We have read in one of O. Henry's books of a citizen of a South American republic, where everybody was "grafting" day and night, who determined to make himself conspicuous by being honest. Greta Garbo, one of the world's great film stars, got pages of publicity by refusing to be interviewed. Shakespeare himself seems to have dodged the publicity man to such an extent that even now there is some doubt whether he wrote all his own works, or whether they were done by somebody else of the same name. Kipling was remarkable in that his life was so very unremarkable.

He hated publicity as his Satanic Majesty is supposed to hate holy water; and in private life he was just a hard-working, commonsense, level-headed man, without any redeeming vices that I could discover. A pity, too, perhaps; for there is nothing so interesting as scandals about great geniuses. Though he was a very rich man, I found him living in an unpretentious house at Rottingdean, Brighton. The only thing that marked it as the lair of a literary lion was the crowd of tourists (mostly Americans) who hung about from daylight till dark trying to look over the wall, or waiting to intercept his two little children when they went out for a walk. By having his car brought into the garden and getting into it from his own doorstep, Kipling was able to dash out through the ranks of autograph hunters even as a tiger dashes out when surrounded by savages.

His wife, a charming and cultivated American lady, was in her own way just as big a disappointment as was Kipling. She did not seek to be a society star, nor to swagger about covered with rubies and emeralds.

"In the States," she said, "when people push their money in your face, we always wonder how they got it."

Kipling's house was a home. And it was a home of hard work, for he allowed nothing to interfere with his two or three hours of work a day. The rest of the time he roved round getting material.

"I must buy a house in Australia some day," he said. "I've a house here, and in New York, and in Cape Town; but I'd like to live in Australia for a while. I've been there, but I only went through it like the devil went through Athlone, in standing jumps. You can't learn anything about a country that way. You have to live there and then you can get things right. You people in Australia haven't grown up yet. You think the Melbourne Cup is the most important thing in the world."

Motoring in those days was just in the stage when the betting was about even whether the car would get its passengers home or whether the wife would sit and knit by the roadside while the husband lay on his back under the car and had his clothes smothered in dust and oil.

Kipling, it appeared, had a new car coming on trial, and our first excursion was to be a run in this new car. One of the newly invented Lanchester cars arrived, driven by a man in overalls, who looked like a superior sort of mechanic. He said that his name was Laurence. When he heard that I came from Australia, he asked me whether I knew his brother in Sydney. It so happened that I *did* know his brother; thereafter things went swimmingly. "I have another brother," he said, "a High Court Judge here. When I take these cars round for a trial I generally drag in something about my brother, the High Court Judge, for fear they'll send me round to the kitchen. Sometimes," he added, "I would prefer to go to the kitchen."

Kipling and I piled into the back of the car, with the great man as excited as a child with a new toy. Out we went, scattering tourists right and left, and away over the Sussex Downs. We were climbing a hill of about one in five with nothing much below us but the English Channel, when Kipling, possibly with a view to getting some accurate copy about motoring, said "What would happen if she stopped here, Laurence?"

"I'll show you," said Laurence. He stopped the engine and let the car, with its illustrious passenger, run back towards that awful drop. I had a look over my shoulder and was preparing to jump when Laurence dropped a sprag and pulled her up all standing. Then he threw in the engine and away we went. I said to Kipling "Weren't you frightened? I was nearly jumping out."

"Yes," he said, "I was frightened. But I thought what a bad advertisement it would be for the Lanchester company if they killed me, so I sat tight."

Away we went through the beautiful English lanes, where the leaves swirled after the car, and one expected to see Puck of Pook's Hill peering out from behind a tree. We passed military barracks, where Mulvaney, Otheris, and Learoyd, with their swagger canes, were just setting out for a walk. We saw the stolid English farm labourers putting in the oak bridge that would last for generations. We saw a sailing ship ploughing her way down the Channel, and noted "the shudder, the stumble, the roll as the star-stabbing bowsprit emerges". It was like looking at a series of paintings — and here at my side was the painter.

Earnest in everything that he touched, he pulled the car up outside a butcher's shop to do a little Empire propaganda. Pointing at the carcass of a lamb hanging in the window, he asked me to guess its weight. Not being altogether inexperienced in the weight of lambs, I had a guess, and he said "I'll go in and buy that lamb, and we'll see if you're right; and we'll see where this butcher is getting his mutton."

It turned out that I was within two pounds of the lamb's weight. This seemed to astonish Kipling very much, and he said to the butcher "This gentleman comes from Australia, where they do nothing but weigh lambs all day long. You must buy all the Australian lamb you can get, and keep the money in the Empire."

The butcher, not knowing in the least who he was, said, "The Empire. Ha! My customers don't bother about the Empire, sir. It's their guts they think about!"

This unedifying incident of the butcher may be some sort of guide as to what Kipling's English contemporaries thought of him. Frankly, they looked upon him as one of these infernal know-all fellows, who wanted to do all sorts of queer things. What right had anyone to come along and suggest that some day there would be a big war, and that England should be prepared for it? Fancy advocating that we should give more time to drill, and less time to sports! The flannelled fools at the wickets, forsooth, and the muddied oafs at the goals — when everybody knew that all battles were won on the playing fields of Eton and Rugby!

Kipling, out of his own pocket, bought enough land for a rifle range, and paid the wages of a retired sergeant-major to teach the yokels drill and musketry. Was he applauded by his neighbours? Not that you would notice it. A local magnate, stodgy as a bale of hay, looked in and confided to me that Kipling was undoubtedly clever but too unconventional.

"All this business about drilling men," he said, "is just putting wrong ideas into their heads. I wouldn't let my men go."

Later on, in the Great War, he was to know more about it. Kipling himself lost his only son in the Great War, and was asked to write an epitaph to be put on a tablet in the centre of the thousands of war graves. He wrote: "Had our fathers not lied to us, so many of us would not be here." And who shall blame him? Needless to say, they did not use it.

So Kipling stalked through the land of little men, as Gulliver stalked through the land of the Lilliputians. He would never have made a political leader, for he was less of a quack, less of a showman, and less of a time-server than any public man I ever met. Had he been a spectacular person like Gabriel d'Annunzio he might have led a great Imperialist movement. But he had no gift of speech, and his nature abhorred anything in the way of theatricalism. He wrote of things as he saw them, bearing in his own way the white man's burden and expecting no fee or reward.

Kipling carried his earnestness into his work, for he must have everything right. Smoking one evening, he picked up some manuscript, and said, "Here's something I am working on, and it brings in your country. Just see if it's right, will you?"

The verse in his hand was, "The scent of the wattle at Lichtenberg, riding in the rain." And the lines that troubled him were:

> My fruit farm on Hunter's River
> With the new vines joining hands.

For some reason or another he was worried as to whether these lines were right.

I said that in Australia we would speak of an orchard, not of a fruit farm; and that we called it Hunter River, and not Hunter's River. But why worry! He wasn't writing a geography or a gardener's guide. Even old Ouida, who was a best-seller in her day, once made one of her guardsman heroes, weighing thirteen stone, ride the same horse to victory in the Derby two years running — and nobody murdered her.

"They should have murdered her," said Kipling. "Writing things wrong is like singing out of tune. You don't sing, do you?"

"No. But how could you tell?"

"Nobody that has the ear for rhythm ever has the ear for music. When I sing, the dog gets up and goes out of the room."

This insistence on photographic accuracy, so unusual in a poet, may have been the one loose bearing in the otherwise perfect machinery of his mind; or it may have been that his training as a sub-editor had bitten so deeply into his system that he looked upon inaccuracy as the cardinal sin. There was no satisfaction for him in a majestic march of words if any of the words were out of step.

I said to him, "You ought to be satisfied. You seem to get things pretty right, anyway. How did you come to get that little touch about the Australian trooper riding into Lichtenberg when the rain brought out the scent of the wattles? Inspiration?"

"No," he said. "Observation. I used to poke about among the troops and ask all the silly questions I could think of. I saw this Australian trooper pull down a wattle bough and smell it. So I rode alongside and asked him where he came from. He told me about himself, and added, 'I didn't know they had our wattle over here. It smells like home.' That gave me the general idea for the verses; then all I had to do was to sketch in the background in as few strokes as possible. And when you're only using a few strokes you must have 'em in the right place. That's why I asked you whether it was right to talk about the fruit farm and Hunter's River."

All very well, but being somewhat in the verse line myself, I knew that only a master could have written those few little verses. Possibly only one man that ever lived could have done it — Kipling himself.

He was sub-editor of a big Indian paper, and all the news of the world came through his hands to be trimmed up and cut down and put under headlines. The worst training in the world for a poet, one would think, yet, it gave him his crisp, clear-cut style. He thought in essentials, and scorned padding, as a sub-editor should. "The Wake a Welt of Light", "He Looked Like a Lance in Rest", "Oak, Ash, and Thorn", "The Joyous Venture". These are all head-lines — not a word wasted. Phil May had this gift of condensation in art, and Kipling has it in literature. Then, as to his gift of vivid description. Here are a couple of lines from the "Ballad of East and West", describing the chase of an Indian raider by an officer on a troop horse:

> The dun he leaned against the bit and slugged his head above,
> But the red mare played with the snaffle bars, as a maiden plays with a glove.

I said, "How on earth did you manage to write that, you who say that you know nothing about horses? It's just a picture of the way the horses would gallop. You can see the well-bred mare getting over the ground like a gazelle with the big, heavy-headed horse toiling after her."

"Observation," he said. "I suppose I must have noticed the action of horses without knowing that I noticed it."

It must have been the same sort of observation that made him call the pompous heads of army departments "little tin gods on wheels". The phrase was not new, but like Homer going down the road, he went and took it. Like all great artists, he was quite dissatisfied with his own work, "If you can write a thing about half as well as it ought to be written," he said, "then perhaps, after all, you may not have written it so badly."

I asked him how he came to write *Kim* with its mass of material and its infinite (and no doubt accurate) detail.

"Oh," he said, "the material was just lying about there in heaps. All I had to do was to take it and fit it together."

And now the reader asks, hadn't the man any hobbies? Did he garden or play cards or shoot or hunt or fish? Not a bit of it. He took a great deal of interest in small improvements to his property, such as you may read about in *Puck of Pook's Hill*, but I think that was mainly on account of the enjoyment he got from watching the habits and customs of the English agricultural labourer, as set forth in the same book. His sight was too bad to allow him to race over raspers in the hunting-field or drop a dry fly over a rising trout: hence his nickname of Beetle in *Stalky & Co.* His only hobby was work. And like Goethe's hero he toiled without haste and without rest. Look at a collection of his works and you will get some idea of the urge that must have driven him to keep working. At the age of forty he had written more books than most men write in a lifetime, and not a line went into one of those books that he did not verify. True, he did once describe the Maribyrnong Plate as a steeplechase; but if he had had an Australian turf guide at hand, he would have corrected the error. I have already quoted the Scotch engineer's objection to Kipling's description of the destroyers lying in wait for their prey in the swirl of the reefs — "and they drawing six feet forrard and nine feet aft". But did not Shakespeare once locate a navy in Bohemia or some other inland country? Apart from his literary work, he felt that the white man's burden was laid on him to advocate in every way this bringing of the British peoples under Empire council, with India as a sort of apprentice nation until it learnt to govern itself. In view of what has happened lately, he might have also questioned the ability of the white parts of the Empire to govern themselves; but he said that, when the Australians grew up, and when the young Africans forgot to be Dutch, there would be such an empire as the world never saw. By way of contribution to the debate, I suggested that the Australians would always put Australia first, and that the young Africans did not care a hoot about the Dutch — they were Afrikanders first, last, and all the time. But the only motherland he had known was that "grim stepmother", India, and he could not conceive that South Africans or Australians would study the interests of their own territories when they might be partners in a great empire. One must concede it to him that he took a large view.

As to the Indians, he said that the Indian peasant could neither understand nor make any sensible use of self-government; and he wrote all sorts of nasty things about the British M.P.s who wandered over to "smoodge" to the Indians. He would cheerfully have seen them get their throats cut.

from *Happy Dispatches*

Lay of the Motor Car

We're away! and the wind whistles shrewd
   In our whiskers and teeth;
And the granite-like grey of the road
   Seems to slide underneath.
As an eagle might sweep through the sky,
   So we sweep through the land;
And the pallid pedestrians fly
   When they hear us at hand.

We outpace, we outlast, we outstrip!
   Not the fast-fleeing hare,
Nor the racehorses under the whip,
   Nor the birds of the air
Can compete with our swiftness sublime,
   Our ease and our grace.
We annihilate chickens and time
   And policemen and space.

Do you mind that fat grocer who crossed?
   How he dropped down to pray
In the road when he saw he was lost;
   How he melted away
Underneath, and there rang through the fog
   His earsplitting squeal
As he went — Is that he or a dog,
   That stuff on the wheel?

A War Office in Trouble

SCENE: War Office, London. Telephones are ringing, typewriters clicking, clerks in dozens rushing hither and thither at express rate. An atmosphere of feverish unrest hangs over everything. In the passages and lobbies crowds of military contractors, officials, newspapermen and inventors of patent guns have been waiting for hours to get a few minutes' interview with those in authority. Mounted messengers dash up to the door every few seconds. In the innermost room of all, a much-decorated military veteran with a bald head, a grizzled moustache and an eyeglass is dictating to three shorthand writers at once, while clerks rush in and out with cablegrams, letters and cards from people waiting. On the table are littered a heap of lists of troops, army-contracts, and tenders for supplies, all marked "Urgent". A clerk rushes in.

CLERK: "Cablegram from Australia offering troops, sir!"

MILITARY VETERAN: "No! Can't have 'em. It has been decided not to use blacks, except as a last resource."

CLERK: "But these are white troops, sir — the local forces. It is officially desired that they be taken if possible."

MILITARY VETERAN: "Who is the Australian Commander-in-Chief? I didn't know they had an army at all. I knew they had police, of course!"

CLERK: "There are seven distinct cablegrams, sir; seven distinct Commanders-in-Chief all offering troops."

M.V. (*roused to excitement*): "Great Heavens! are they going to take the war off our hands? *Seven* Commanders-in-Chief! They must have been quietly breeding armies all these years in Australia. Let's have a look at the cables. Where's this from?"

C: "Tasmania, sir. They offer to send a Commander-in-Chief and" (pauses, aghast) "and *eighty-five* men!"

M.V. (*jumping to his feet*): "What! Have I wasted all this time talking about eighty-five men! You must be making a mistake!"

C: "No, sir. It says eighty-five men!"

M.V.: "Well I *am* damned! Eighty-five men! You cable back and say that I've seen bigger armies on the stage at Drury Lane Theatre. Just wire and say *this* isn't a pantomime. They haven't got to march round and round a piece of scenery. Tell 'em to stop at home and *breed*!" (*Resumes dictation.*) "At least five thousand extra men should be sent from India in addition to —"

c: "Cabinet instructions are to take these troops, whether they're any good or not, sir. Political reasons!"

m.v. (*with a sigh*): "Well, let 'em come. Let 'em *all* come — the whole eighty-five! But don't let it leak out, or the Boers will say we're not playing 'em fair. Tell 'em to send infantry, anyhow; we don't want horses eating their heads off."

c. (*interrupts again*): "These other colonies, sir — are we to accept 'em all?"

m.v.: "Yes. Didn't I say let 'em *all* come? There'll be plenty of room for 'em in South Africa. They won't feel crowded." (*Resumes dictation*.) "The expenditure of a hundred thousand pounds at least will be needed to —"

c: "They want to know, if they pay the men's fares over, will the British Government pay their return fares?"

m.v.: "Yes, I should think we would. We'll put 'em in the front and there won't be so many of 'em left to go back. If the colonies had any sense *they'd* have paid the return fares. Now, please go away and let me get to work."

(*Ten minutes later, clerk timidly reappears.*)
c: "If you please, sir, another cable from New South Wales. They say they would sooner send artillery!"

m.v.: "Oh, blast it all! What does their artillery amount to?"

c: "One battery, sir."

m.v. "*One* battery! Well, they've got to come, I suppose. 'Cry havoc and let slip the dogs of war.' Stop their one battery if you can; but if not, let it come. And now go, and don't let me have any more of you." (*Resumes dictation, and has just got to "the purchase of ten thousand horses" when the Clerk reappears.*)

c: "Fresh cable, sir! Two circus proprietors in Sydney have presented six circus horses —"

m.v.: "Shivering Sheol! This is the climax! Six circus horses! Didn't they say anything about a clown and pantaloon? Surely they wouldn't see the Empire hurled to ruin for want of a clown. Perhaps they could let us have a few sword-swallowers to get off with the Boers' weapons? Look here, now — hand the whole thing over to one of the senior clerks, and tell him to do exactly what he d——well pleases in the matter, but that if he comes in here to ask any questions about it, I'll have him shot! Now go, and don't you come here any more, or I'll have *you* shot too. Take this cheque for a hundred thousand to the petty cash department, and tell that contractor outside that his tender is two millions over the estimate, and don't let me hear any more of this blessed Australian army."

Cable message: Some difficulty exists in ascertaining from the War Office whether the colonial troops will be expected to take their own saddles or not, and whether the officer commanding shall take one horse or two. It is not definitely known whether the offer of Fitzgeralds' six circus horses will be accepted. Great enthusiasm prevails.

Driver Smith

'Twas Driver Smith of Battery A was anxious to see a fight;
He thought of the Transvaal all the day, he thought of it all the night —
"Well, if the battery's left behind, I'll go to the war," says he,
"I'll go a-driving an ambulance in the ranks of the A.M.C.

"I'm fairly sick of these here parades, it's want of a change that kills
A-charging the Randwick Rifle Range and aiming at Surry Hills.
And I think if I go with the ambulance I'm certain to find a show,
For they have to send the medical men wherever the troops can go.

"Wherever the rifle bullets flash and the Maxims raise a din,
It's there you'll find the medical men a-raking the wounded in —
A-raking 'em in like human flies — and a driver smart like me
Will find some scope for his extra skill in the ranks of the A.M.C."

So Driver Smith he went to the war a-cracking his driver's whip,
From ambulance to collecting base they showed him his regular trip.
And he said to the boys that were marching past, as he gave his whip a crack,
"You'll walk yourselves to the fight," says he — "Lord spare me, I'll drive you back."

Now, the fight went on in the Transvaal hills for the half of a day or more,
And Driver Smith he worked his trip — all aboard for the seat of war!
He took his load from the stretcher men and hurried 'em homeward fast
Till he heard a sound he knew full well — a battery rolling past.

He heard the clink of the leading chains and the roll of the guns behind —
He heard the crack of the drivers' whips, and he says to 'em, "Strike me blind,
I'll miss me trip with this ambulance, although I don't care to shirk,
But I'll take the car off the line to-day and follow the guns at work."

Then up the Battery Colonel came a-cursing 'em black in the face.
"Sit down and shift 'em, you drivers there, and gallop 'em into place."
So off the Battery rolled and swung, a-going a merry dance,
And holding his own with the leading gun goes Smith with his ambulance.

They opened fire on the mountainside, a-peppering by and large,
When over the hill above their flank the Boers came down at the charge;
They rushed the guns with a daring rush, a-volleying left and right,
And Driver Smith with his ambulance moved up to the edge of the fight.

The gunners stuck to their guns like men, and fought like the wild cats fight,
For a Battery man don't leave his gun with ever a hope in sight;
But the bullets sang and the Mausers cracked and the Battery men gave way,
Till Driver Smith with his ambulance drove into the thick of the fray.

He saw the head of the Transvaal troop a-thundering to and fro,
A hard old face with a monkey beard — a face that he seemed to know;
"Now, who's that leader," said Driver Smith, "I've seen him before to-day.
Why, bless my heart, but it's Kruger's self", and he jumped for him straight
    away.

He collared old Kruger round the waist and hustled him into the van.
It wasn't according to stretcher drill for raising a wounded man;
But he forced him in and said: "All aboard, we're off for a little ride,
And you'll have the car to yourself," says he, "I reckon we're full inside."

He wheeled his team on the mountainside and set 'em a merry pace,
A-galloping over the rocks and stones, and a lot of the Boers gave chase;
But Driver Smith had a fairish start, and he said to the Boers, "Good-day,
You have Buckley's chance for to catch a man that was trained in Battery A."

He drove his team to the hospital and said to the P.M.O.,
"Beg pardon, sir, but I missed a trip, mistaking the way to go;
And Kruger came to the ambulance and asked could we spare a bed,
So I fetched him here, and we'll take him home to show for a bob a head."

So the word went round to the English troops to say they need fight no more,
For Driver Smith with his ambulance had ended the blooming war:
And in London now at the music halls he's starring it every night,
And drawing a hundred pounds a week to tell how he won the fight.

Right in the Front of the Army

"Where 'ave you been this week or more,
'Aven't seen you about the war?
Thought perhaps you was at the rear
Guarding the waggons." "What, us? No fear!
Where have we been? Why, bless my heart,
Where have we been since the bloomin' start?
    Right in the front of the army,
      Battling day and night!
    Right in the front of the army,
      Teachin 'em how to fight!"
Every separate man you see,
Sapper, gunner, and C.I.V.,
Every one of 'em seems to be
Right in the front of the army!

Most of the troops to the camp had gone,
When we met with a cow gun toiling on;
And we said to the boys, as they walked her past,
"Well, thank goodness, you're here at last!"
"Here at last! Why, what d'yer mean?
Ain't we just where we've always been?
    Right in the front of the army,
      Battling day and night!
    Right in the front of the army,
      Teaching 'em how to fight!"
Correspondents and vets in force,
Mounted foot and dismounted horse,
All of them were, as a matter of course,
Right in the front of the army.

Old Lord Roberts will have to mind
If ever the enemy get behind;
For they'll smash him up with a rear attack,
Because his army has got no back!
Think of the horrors that might befall
An army without any rear at all!
    Right in the front of the army,
      Battling day and night!
    Right in the front of the army,
      Teaching 'em how to fight!

Swede attachés and German counts,
Yeomen (known as De Wet's remounts),
All of them were by their own accounts
Right in the front of the army!

"To Bloemfontein"

The Australian Horse — Ahead of Everybody — The Chief
Place of Distinction — What Shrapnel Did — Flight of the Boers
— Surrender of the Town

BLOEMFONTEIN, Mar. 13

My last letter was from Poplar Grove, a place where the army camped after chasing the remains of the Boer army out of a strong position at the back of the Seven Kopjes. This engagement was followed by an easy day, as we moved on to a beautiful camp on a big well-grassed flat with the Modder River running by it. As we marched up to this camp the First Australian Horse were given the post of honour, right out in the front of the army, ahead of the Rimington scouts, ahead of everybody, the nearest men of all to the enemy. They spread out in good style, too, their fresh well-filled-out horses evoking great praise as they swung along with the true Waler stride. They saw the Boers in the distance — one generally has to be content with seeing them at a good distance — and reported accordingly; also they were told to try and discover a ford across the Modder River, and they not only discovered it but guided the troops successfully over it, a thing that may seem a small matter to you in Australia, but which would be a long way beyond the scope of the average English Tommy, who would not find the ford in the first place, and would infallibly lose the way to it if by any accident he did find it. Major Lee has been made Provost Marshal of the Army, and has to see that no looting or pillaging goes on, so that he has to keep well up in the front. With him, we found one of the First Australian Horse, riding up and down on a kind of sentry go by himself. We thought at first he had discovered a pig or a patch of watermelons, or some other edible treasure, and was keeping watch over it, but when we asked what he was doing, he said, "I'm waiting to show the troops the crossing place." We suggested that the Boers might be hiding in the river timber — a very likely contingency — but he said, "Oh, I ain't afraid," so we rode on and left him by the river.

HOW FORAGE WAS GOT

At a big farm, near the camp, we met a lot of the New South Wales Mounted Infantry — Colonel Knight's men — each laden with a bag of horse feed that they had got out of a stable at the back of the farm. By the unwritten law of the army it is no offence to take anything necessary for a horse or man; so we rode round to the front and found a General and his chief staff officer sitting in the verandah. Major Lee suggested that he might leave a sentry over the farm to prevent pillage, but the chief staff officer assured him that it was quite impossible for anyone to take anything from the farm while he was there — and all the while the New South Wales men, like a string of ants, were toiling away with the forage out of the back of the house! We rode on and left him in the full belief that no one would venture near the house while he was there. It was a very creditable beginning for the new arrivals, as there were at least 10,000 men who would have jumped at the chance of getting at that forage, so it was not at all bad for them to be smart enough to get in first. We rested all next day, swam in the Modder, cooked ducks and goats purchased from the Kaffir huts, and generally enjoyed ourselves.

HORDES OF MEN, GUNS, AND HORSES

On the 12th the army moved again. There were countless hordes of men and guns and horses, and once more the Australians were well in the front — in fact the front line of the 1st Brigade was almost as much Australian as English. The country is something lovely now — green and rippling with grass — and as we rode along we saw countless herds of bucks, but the Free Staters have moved most of their cattle. One buck seemed lame, so at the urgent solicitation of several hungry officers, I gave chase to him, but with very faint hopes, as a buck on three legs can go faster than most other animals with four. However, luck was on our side, and a short dash succeeded in wheeling the animal into a wire fence, where he got tangled up and was soon despatched with a small penknife. This may seem a trifling matter, but there were thousands of spectators of the chase, and every man would have given anything for the venison. After one has been campaigning a while the fighting becomes of vastly less importance than the victualling department.

BOERS IN FRONT

It was not supposed that any fight would take place that day, and the vast force spread out, and tramped gaily along until a scout reported that a few Boers were on a kopje right in front of us. All were halted, and the New South Wales Lancers, First Australian Horse, and a troop of the Carbineers were sent out to reconnoitre. The Boers, with their usual cunning, let them get up quite close, then they opened fire with rifles, and with the famous "pom-pom" guns, the Vickers-Maxim, which all troops hold in such detestation. The "pom-pom" shells fell right among a troop of the First Australian Horse, and they withdrew in good order. The Lancers and Carbineers came in for the rifle fire, and one of the latter was killed, and another wounded. The Lancers, as usual, escaped scatheless; their luck is something wonderful. After this cheerful beginning the cavalry were ordered to occupy some small hills on the right of the big sloping hill held by the Boers, and as they galloped up the Boers ran away, but as soon as the cavalry, which included the Australians, had settled snugly in among the rocks of the kopje the Boers started shrapnel on them, bursting their shells overhead with great accuracy, but the bullets with which the shells are filled all went in too far, and failed to kill anybody, though they frightened a good many. The guns came clattering up, and opened fire on the Boer hill, but the Transvaalers stuck stubbornly to their position, and some of them came gaily out into the open to gather in the horses of the dead and wounded Carbineers. This gave our men something to shoot at, and a perfect hail of bullets went whistling over to the venturesome Boers, but they got safely in with their prey.

ATTACKING A BIG HILL

Then an order was given that a troop of Carbineers and two troops of the First Australian Horse should leave their horses and advance up the big hill held by the Boers. This was a very exciting moment. Lieutenants Mackellar and Wilkinson were sent with their troops, and curiously enough the Carbineer officer was Lieutenant Rundle, also an Australian. Our men advanced gaily, working along through the long grass as though they were going to shoot quail. For a great part of their advance they were hidden from the Boers by the swell of the hill above them, and they looked as though they were going to win the fight off their own bat, so to speak. But all of a sudden they came in sight of the Boers at about 800 yards range. The way they dropped down and melted into the grass was astonishing, as at one moment the hillside was alive with men; at the next moment the khaki uniforms had blended with the brown grass, and there wasn't a man to be seen; but the sharp cracking of the rifles told that they were busily at work. All the while the Boer cannons on the far end of the big hill were keeping up an incessant fusillade — now firing at the horses that were huddled in under the shelter of the small hills, now blazing at our guns which were working away in the open, and at last they pushed a gun forward and put a shell among the mule waggons, knocking one mule to ribbons, and setting all the mule drivers plying their whips with shrill cries of "Ahk! Ahk!" which, in mule driver language means, "Put your best leg foremost." They scattered like a covey of partridges, and the next shell only struck a bare and lonesome hillside.

SHRAPNEL FOR THE ENEMY

Meanwhile our boys upon the hill and the Boers were blazing away at each other without doing much damage. Then our men were recalled in order to let the guns have a clear shot at the kopjes, and we simply showered shrapnel on it till suddenly the Boers rose from their hiding places, jumped on their horses, which had been hidden behind a wall, and started to gallop off. We could see all this through the glasses, the men looking like little dolls, and the horses like toy horses. General French ordered a gun on the right to shoot at them. The gunners were slow getting into action, and the General expressed his sentiments very freely. "Shoot, will you, shoot," he cried. "Even if you don't hit anything, shoot at once." At last they sent the first shell whizzing on its way, and it fell right among the retreating Dutch. "That's the style," said the General. "Now go on shooting for 50 rounds, even if there isn't a man to shoot at." This order was not strictly adhered to, but before long the cavalry were ordered to go on along the Boer flank. The remainder of the fight in the front of the Boer position did not concern the Australian contingent. These moved on at a swinging canter round the long line of hills where the Boers were, and they came right away round to the back of the Boers.

AUSTRALIANS EVERYWHERE

As we galloped along we passed a big contingent of Queenslanders waiting for orders by a dry salt pan, and soon after we saw the New Zealanders also holding a position under some hills. The army seemed to be half Australians. As we pushed on we crossed a body of men dashing along at full speed to occupy some hills right close up to the enemy's guns, and lo and behold these also were Australians, Colonel Knight and Captain Antill with their merry men, as full of fight as one could ask, dashing along to make a name for themselves. The two brigades had crossed each other by this time, the Cavalry working away to the right till they quite overlapped the Mounted Infantry, who were going straight on against the Boer position. They seized the hills close to the Boers, and waited there to make a dash. We moved on, and got into a big open plain with a Boer gun on some hills on our left, and a lot of loose unattached Boers roaming about in some kopjes on the right. The gun started to shell us, and sent some shells whizzing over the column; then as we drew out to avoid it the Boers in the hills opened rifle fire, and made us draw in again. We were between the devil and the deep sea for a while, and it was a miracle that only one man was hit — a trooper of the Australian Horse, and he was slightly wounded in the shoulder. Previously a trooper named Parry, from Goulburn, had his leg broken by his horse falling in an ant-bear hole, and he was picked up by an Australian Ambulance under Captain Roth.

THE INEVITABLE WHITE FLAG

We did not charge the gun that was playing on us, but a battery of our guns came toiling round and set to work to silence it, and before long up went the white flag, and a staff officer came down at the gallop to say that the Boers were flying, and that we should advance at once. The English Cavalry were

From every coast, from every clime, they met in proud array,
To go with French to Kimberley to drive the Boers away.

With French to Kimberley, p. 142

If ever they want us to stand the brunt
Of a hard-fought, grim campaign,
We will carry our own flag up to the front
When we go to the wars again.

Our Own Flag, p. 147

simply unable to move, and regiment after regiment sent in to say that they could not possibly pursue — their horses were absolutely tired out. The First Australian Horse and the Lancers were fit to go on, and they galloped about a mile in the gathering darkness, but were recalled, much to Captain Thompson's disgust. The Boers had got too much start. It is marvellous how they get their guns away. The smoke had hardly cleared away from their gun when they hoisted the white flag, and yet they had slipped the gun away over a hill and away to the north before our cavalry could get up. While we were trying our hands at the business at the rear, the infantry had taken on the business of clearing the Boers out of the front position where we began fighting. They marched up under cover of shell-fire, a steady attack, the Buffs and the Essex Regiment taking the lead. They simply swarmed up the hill like a colony of ants, moving up steadily and surely. The infantry have to do such a lot of walking for so very little fighting that no wonder they make the most of their shooting when they get any. The "Footies" or "Toe-eys" as they are called, do fight in grim earnest when they get a chance. The Boers held the trenches till the last moment. They shot till the infantry were within a few yards of them, and then hoisted a white flag, but it was too late for white flag business then, and a desperate bayonet charge by the Welsh cleared the Boers out at the point of the bayonet, and as night fell the last of them fled north. The troops bivouacked out in the veldt, and all hands straggled into camp as best as they could. The ambulances, under Major Fiaschi, were out all night getting in wounded, and they got load after load. We lost 80 killed and 300 wounded, and our men buried over 120 Boers. They lay about the trenches, grimy figures stiff in death, their saddles bloodstained and torn by bullets lying round them. It was a terrible sight. Gordon wrote, "He lay as only dead men lie," and there is no mistaking the stiff uncouth posture of the dead man. The horrors of war are not brought home to one till one sees the dead lying like bundles of old clothes in the trenches in the grey dawn. This was one of the most serious engagements in the war, but not so far as Australians were concerned. It was called Driefontein, which means three fountains.

CAPTURE OF A LEGISLATOR

After this we moved on a long march of about 25 miles to Bloemfontein, and this was very exciting. As we drew near Bloemfontein, the capital of the Free State, excitement ran high. Would they fight? Would we walk in *à la* Kimberley? Out on the veldt we saw a Cape cart drawn by a couple of slashing horses making the best of its way to the town, and Lieutenant James Osborne (late of the First Australian Horse, but now of the 16th Lancers and on General French's staff) was the first man to intercept the fugitive. The occupier of the cart turned out to be a Mr Palmer, a member of the Free State Legislature. He was very disconcerted at being captured in such a summary fashion. He was given an ultimatum, signed by Lord Roberts, calling on the town to surrender within 24 hours or the town would be bombarded. He sold a lot of cattle to the army en route, and went on his way rejoicing, with the ultimatum in his pocket. When we came over we expected, on getting into the Free State, to be able to help ourselves to anything we fancied, but one Free State burgher (only just returned from fighting against us) was actually paid £5000 for 500 head of cattle taken for the use of the army. It looks like encouraging them to go to war again.

POM-POMS

We marched on after sending this envoy ahead, and it was supposed that no resistance would be offered by the Bloemfontein people, but just as our New South Wales Lancer patrol, which was right in the front, got close to a big range of hills the rattle of musketry from the hills told us that Brother Boer did not mean to give up his capital of the Free State without a struggle. The Lancers were nicely caught, as they were within about 400 yards, and bullets came whistling in all directions; and Sergeant Gould, who was in charge of the patrol, had to bring his men out as best he could. They all got away safely to the shelter of a hill, and just as they got to the hill a horse was shot dead at about 2000 yards range. It was strange that a horse should be killed at this range after all the patrol being absolutely missed at 400 yards. Major Allenby, of the Inniskillings, is in charge of the Lancer squadron since Major Lee is Provost Marshal, and he was much amused at the cool way in which the men treated the risk they had run. The whole army camped for the night, and just as it got dark there was a flicker of light on a hill like a flashlight signal working, and soon we heard the well-known "pom, pom, pom" of the Vickers-Maxim, and the shells came bursting in little lines of flame across the veldt close to our massed troops. This set the column uneasy, and they moved away at the best pace till out of range.

PEPPERING THE HILLS

All hands slept out that night holding their horses, and lying with their heads pillowed in their arms, and at last the morning of the 13th dawned. A few shots were fired at daylight by the Boers, but before long we saw them leaving their hills and rushing away north. General French was in charge of the attack, and he sent shell after shell after them, but shell fire at long range is not very effective. We were up on a big flat hill, and could see the town of Bloemfontein spread out below us, a big solid stone-built town with church spires and factory chimneys rising out of a bower of green trees. Not a sign of life came from the town, and General French ordered the cannon to keep on shelling the hills all round the town, and all the time he kept on pushing his troops nearer and nearer. From the hills the town looked the most peaceful place in the world, and it seemed only necessary to ride in a leisurely way over the beautiful green flat that led to the town, and the capture of Bloemfontein would be complete. But from the hills around the west side of the town there still came the occasional snarl, or rather bark, of the "pom pom" gun, showing that the Boers were still on the alert. The General rode about on the top of the hill, sending orders here, there, and everywhere. "Close in", "Occupy such and such a kopje", "Push on", until a regular half-circle of troops was drawn round the town on the south and west, while by the roads leaving the town north and east we could see the Boer waggons moving off at a great pace, and at last their guns, drawn by horses, dashed across a small open place among the hills, and were shelled at, but missed.

FIRST INTO BLOEMFONTEIN

In another five seconds two other correspondents and myself were racing for the honour of being first into Bloemfontein. There was still a risk that the Boers had not all gone, but we chanced that, and galloped along at a great pace over the open veldt. As we drew near the town my Australian-bred colt, by Myles-na-Coppaleen, proved himself much better than the other two horses, and we dashed into the town in a string, riding over a lot of rugs and gear of various sorts that the Boers had dropped. Once in the town we slowed to a walk, and were warmly welcomed by the townsfolk, who all shook hands with us, and hoorayed as though they liked having their town captured. The fact is that the Boer — the man we are fighting — is not a townsman at all. In these towns the names of the shops and the trades are all in English — Clothing Hall, Grocery Emporium, and so forth, and the townsfolk of Bloemfontein are 80 per cent English — at any rate they are nearly 100 per cent English tonight, as the Dutch element has run away. Riding through the town, all sorts of people came up with all sorts of questions; but most of them wanted to know when they could see Lord Roberts. We arrived at the Bloemfontein Club with a long string of excited and gesticulating followers, and here we were made welcome in great style, and introduced to Mr Fraser (the Mayor), the town clerk, and various other dignitaries, and after some refreshments we agreed to guide them out to surrender the town to Lord Roberts.

A QUAINT PROCESSION

It was a quaint procession — we three sunburnt, travel-stained, unshaven knights of the pen, on our weary horses, jogging along in front of two Cape carts, which contained the grave and reverend seigneurs of the town. Mr Fraser was the man that struck us most; he is a square-built, grey-bearded man of Scotch type. He is the man who was against the war, and contested the Presidency with Steyn. He told us that Steyn had only just left the town, and that he had driven so fast to get away that the horses had nearly died. As we got near the English lines a staff officer came down and took over our convoy from us, and said to them, "Field-Marshal Lord Roberts is on this hill, and will be pleased to see you." The grave and reverend seigneurs had to toil up a remarkably steep rocky hill, but at the top they were received with great state by the little wiry hard-faced man who is at present the greatest figure in the English Union. The Mayor spoke first. He took off his hat and addressing Lord Roberts said, "We have come, sir, to hand over the town to you. We ask protection for life and property." The others all followed, each surrendering his particular trust — the Town Hall, the Consular papers, and so on. The keys of the public buildings were handed over, and then Lord Roberts said, "I am very pleased to see you. I guarantee to protect both life and property." He is a fine-featured old man, with an essentially combative look on his face; he has the steel-grey eyes of a born fighter. His staff and General French's staff gathered round the little knot of civilians, and there, on the top of the big hill overlooking the town, the conquest of the capital of the Free State was concluded.

LORD ROBERT'S ENTRY INTO THE TOWN

Lord Roberts arranged to enter the town in state. The troops were camped outside the town and a long procession was formed with the Field-Marshal in the lead, then his staff, then the intelligence department, whoever they are, then the foreign attaches — a German, an American, a Japanese, a Spaniard, and a Russian — and then we three war correspondents, with a tail of about a thousand armed men stringing after us. As we got to the town the Kaffirs had started to loot a hospital or some public building, and were carrying away beds and bedding with great vigour. A lot of English Lancers were let loose among them, and the beds were pretty well all recaptured. The townsfolk lined the streets and cheered themselves hoarse, but half of them would have cheered either side. We rode round to the Presidency, and here the English flag was hoisted with great formality, and the onlookers sang "God Save the Queen" with great vigour. Then they struck up "Tommy Atkins", and the crowd dispersed. All provisions are plentiful; clothes are cheap. The Boers have left the town absolutely uninjured, though it is as English as any town in Australia. The town is absolutely quiet, and this hotel is exactly like a good sort of country hotel in a town, say, as large as Goulburn. The people here say the Boers will fight on about Croonstad. I will close this letter now, and may follow it up from here as soon as the line is repaired down south.

from the *Boer War Dispatches*

The Boers in Flight

General French in Pursuit — The Ambulance in the Enemy's
Camp — "How Long will the War Last?" — The Boers' Answer
— The Commandeered Pony — "Well Done, New South
Wales"

BLOEMFONTEIN, May 2

Next day we started early to get round behind the Boers, who were fighting Rundle. They were holding a great big range of hills, and behind them was a lovely valley — the headwaters of the Modder River. We marched up this valley through fields of maize, sorghum, Kaffir corn, melons, and pumpkins, all growing splendidly. This is a very high plateau hereabouts, and the land is very fertile, and the water supply certain. The climate is very like Orange, New South Wales, but like Orange at its very best. We got bread, butter, horse forage, vegetables, and all supplies at the farmhouses. Every farm had a storehouse filled with grain and horse feed.

As we approached De Wetsdorp, we found that the Boers had run in the night from the hills where they had been, and Rundle came over the hills into the town just as we marched up from the back. The two Generals met and rode into the town together. This is a quaint little place, where in ordinary times a man might live to be a hundred for all there would be in the way of novelty or excitement to wear him out. The folk said that the Boers had just run away — 6000 of them — and that if we would follow after them we could catch them. It was also ascertained that the Boers at Wepener had joined the fugitives, and that Brabant was following them up, and that they were all making for Thaba'nchu.

It didn't take General French long to make up his mind. He decided to go after them, although our supplies had run out, and orders were given that the troops should be allowed to feed themselves during the march and take what they wanted from the houses. Hitherto all taking of poultry was unauthorised. It was an important matter to get supplies at once, as we understood we were to follow Pole-Carew's division on the march to Thaba'nchu, and he had a lot of Highlanders with him, and there is a poor prospect of getting anything in the wake of a Highland regiment. Therefore when the order was given that we could feed ourselves I was standing by a kraal full of small pigs, and I jumped in over the wall on one side just as a wave of Tommies surged over the opposite wall, and I got a fine fat pig round the waist just in time to wrestle him clear of the Tommies and march him off to the waggon. On the way there a nigger on horseback came along galloping after a wounded partridge, and as the bird flew straight at me I caught him and put him in the waggon also, so we made a good start. But before long we found that Pole-Carew was to wait and we were to go first as usual, so all the way to Thaba'nchu we lived on the fat of the land. We had turkeys, ducks, geese and pumpkins, and the march was more like a picnic than a war.

Strategically our movements resembled a pig hunt by a lot of Tommies, the Boer army representing the pig. The country was alive with our troops, who were trying to catch the Boers and bring them to a stand or get their waggons, and every effort was made to get on their tracks. It was thought that if we could only find them we would bring them to grief. All scouts were interrogated as to the last news of the Boers, and all agreed that they were ahead of us going to Thaba'nchu. We pushed on, enjoying the most lovely weather and seeing no enemy for two days, when we came to Thaba'nchu itself, a town that was once the greatest Kaffir settlement in the country. Even now there are thousands there. The town is nestled in among a huge chain of hills, and these are only passable through narrow "poorts" or passes.

REARGUARD OF THE BOERS

The General left the troops behind and rode into the town, and just as we came into the "poort" we heard the crack-crack of the Mausers on the hill above our heads, and knew that at last we had come on the rearguard of the Boers. They were hiding in the hills and sniping our men who passed by. We found General Hamilton in the town, and he had among his troops a couple of Australian ambulances under Lieutenant Horsfall, and a company of New South Wales Mounted Infantry under Captain Holmes. Also the New Zealanders were with him, so that there was quite a gathering of old friends.

Our brigade did not come into the town that night, but camped outside it, and at grey dawn we moved off to the east to get behind the big hills and see if we could find the Boer waggons. On our march we had been joined by the two Sydney consulting surgeons — MacCormick and Scot-Skirving. These two gentlemen, with Sergeant Dart and myself, went forward after the troops, leaving the ambulances some distance behind. We heard some shelling, and were told that there had been a few Boers behind a big kopje, but that they had run, and that there was no doubt that the Boers had got away altogether, either east to Ladybrand or north to Karee, and we would see no more of them. We thought it was bad luck after chasing them so far.

They had managed to shoot a trooper of the 17th Lancers as they fled, and we went down to see him, and found him in a bad way. The bulk of the force was halted, but two troops were sent on to reconnoitre. We followed them a little way, and then dismounted and lay under a haystack and agreed what a dull business war was. All the troops had gone out of sight. It was a heavenly afternoon, and the most absolute silence reigned, when all of a sudden, looking away across the plain, we saw the two troops that had been reconnoitring coming back at the gallop as hard as ever their horses could travel, while behind them were little dots on the plain that momentarily grew larger and larger, and we knew that these were the missing Boers in hot pursuit of our men. We could hear faint rifle shots, and saw a bullet or two kick up the dust beside the galloping men.

THE BOERS AT WORK

As they advanced towards us, it was curious to notice that while the English all rode straight the Boers seemed to cross each other's track every now and again. No doubt the trained troop horses kept their direction, while the Boers' ponies picked the best ground, but the effect was very curious; the Boers seemed to be riding wildly, in all directions at once, and the whole show, coming along in absolute silence except for the faint rifle fire, looked like a cinematograph more than the reality. A bullet or two coming on ahead of them convinced us that it was time to make a move, so we caught our horses and cantered on ahead, looking over our shoulders as we went. It was a most exciting thing to watch. A horse went down, shot dead, and the man on him, the moment he touched the ground, threw his head back and started to run as hard as ever his legs would carry him. A mate stopped and took him up behind him; another dismounted man, running along, threw up his hands, pitched forward, and fell headlong. Horse after horse went down, but the men caught hold of their comrades' stirrups and came along. They drew near the main body, which had with it two 12-pounder guns and a Maxim, and as we got near this Dart and I, being wise, drew out on the flank, as we knew the Boers would not waste powder on a single man, but the two surgeons, fearing that they would be cut off, joined in with the mass of troops, and had the satisfaction of hearing a bullet or two whistle over them.

The Boers were now quite close, that is to say, quite close for men who carry a rifle that throws 2500 yards, and we began to feel uncomfortable but at last our Maxims and 12-pounders got to work, and the Boers halted, wheeled, and dashed behind a big kopje. Soon we saw them bringing up a long-range gun behind the shelter of this kopje, and as this gun could out-range ours by a mile or two it was not much good arguing with it. The first shell went right over our guns, and burst near the ambulances and transport waggons at the back, causing no end of a scatter.

Our guns and troops were then retired rapidly, and we were retiring rapidly too when we met one of our ambulances on its way down to pick up the wounded 17th Lancer, who had been shot by the Boers earlier in the day. Sergeant Bond was leading the way, and Surgeon-Captain Marshall was in charge of the party. I said, "You can't go down there now. The Boers are there. I know where the man is, but the Boers have got him." The sergeant was quite excited, and he said he would go down at any cost, so in the long run we four, viz., Drs MacCormick, Scot-Skirving, Dart, and myself joined them, and went down to the laager after this wounded man. The ambulance drivers were Willey and Easby, two men "trained in Battery A", while Corporal Donnellan, the crack singer of the A.M.C., was in charge of the waggon under Captain Marshall's directions.

It was just falling dusk as we faced slowly down the hill. The Boers came past us in droves, all galloping on their wiry little ponies to reach the top of the hill, and get a shot at our retreating troops. They took no more notice of us than if we were part and parcel of the cornfield we were driving through. From the foot of the kopje in front they got two black-powder guns at work, and the shells whizzed over us and burst among our troops far away. The two sergeants rode on ahead with Captain Marshall. The two consulting surgeons came next, probably thinking what a frightful gap there would be in Sydney medical circles if the Boers decided to make them prisoners. The battery drivers and Donnellan, in the waggon, exchanged jokes as the shells went over — it takes a lot to bustle a battery driver — and I slunk in the rear, having just awakened to the fact that I was riding a pony which I had that day taken from a deserted Boer farm, and I thought it was quite likely I would meet the owner in the laager. It was too late to go back then, so I borrowed a Red Cross badge from Easby to signify that I was one of the ambulance party, and on we went.

"HERE YOU ARE — THIS WAY"

For all the notice the Boers took of us, we might have driven that ambulance right through the laager and out the other side, but every time they let off their black-powder gun she made such a whirl of smoke, and such a nasty noise, that we thought infallibly sooner or later a shell would come crashing into us. The Boers behind us had now dismounted, and were shooting away at our troops, who by this time were some miles away from us. When we got close up to where the gun was working, Dart and Dr Scot-Skirving went over to the Boers there, and met the Boer general. They were told they might go and get any wounded men, and we were directed to a farmhouse. As we drove up to the farmhouse we saw a crowd of Boers round it, and several sharp authoritative voices called out in English, "Here you are! This way!" We drove up, halted the ambulance, got off the horses, and were at last in the ranks of the enemy.

We saw a crowd of rough, dirty, bearded men, just like a lot of shearers or farm hands, as no doubt most of them were. Each man was leading a pony and carrying a rifle. The rifle was the only thing neat and workmanlike about them. Their clothes were poor, ready-made slops, their hats every kind of battered old felt, their saddles wretched things worn out of shape; no two men were dressed alike; they were all ages, all sizes, and all classes; all were dirty, with rough unshaven faces, but we did not take much notice of that, as campaigning is not clean work, and we ourselves had not had our clothes off for a week, and would not have taken a prize for neatness of turnout. Their horses were splendid, wiry, half Arab, half Basuto animals, about 14.2 in height; they had any amount of shape, strength and quality. The brutes we had been buying or commandeering at the farms were simply the refuse that the Boers would not take. The Boers came stringing up to the farm, and each went into the barn, came out with a bundle of horse forage under his arm, and walked away leading his pony. Each had a blanket on his saddle. Some had a white blanket, some blue, some red, some gaudy-coloured rugs. The guns were still working, and away up on the hill the riflemen still fired, but these men lounged about talking to each other in guttural Dutch, apparently quite at their leisure.

THE STRETCHER BEARERS

Behind the barn with a group of Boers round him, we found the wounded man, and behind him, with solemn faces, and looking ridiculously wooden and machine-like in that motley crew, were four Tommies. They rolled their eyes towards us appealingly as the Boer leader came up. He was a young man, thin and slight, with a straggling sandy beard, and he wore a "hard-hitter" hat, a suit of dirty grey tweed, and a huge belt of cartridges buckled in a slovenly way round his waist. He looked like an assistant in a second-hand clothes shop out for a day's shooting. He spoke quite good English, and opened the conversation by asking for our leader. We pushed Captain Marshall forward. "You can take the wounded man," said the Boer. "But these others, no!" "These others" looked remarkably sick but said nothing. "What are they," said Captain Marshall, "are they prisoners?"

"Please, sir, we're the stretcher bearers, sir," said the four Tommies in chorus.

It must be explained that each regiment has its own doctor, who has four men detailed to assist him, and to be ready to carry the wounded. These men do not carry arms, and they wear a red cross, and are supposed to be exempt from capture. It seemed that these four men had been carrying, or preparing to carry, the wounded man along when the Boers swooped down on them.

"You are not going to arrest stretcher bearers, surely?" said Captain Marshall. The gentleman in the pot hat and the cartridge belt got quite excited. He was evidently a bit of a bush lawyer, and liked to hear himself speak. "They are not ambulance men," he said. "Where are their ambulance certificates? They have none."

This made me feel dismal, as I, of course, had no ambulance certificate, and it looked as if all without them were booked for Pretoria. Also, the matter of that horse was weighing on my mind. Each Boer that went past seemed to my excited imagination to be looking at him with an eye of recognition.

"We don't carry ambulance certificates either," said Captain Marshall, and at this I felt more comfortable. "But look here, my man," said the Boer leader (he was a field cornet), "it's no use to talk. By the Geneva convention all non-combatants must keep three miles away from the fighting line. Now, I myself was fired on when standing by these men. A bullet went by my head. They are within the fighting line, and are liable to be made prisoners." At this Dr Scot-Skirving took a hand, and made a brilliant effort to argue the field cornet into letting the men go. Like the man in the *Bab Ballads*, he argued up, he argued down, he likewise argued round about him. He rather cornered the field cornet, who fell back on his Geneva convention, a document with which none of us had any acquaintance. At last he said that he would refer the matter of the four stretcher bearers to the General, and they would be decided upon in the morning. Meanwhile, we could take our wounded man, but must not go to look for any more wounded. We must go back to our own lines at once. If there were any more wounded the Boers would find them and let us know in the morning.

While the talk was going on I had a look into the farmhouse. About a dozen large hairy Boers were sitting round the room smoking silently. A little girl was nursing a baby in a corner. A teapot and cups were on the table. It reminded me of the pictures of the "Cotter's Saturday Night" in Burns's poems. One particularly big man was seated by the fire half asleep in his chair, and the rest were absolutely silent, all evidently tired and sleepy. The men outside the farm were leaning on their rifles talking among themselves in Dutch. We asked them a few questions, but got very little out of them, and then we picked up the wounded man, put him in the ambulance, and started off, glad to be so well out of it.

We hadn't gone a quarter of a mile when a messenger came after us to know why we had not gone to look for the wounded on the veldt.

We said that the General had forbidden it.

He said yes, that was right enough, but that another general (evidently a superior person) had ordered that we should go. They seemed to have nearly as many generals as we had, but we wheeled the ambulance round and went back and two Boers came with us as guides. They said they knew where there was a wounded man, and we lumbered along after them; their neat, active ponies ambling at a great pace.

"MY NAME IS STEYN"

It was now almost dark, and the stars were coming out, so I had little fear of the pony being recognised. I had taken him from the farm of a man named Steyn, and the nigger at the farm had said that his master was away in the commando; but I thought it would be very bad luck if I struck Steyn out of all the men in the commando, so I went alongside the nearest Boer and had a talk to him. I asked him whether he was a Free Stater or a Transvaaler, and he said he was a Free Stater. I got him to lend me his carbine, and I showed him how to carry it as the Australian buffalo shooters carry it, i.e., under the thigh pressed against the saddle. He tried the method and approved of it. Then I said, "You mustn't shoot me next time we meet, because I have shown you that." He said, "I will not shoot any more today, anyhow; I am very tired." I said "What is your name?" He said, "My name is Steyn." I pulled the pony back to the rear of the procession and remained there till he disappeared. My luck was evidently bad that day.

One of the Boers was quite a youngster, only 15 years of age. A talkative youngster, chattering away volubly. He took himself very seriously, as boys of that age are apt to do. We asked him how long the Boers would go on with the war. He raised his hand and struck an attitude.

"Till the last Afrikander is dead," he said, "If there is only he and I left," he went on — touching the man next to him — "we will fight till we are both killed. Then you will have the land. Till then, no!"

He was evidently a youngster of some position in life, and the two men with him were apparently his followers in some way — his farm hands, probably. They seemed to be half-amused at, and half-proud of, his tall talk. "I am a wonderful fellow," he said. "I cannot miss a man up to 800 yards. The Boers can all shoot well. The English cannot shoot; they are brave enough, but they cannot shoot. Ah, this man shooting, it is difficult! Buck shooting is easy; but the buck does not fire back. I do not want to be wounded, to be in the ambulance. I would sooner be killed. It was worse to fight the Kaffirs than you English," he said. "If you were wounded then, there was no ambulance, no. They came with the spear and cut you to pieces. My father told me!"

"WE MUST FIND THE WOUNDED"

We said we hoped he wouldn't get wounded, and indeed one could not help liking the youngster, he was such an outspoken young swashbuckler. He was riding a splendid grey horse, of which he was very proud. "This is a splendid horse," he said, "I took him from one of Brabant's troopers. I have ridden him today already eight hours, and he is not tired. I have been everywhere. I will sleep out tonight on the veldt. We all sleep out on the veldt when we camp. I am never cold at night; but we must find this wounded man. It is terrible to be wounded on the veldt these nights. The cold — ah, a man would die!"

While he was talking, we had drifted on past the camp, by the little fires where the Boers were lying, and we came away up the flat where the pursuit had been; we found the place where the man had fallen, and, much to our disgust, we found a lot of crumbs of bread and an empty box of beef lozenges. Now, a badly wounded man doesn't eat bread and beef lozenges, so we guessed that there was not much the matter with him, and anyhow he had disappeared, so after a long hunt we turned back. The boy accompanied us back to the farm, and in the firelight I had a good look at him; a slight, active, excitable youngster, very different from the phlegmatic Dutch type. He said his name was Verry, a French name, and indeed there is a large strain of Huguenot blood in these people. Cellier, Du Poit, Du Plessis are all Boer names, and are, of course, of French origin.

The young Afrikander is very like the young Australian — slight, fibrous, and of nervous temperament; running to length of limb rather than breadth of chest. He said, "I hope we meet again, but I do not want to be a prisoner at Cape Town and eat fish. I have a brother who was taken prisoner with Cronje. He is at Cape Town and eats fish. If they give me a hook and line I will catch all the fish."

It must be explained that this joke about eating fish is the one Boer joke (if it is a joke at all). When we took out the elders of Bloemfontein to sur-render the town to Lord Roberts, one of them said that he had sent a lot of sick men away before the English came, because they were afraid the English would take them, and they didn't like eating fish. All the other burghers laughed, and Lord Roberts didn't know it was a joke, so he didn't laugh. This youngster said that they had better fighting generals than Cronje. One of their crack generals is Olivier, and a young Olivier came out of this farm to look at us. He was another slight, wiry youngster; someone made a remark about Pretoria and he said, "Yes, it is not far to Pretoria — to march there. But it is a long way to fight there!"

This epigram closed the conversation, as we thought. It was now pitch dark. We did not know which way our troops had gone, and we debated among ourselves the advisability of camping where we were, and going home in the morning after another search for wounded. Things were going so swim-mingly that we thought it would be rather a fine thing to camp in the Boer lines all night. Young Olivier apparently thought we had decided about it, and sent some message to the field cornet with the result that a messenger with an unmistakable Irish brogue came down to say that we were to camp near the kraal; that we could have the captured stretcher bearers for company, that guards would be put round us, and that, in the morning, there would be further orders concerning us!

This put things in a new light altogether. It was all very fine to talk of stopping voluntarily in their lines, but when they talked of putting guards over us it became a different matter. With one accord we raised a chorus, "But we want to go home!" "You have no right to keep us!" and so on.

Now, I firmly believe that if it hadn't been for that Irishman they would have kept us all night, and possibly for good, because the English have more than once detained their ambulances when it appeared politic to do so. But our Irish friend was obviously anxious to see us off the premises. He didn't want to be recognised in the daylight, so he said he would go to the field cornet and get further orders. He came back soon, saying that we could go if we liked, and the drivers didn't waste much time in getting under way. A guide came to see us past their pickets. He gave no countersign, but, as he approached the pickets, we lit three matches, and they let us through without a word. Then he said goodnight and turned back and we were out on the open veldt, with four tired horses dragging a heavy ambulance over ploughed ground, with a dying man in the ambulance, without the faintest idea where our troops were, and with nothing but the clothes we stood up in to keep the cold out.

THE WHITE FLAG

We travelled the ambulance for a couple of hours, not being very particular which way we went so long as we went away from the Boers, and at midnight we came to a farmhouse at which I knocked, and the inhabitant opened the door about an inch, and poked out a white flag on a stick so suddenly that he nearly poked it down my throat. He was a rail sitter, according to himself, a farmer who didn't believe in the war, but he was afraid to take us in for fear the Boers would have revenge on him. However, there were six of us, so we persuaded him to get up and to make a fire, and his wife made us coffee and gave us bread and milk, and we had quite a jovial evening. Dr MacCormick and I slept in the stable on some oat sacks and hay, which the horses ate from under us while we slept.

But the things we saw and did at the farmhouse and our subsequent adventures at Thaba'nchu must keep till another letter. I will merely mention here that there was a sharp fight next day, in which our company of Mounted Infantry, under Captain Holmes, with Lieutenants Dove and Harriott, behaved exceedingly well. They were stuck on an outlying kopje, within easy range of rifle fire and pom-pom fire from the Boers, and there they stayed for a day and a half without any food, and they held the position and kept the Boers off it till they were withdrawn. They lost many horses, and had some few men wounded.

"WELL DONE, HOLMES"

I happened to be talking to Captain Holmes when Colonel De Lisle, the officer in command, came up. He said, "Well done, Holmes. Well done, you New South Wales men. I never saw a more stubborn defence." This was high praise for a commander to give, as the British Army is very sparing in compliments, and we of the old colony held our heads a little higher as he rode away. Then I turned my horse's head and set out on my 38-mile ride to Bloemfontein, leaving French's troops to hunt the Boers round and round those big hills; for after all our pursuit, when we did catch them we could not do much with them. They got their guns up to the top of the mountain and shelled French's headquarters. They stuck to their cover among the stones, and one day when the Highlanders were on one peak and the Boers on another a Boer walked out in the open with his hands in his pockets. All the crack shots had a go at him at about 2000 yards range, and though they made him duck his head once they couldn't make him take his hands out of his pockets. It was not likely that anything decisive would be done at Thaba'nchu, so I have come back to Bloemfontein to find it a deserted city.

The troops have gone on; the tents are here, but they are all empty; the waiters at the club are sitting on the bar counter yarning instead of having to serve rows of customers four deep; a few farmers are playing billiards in the billiard room. It is reported in town that we have taken Brandfort, and that the Victorians were engaged and suffered severely; so as soon as my horses are fit to travel I must follow on, and my next letter may be from Johannesburg or from Pretoria itself. The army has moved bodily as it always moves, and we are glad, because the sooner it gets its business over the sooner we will be back in Australia.

from the *Boer War Dispatches*

With French to Kimberley

The Boers were down on Kimberley with siege and Maxim gun;
The Boers were down on Kimberley, their numbers ten to one!
Faint were the hopes the British had to make the struggle good,
Defenceless in an open plain the Diamond City stood.
They built them forts from bags of sand, they fought from roof and wall,
They flashed a message to the south, "Help! or the town must fall!"
And down our ranks the order ran to march at dawn of day,
For French was off to Kimberley to drive the Boers away.

He made no march along the line; he made no front attack
Upon those Magersfontein heights that drove the Scotchmen back;
But eastward over pathless plains by open veldt and vley,
Across the front of Cronje's force his troopers held their way.
The springbuck, feeding on the flats where Modder River runs,
Were startled by his horses' hoofs, the rumble of his guns.
The Dutchman's spies that watched his march from every rocky wall
Rode back in haste: "He marches east! He threatens Jacobsdal!"
Then north he wheeled as wheels the hawk and showed to their dismay,
That French was off to Kimberley to drive the Boers away.

His column was five thousand strong — all mounted men — and guns:
There met, beneath the world-wide flag, the world-wide Empire's sons;
They came to prove to all the earth that kinship conquers space,
And those who fight the British Isles must fight the British race!
From far New Zealand's flax and fern, from cold Canadian snows,
From Queensland plains, where hot as fire the summer sunshine glows;
And in the front the Lancers rode that New South Wales had sent:
With easy stride across the plain their long, lean Walers went.
Unknown, untried, those squadrons were, but proudly out they drew
Beside the English regiments that fought at Waterloo.
From every coast, from every clime, they met in proud array,
To go with French to Kimberley to drive the Boers away.

He crossed the Reit and fought his way towards the Modder bank.
The foemen closed behind his march, and hung upon the flank.
The long, dry grass was all ablaze, and fierce the veldt fire runs;
He fought them through a wall of flame that blazed around the guns!
Then limbered up and drove at speed, though horses fell and died;
We might not halt for man nor beast on that wild, daring ride.
Black with the smoke and parched with thirst, we pressed the livelong day
Our headlong march to Kimberley to drive the Boers away.

We reached the drift at fall of night, and camped across the ford.
Next day from all the hills around the Dutchman's cannons roared.
A narrow pass between the hills, with guns on either side;
The boldest man might well turn pale before that pass he tried,
For if the first attack should fail then every hope was gone:
But French looked once, and only once, and then he said, "Push on!"
The gunners plied their guns amain; the hail of shrapnel flew;
With rifle fire and lancer charge their squadrons back we threw;
And through the pass between the hills we swept in furious fray,
And French was through to Kimberley to drive the Boers away.

Ay, French was through to Kimberley! And ere the day was done
We saw the Diamond City stand, lit by the evening sun:
Above the town the heliograph hung like an eye of flame:
Around the town the foemen camped — they knew not that we came;
But soon they saw us, rank on rank; they heard our squadrons' tread;
In panic fear they left their tents, in hopeless rout they fled;
And French rode into Kimberley; the people cheered amain,
The women came with tear-stained eyes to touch his bridle rein,
The starving children lined the streets to raise a feeble cheer,
The bells rang out a joyous peal to say "Relief is here!"
Ay! we that saw that stirring march are proud that we can say
We went with French to Kimberley to drive the Boers away.

A General Inspection

"When's the General's inspection?" inquired the cook, uneasily, of the Orderly Room Sergeant. The Sergeant, being Scotch, and in daily converse with "The Heads", was always supposed to know everything about everybody in the military world.

"What are you worrying about?" he said.

"You never know what a General'll want," the cook explained. "One's all for drill, another for shootin'; and all that. One come one day, and it seems his dream was to have every officer know the men's names and all about 'em. Our captain had been put fly to this, so he sez to us, just before the General came round, 'Whatever name I give you men today, see you answer to it', he says. So the General come along the line, lookin' at our boots and feelin' our toonics between his finger and thumb, because some of 'em were different issue to the others; and all of a sudden he points to me, and he sez, 'What's that man's name?', he sez. An', of course, our Captain knew my name all right; but bein' ast sudden that way, he got rattled and outs with the first name he can think of. 'His name's McFarland,' he says. Well, there was a McFarland about ten paces further down the line; and just as the General comes opposite to him, he halts and snaps out, 'Trooper McFarland, two paces to the front, march!' He wanted to see if our Captain had give me the right name or not. So o' course, this real McFarland, he steps out, and I steps out, too. And the General lamps us a bit, and he says, 'What's this?' he says. 'Is there two McFarland's, are you brothers?' he says. So I says 'Yes, sir', and the other real McFarland he says, 'No, sir', both together, just like that: and, of course, the General went off a treat. So you see, Scotty, you want to know what this one will ask?"

The Orderly Sergeant was quite in the dark as to what form the General's questions were likely to take, so he side-stepped the problem.

"Nobody keers whit happens tae a kuk," he said.

"Oh! don't they!" said the cook. "That's all you know. I bet you the General'll ask me more questions than any man in the Regiment."

All this Scotty pondered till you could almost hear his brain working; and then he put forward a valuable suggestion.

"He'll go tae the Light Horrse lines before he comes here," he said. "You step over to yon Light Horrse kuk-house, and find out what he asks them, an' ye'll be a' richt!"

It was a quarter of a mile to the Light Horse cook-house; and a half mile walk on a hot day over loose desert sand did not appeal to our cook, who is a credit to his own cooking: but he saw nothing else for it, so he set off doggedly to plod over the sand in the blazing heat and disappeared among the Light Horse tents. Soon we saw the cavalcade of the inspecting General moving slowly up the Light Horse lines, and with our mental vision, we could

For the "ringers" have cast the machines aside
And answered the call for men.

Australia Today 1916, p. 148

The man who used to "hump his drum",
On far-out Queensland runs,
Is fighting side by side with some
Tasmanian farmer's sons.

"We're All Australians Now", p. 150

see, and with the ear of imagination we could hear, the General pointing with his cane and asking why the tent flaps were not rolled evenly, and why there were so many Egyptian beds in the tents.

There came a long halt before the Light Horse cook-house: and it is a singular fact that Generals often show great interest in the doings of cooks. One has been known, after shaking everybody from the C.O. to the Company Sergeant Major to their foundations, to speak quite pleasantly with the cooks, and ask them what they did for a living before the war. Possibly the reason for this is, that an army travels on its stomach, and the cook is really a very important man. "No cook, no company" would be a very good military maxim to be elaborated in lectures at Duntroon and elsewhere.

At last the General moved away from the Light Horse cook-house, and soon afterwards we could see our own cook in the distance ploughing his way back through the sand. When he arrived he was sweating profusely, but wore a contented look. The Orderly Room Sergeant had made a job for himself to take some papers to the Quartermaster's, so as to escape for a while from the state of high nervous tension that prevails in orderly room when a general inspection is on. He hailed the cook as he passed.

"Find oot onything?" he said.

"I think so," said the cook. "I went to both cook-houses after the Head had been there; and he ast each of 'em whether they gave the men roast meat or only stoos. He roared one of 'em up a treat for not having an oven to roast meat in. Roast meat!"

By this time the General rode up, with his A.D.C., and the local Commandant the regulation distance behind him. He noted whether the Officers' Mess room was in good order, and whether the mess orderly was tidy. For it is by details that military shows are judged: and incident to this it may be mentioned that one of the greatest station inspectors in Australia once said that he always judged a station manager by his gates. If the gates were in good order, then everything else was likely to be in good order: by their gates ye shall know them! But to return to the inspection.

The General, having immediately awarded full points for neatness of turn-out to the officers' mess, and for speed, style and action to the mess orderly, set off round the camp. At the first squadron, the squadron leader rode up and saluted and fell in beside the General to receive whatever of praise or blame might be coming his way. Now, the squadron leader had put in a couple of anxious hours going about his lines, seeing that the white stones round the camp were nicely whitewashed, all dunnage and litter out of the road, everybody dressed correctly, and so on. But he had made his inspection on foot, and, not being able to see to the roofs of the sheds, had missed the fact that all the natives employed in the lines had stacked their *gallabiehs* on the roof of one of the sheds. The General's eagle eye fell on this: "What have you got up on that roof," he said, "an old clothes store?" Then he found a fire bucket empty and volunteered the remark, that fire buckets without water in them would not be of much use in case of a conflagration. "You can't put out fires with 'eye-wash', you know," he said, pointing to the rows of beautifully whitewashed stones on which such hopes had been built. In fact, things were going badly all along the line, and it was felt that it rested with the cookhouse to redeem the day. Had not all the cook-house staff once been awarded a prize of two pounds for the best and cleanest cook-house in camp? All was not yet lost!

The General rode up to the cook-house and the cook came out, saluted, and stood to attention. The General asked the usual questions as to how long the cook had been at the job and whether he was a cook in civil life, to which latter question he received the reply that the cook, in private life, was a revolving window shutter manufacturer! Not being able to carry the conversation further in that line, the General turned to the cook-house.

"Very good," he said. "No flies. Sink in good order. Brick floor. Very clean. What did the men have for breakfast this morning?"

"Porridge and bacon, Sir; and most of 'em buys a few eggs, and I fry 'em."

"Very good. And what did they have for dinner?"

Now the men had had stew for dinner, but the cook wasn't going to say so. He had not walked half a mile in the heat and sand for nothing.

"They had roast meat and baked potatoes and puddin'," he said.

"Very good, very good. That's it. Not too much stew. Feed men well, and they'll do well at any job. Very satisfactory."

The day was saved. Our cook had redeemed the honour of the Regiment; but alas, just as the General drew his bridle to move off, his eye lit on the cook's bare, hairy chest, which was exposed by an open shirt.

"Where's your identity disc?" said the General.

A personal search revealed, that not only the cook, but two of his assistants were minus their discs. The General moved on without a word. And thus it was that our report of the inspection contained the dreadful sentence: "A little more attention to details would be desirable". And thus it was that our cook trod the orderly room tarpaulin next morning on a charge of "neglect, to the prejudice of good order and military discipline in that he omitted to wear his identity disc".

"There you are," said the cook, "me walkin' all that way to the Light Horse for nothin'. I wish I'd told him the men had stoo for dinner. He'd a gone that wild, he wouldn't ha' noticed the identity disc!"

Our Own Flag

They mustered us up with a royal din,
  In wearisome weeks of drought.
Ere ever the half of the crops were in,
  Or the half of the sheds cut out.

'Twas down with saddle and spurs and whip
  The swagman dropped his swag.
And we hurried us off to an outbound ship
  To fight for the English flag.

The English flag — it is ours in sooth
  We stand by it wrong or right.
But deep in our hearts is the honest truth
  We fought for the sake of a fight.

And the English flag may flutter and wave
  Where the World-wide Oceans toss,
But the flag the Australian dies to save
  Is the flag of the Southern Cross.

If ever they want us to stand the brunt
  Of a hard-fought, grim campaign,
We will carry our own flag up to the front
  When we go to the wars again.

Australia Today 1916

They came from the lower levels
  Deep down in the Brilliant mine;
From the wastes where the whirlwind revels,
  Whirling the leaves of pine.

On the western plains, where the Darling flows,
  And the dust storms wheel and shift,
The teamster loosened his yokes and bows,
  And turned his team adrift.

On the western stations, far and wide,
  There's many an empty pen,
For the "ringers" have cast the machines aside
  And answered the call for men.

On the lucerne flats where the stream runs slow,
  And the Hunter finds the sea,
The women are driving the mowers now,
  With the children at their knee.

For the men have gone, as a man must go,
  At the call of the rolling drums;
For the men have sworn that the Turks shall know
  When the old battalion comes.

Column of companies by the right,
  Steady in strong array,
With the sun on the bayonets gleaming bright,
  The battalion marched away.

They battled, the old battalion,
  Through the toil of the training camps,
Sweated and strove at lectures,
  By the light of the stinking lamps.

Marching, shooting, and drilling;
  Steady and slow and stern;
Awkward and strange, but willing
  All of their job to learn.

Learning to use the rifle;
　Learning to use the spade;
Deeming fatigue a trifle
　During each long parade.

Till at last they welded
　Into a concrete whole,
And there grew in the old battalion
　A kind of battalion's soul.

Brotherhood never was like it;
　Friendship is not the word;
But deep in that body of marching men
　The soul of a nation stirred.

And like one man with a single thought
　Cheery and confident;
Ready for all that the future brought,
　The old battalion went.

Column of companies by the right,
　Steady in strong array,
With the sun on the bayonets gleaming bright,
　The battalion marched away.

How shall we tell of their landing
　By the hills where the foe were spread,
And the track of the old battalion
　Was marked by the Turkish dead?

With the dash that discipline teaches,
　Though the hail of the shrapnel flew,
And the forts were raking the beaches,
　And the toll of the dead men grew.

They fixed their grip on the gaunt hillside
　With a pluck that has won them fame;
And the home-folks know that the dead men died
　For the pride of Australia's name.

Column of companies by the right,
　To the beat of the rolling drums;
With honours gained in a stirring fight
　The old Battalion comes!

"We're All Australians Now"

Australia takes her pen in hand,
   To write a line to you,
To let you fellows understand,
   How proud we are of you.

From shearing shed and cattle run,
   From Broome to Hobson's Bay,
Each native-born Australian son,
   Stands straighter up today.

The man who used to "hump his drum",
   On far-out Queensland runs,
Is fighting side by side with some
   Tasmanian farmer's sons.

The fisher-boys dropped sail and oar
   To grimly stand the test,
Along that storm-swept Turkish shore,
   With miners from the west.

The old state jealousies of yore
   Are dead as Pharaoh's sow,
We're not State children any more
   We're all Australians now!

Our six-starred flag that used to fly,
   Half-shyly to the breeze,
Unknown where older nations ply
   Their trade on foreign seas,

Flies out to meet the morning blue
   With Vict'ry at the prow;
For that's the flag the *Sydney* flew,
   The wide seas know it now!

The mettle that a race can show,
   Is proved with shot and steel,
And now we know what nations know
   And feel what nations feel.

The honoured graves beneath the crest
   Of Gaba Tepe hill,
May hold our bravest and our best,
   But we have brave men still.

With all our petty quarrels done,
   Dissensions overthrown,
We have, through what you boys have done,
   A history of our own.

Our old world diff'rences are dead,
   Like weeds beneath the plough,
For English, Scotch, and Irish-bred,
   They're all Australians now!

So now we'll toast the Third Brigade,
   That led Australia's van,
For never shall their glory fade
   In minds Australian.

Fight on, fight on, unflinchingly,
   Till right and justice reign.
Fight on, fight on, till Victory
   Shall send you home again.

And with Australia's flag shall fly
   A spray of wattle bough,
To symbolise our unity,
   We're all Australians now.

The Last Parade

With never a sound of trumpet,
  With never a flag displayed,
The last of the old campaigners
  Lined up for the last parade.

Weary they were and battered,
  Shoeless, and knocked about;
From under their ragged forelocks
  Their hungry eyes looked out.

And they watched as the old commander
  Read out, to the cheering men,
The Nation's thanks and the orders
  To carry them home again.

And the last of the old campaigners,
  Sinewy, lean, and spare —
He spoke for his hungry comrades:
  "Have we not done our share?

"Starving and tired and thirsty
  We limped on the blazing plain;
And after a long night's picket
  You saddled us up again.

"We froze on the windswept kopjes
  When the frost lay snowy white.
Never a halt in the daytime,
  Never a rest at night!

"We knew when the rifles rattled
  From the hillside bare and brown,
And over our weary shoulders
  We felt warm blood run down.

"As we turned for the stretching gallop,
  Crushed to the earth with weight;
But we carried our riders through it —
  Carried them p'raps too late.

"Steel! We were steel to stand it —
We that have lasted through,
We that are old campaigners
Pitiful, poor, and few.

"Over the sea you brought us,
Over the leagues of foam:
Now we have served you fairly
Will you not take us home?

"Home to the Hunter River,
To the flats where the lucerne grows;
Home where the Murrumbidgee
Runs white with the melted snows.

"This is a small thing, surely!
Will not you give command
That the last of the old campaigners
Go back to their native land?"

They looked at the grim commander,
But never a sign he made.
"Dismiss!" and the old campaigners
Moved off from their last parade.

Winston Churchill

Winston in embryo — Army's opinion of him — More feared
than liked — His brush with General French — The world's
greatest advertiser — Ability and swagger — Relief of
Kimberley — Rhodes and Kekewich were quarrelling — French
makes a speech — Alexander of Teck as an officer.

A war correspondent, in army eyes, is an evil to be tolerated; in fact,
he is distinctly nah-poo, as we used afterwards to say in France. Being
an Australian, a steeplechase rider and polo player, I had a (possibly
fictitious) reputation as a judge of a horse, and was constantly asked to go
and pick horses for officers out of the remount depots.

In that way I got to know such celebrities as Lord Roberts, French, Haig,

Winston Churchill and Kipling, and I attained a status in the army that I would never have reached as a correspondent. The horse may be the natural enemy of man, as some people think, but he is the key to more valuable acquaintanceships and good friendships than either rank or riches. I acquired more merit in the army by putting a Cavalry regiment on to back the Australian horse The Grafter, in the City and Suburban, than by the finest dispatches that I ever sent to Reuter's. Generals, as a rule, were "off" correspondents. If they were civil to them it looked as though they were trying to advertise, and if they treated them roughly — well, the correspondents had their own way of getting back at them. One miscreant, a correspondent from an obscure Cape paper, was stopped by a railway staff officer named King Hall from going somewhere or other. Probably King Hall was quite right — but look what the correspondent did to him!

He printed an article in his sausage wrap of a paper to say that, from the top of his head to the soles of his feet, from his immaculately fitting tunic to his beautifully cut riding pants and his spotless boots, King Hall was *beau sabreur*, the sartorial ideal of a British officer.

How did the army eat it up!

Wandering generals would get off the train, poke their heads into King Hall's office and say, "Well, how's the *beau sabreur* today?" Colonels on lines of communication, having little else to do, would ride up to the railway station and inquire of King Hall who made his breeches. Even subalterns, who dared not "chip" a senior officer, would look meaningfully under the table at those boots, as they departed with their railway warrants. If King Hall had been made press censor, every correspondent in South Africa would have been sent home by the next day's boat — unless there was one leaving earlier.

Not that all the correspondent fraternity were casteless in the eyes of the army. *The Times* staff, headed by Lionel James, were persons of consequence. With the English passion for regimentation, they all wore a toothbrush stuck in the band of their hats as a sort of caste mark. If you were a *Times* man you wore a toothbrush; if you were not a *Times* man you didn't dare do it. No, sir!

Winston Churchill (afterwards to be, well, pretty well everything in British governments) was over as correspondent for the *Morning Post*. With his great social influence, his aggressiveness and undoubted ability, he was a man to be feared if not liked. He would even take a fall out of General French; and that, for a correspondent, was about equal to earning the V.C. twice over. One day, when something had gone wrong and Johnnie French was in a particularly bad temper, Churchill said to me, "Come along up to H.Q. I am going to give French a turn. He was very rude to me last time we met."

On that particular day I would as soon have faced a Hyrcanian tiger, and said so. But Churchill insisted. So off we went, Churchill striding along in front with his chin well stuck out, while I shuffled protestingly behind. Arrived at headquarters, Churchill saluted and said, "General, I want to ask whether I am to report today's operations as a success or a failure?"

FRENCH (choking down a few appropriate words that he would have liked to say): "Well, Churchill, that depends on how you look at it."

CHURCHILL: "I am afraid that my point of view would not carry much weight, sir. What I want to know is, whether from *your* point of view, the affair was a success or a failure?"

FRENCH (very dignified): "If you apply to Major Haig, he will let you see the official report. Good morning."

It was a victory for the press, but one felt that a few such victories would mean annihilation. Churchill was not then in parliament — in fact, he had been hooted and badly defeated at his only attempt — but he expounded his plan of campaign.

"This correspondent job," he explained, "is nothing to me; but I mean to get into parliament through it. They wouldn't listen to me when I put up for parliament because they had never heard of me. Now," he said, "I am going to plaster the *Morning Post* with cables about our correspondent, Mr Winston Churchill, driving an armoured train, or pointing out to Lord Roberts where the enemy is. When I go up for parliament again, I'll fly in."

All of which things he did. Persons burdened with inferiority complexes might sit up and take notice.

Churchill was the most curious combination of ability and swagger. The army could neither understand him nor like him; for when it came to getting anywhere or securing any job, he made his own rules. Courage he had in plenty, as will be shown later on; but, like the Duke of Plaza-Toro, he felt that he should always travel with a full band. As one general put it, "You never know when you have got Churchill. You can leave him behind in charge of details and he'll turn up at the front, riding a camel, and with some infernal explanation that you can't very well fault."

Even his work as a correspondent jarred the army to its depths. When there was nothing doing at the front, he always managed to get himself into the news. The Duke of Norfolk's horse fell with him in an ant-bear hole (everybody's horse fell with him in an ant-bear hole at some time or other) and the matter was too trivial for comment. But the *Morning Post*, when it arrived, had a splash heading: "Our Mr Winston Churchill saves the Duke of Norfolk from being crushed by his horse." As the Duke of Norfolk was the great Catholic peer, Churchill no doubt reckoned that this would be worth thousands of Catholic votes to him at the next election.

Churchill and his cousin, the Duke of Marlborough, each drank a big bottle of beer for breakfast every morning — an unholy rite that is the prerogative of men who have been to a certain school or college. It was like *The Times* toothbrush or the I Zingari colours — only the elect dare use it.

Marlborough, by the way, was just as retiring as Churchill was aggressive. He could not get much higher than the House of Lords, so he had no necessity to advertise himself; but he was a duke, so he had to act up to it when under public observation. He was riding one day on the flank of an Australian patrol, when it was found that the Boer bullets, fired at extreme range, were just about able to reach the patrol. The common or garden Australians swerved hurriedly out of danger, but the Duke rode on impassively, while the bullets whipped up the sand in front of and behind his horse. Said an Australian trooper, "If I had that bloke's job, I wouldn't do that."

Churchill, on the other hand, had such a strong personality that even in those early days, when he was quite a young man, the army were prepared to bet that he would either get into jail or become Prime Minister. He had done some soldiering, but he had an uncanny knack of antagonising his superior and inferior officers. As he said himself, "I could see nothing in soldiering except looking after the horses' backs and the men's mess tins in barracks. There's not enough wars to make soldiering worthwhile."

The soldiers tried to retaliate by stirring him up in their own crude way. Once, when he went as a subaltern in charge of some expedition, they sent him a wire: "Don't make a bigger fool of yourself than you can help." But, trying to get through the hide of the pachydermatous Churchill with a telegram was like shooting "old man rhinossyhoss" with paper darts.

Here are some extracts from a diary of this march.

At the Modder River. There was a camp of tents extending for miles and miles, as far as one could see for the dust. The horses were dying of cold and of dust on the lungs, and the men were dying of enteric. Left this place and joined in with French's force on the march to Kimberley. We passed seven miles of mule and bullock waggons. A staff captain — a V.C. man at that — came up and said he had lost touch of the whole of the supply waggons for a certain brigade. We asked him how many waggons there were.

He said, "There ought to be a few miles of it. There are three thousand five hundred mules, besides a lot of bullock waggons." This trifling item was absolutely lost and swallowed up in the mass of mounted men, waggons and guns.

Passed some infantry that had been on the march for days and were pretty well exhausted. It was pitiful to see them, half delirious with heat and thirst, dropping out of the ranks and throwing themselves down in the sun, often too far gone to shelter their heads from the sun, but letting their helmets roll off and lie beside them.

Crossed Reit River and camped, moving off at eight next morning. Here we dropped all Infantry, all transport, and all convoys. This was French's force for the relief of Kimberley, a force of five thousand, all Cavalry and horse artillery, all the squadrons moving abreast across the open veldt. We had three days' rations; no horse feed; and no chance of getting water at the end of the march, unless we could drive the Boers away from the Modder River, which we were to strike at the end of the day. The Boers had fired the grass, and we moved through smoke and dust and blinding heat. The Scots Greys were next to us and were well mounted; but their big English horses were not standing it as well as our leathery Walers. The gun horses were dropping in their harness. Every here and there along the line a pistol shot rang out, telling where some good horse had been dispatched to put him out of misery. Horses and men were about all in, when we reached the Modder; and there was no need to order the troops to clear the Boers off the crossing. The horses just simply bolted for the water; if the Boers had tried to stop them, they would have run over them.

Next day we moved on for Kimberley. Very strict orders — no transport to accompany troops. Our two mule waggon kaffirs, Henry and Alick, with teams of six mules each, had somehow managed to dodge the provost marshal on the first day, and joined us in camp. For the second day the quartermaster told them that they must not accompany the troops, but that they could follow us to Kimberley if they liked. Hardly had we moved off when we saw Henry and Alick hustling along with the best, shoving their teams in before the R.H.A., or the Household Cavalry, or anybody else.

Henry is very black. His principal points are a pair of black puttees and a broken ostrich plume which he wears in his hat. The white plume in the helmet of Navarre was not watched with half as much interest as the ostrich feather of Henry the kaffir on this march. If Henry could keep up, we might have something to eat next day; if not, or if the provost got him, we might have to do a perish for two or three days. Whether we trotted or cantered, Henry, with his team of six little game mules, was scuttling along at our heels.

When the artillery halted on a rise to breathe their horses, Henry swung his team in among them, and the provost must have seen him. Just at that moment, however, the Boers opened on that ridge with a very big gun. Squadrons wheeled right and left, and the gunners swung round like machines. But nothing on the ridge swung round quicker than Henry and Alick swung their respective teams, and nothing got out of danger faster. The quartermaster said, "I was afraid the guns or the Cavalry would run over those boys; but nothing in the army would run over them with guns behind them."

That march to Kimberley was a sort of baptism of fire for my future career as a remount officer, as I saw all sorts of troop and transport animals thoroughly tried out. It was the first time I had seen mule teams in any number, but later on I was to have thousands of mules through my hands. Luckily, I didn't know it.

After the march, I asked Colonel Haig (afterwards Field-Marshal and Commander-in-Chief in France, of whom more anon) which lot of horses had come out of the test with the greatest percentage of efficients.

"Of all people," he said, "who do you think have the most horses fit to move on again if wanted? The Tinbellies."

The Tinbellies are the Life Guards, whose magnificent black horses are seen on sentry duty outside the palaces in London, and the general estimate of the Tinbellies was that they were chocolate soldiers; they were too decorative to be very destructive and yet they had come out on top after one of the most trying marches in history. It was incredible. I told him I thought their horses were too big and too pampered to stand this sort of job.

"Well," he said, "anyone would think so. But they're in great condition, and they're very strong — they can hump the weight. Anyhow, there you are. If I have to send a squadron to clear the Boers off the hills, I'll have to send Her Majesty's Life Guards after them. Bit of a compliment to Johannes Paul Kruger, isn't it?"

French and Haig would have made good poker players. Neither success nor defeat wreathed any smiles on their mask-like faces, or cut any lines on their brows. Here at Kimberley, with a howling, shrieking, cheering crowd almost pulling them off their horses and trying to kiss their very boots as they rode along, everything looked set for a bit of theatricals. But it turned out that Kekewich, the military commander, and Cecil Rhodes, the civilian despot, had quarrelled bitterly and had gone out in separate directions to meet French and get in first with their hard luck stories.

French was officially received by a Jewish gentleman, who probably owned a diamond mine, and his opening sentence was, "Vell, general, vy didn't you come before?"

French was never a good mixer at any time and, according to all reports, he was particularly unenthusiastic about the un-lost tribes. Like the great Duke of Marlborough, his troubles through life had been mostly female and financial. It must be admitted that the world owes a great deal to the Jewish race; French at one time and another had owed them a good deal, too. He made a brief, halting speech, punctuated with sips of champagne.

"Very glad to be here (sip); had a hard march (sip); hope everything will go well now (sip); must go and see about refitting (sip); when Colonel Kekewich comes back, let me know." With that he finished the fizz and bolted off.

One pauses to think how differently Baden-Powell would have handled such an opportunity.

Kimberley. Day after relief. Went round and saw the wreckage of transport and troop animals. Horses that have collapsed through heat and overwork are being shot in all directions. The people here have been living on horseflesh and thousands of starving kaffirs are hanging round the lines. When a horse is shot, they fling themselves on it like a crowd of vultures, and in ten minutes there is not a scrap left. My friend, the Duke of Teck, will have to step lively to keep this column supplied with horses, as they have to be led up, and there is every chance of their being cut off by the enemy. I never knew there was a remount service before this war. It has its hands full now.

Our mule drivers, Henry and Alick, are the only two boys to get up with their officers' waggons, as the English Cavalry officers obeyed orders strictly and would not let their boys come along. We are the only officers' mess that have food and blankets. Prince Alexander of Teck, a subaltern with the Inniskillings, didn't even have an overcoat. He wouldn't take anything from us, as he said it wasn't playing the game to take anything while his mates were doing a perish. Later on, he was attached to our Australian Lancer squadron and was a good soldier. One of our newly-arrived Australian officers asked him what he would do and what orders he would give if he found his command surrounded by Boers.

"I would lie flat down on my guts," he said. There was no theatricalism about Alexander of Teck.

Henry and Alick are the heroes of the local kaffir population. They drew some money today, and as Henry was on duty he gave his share to Alick to buy some dop, a very villainous kind of Cape brandy. Alick fell in with a crowd of hero-worshippers, and among them they drank all Henry's dop. Alick also lost all Henry's money playing the Kaffir equivalent for baccara. At lunch-time the quartermaster heard a fearful row in the lines and arrived just in time to prevent Henry (much the bigger man) from choking Alick to death. He had them separated and put to work at different ends of the line, Alick with tears streaming down his face, saying, "One more chance, quartermaster, one more chance. He kickit my mules." In ten minutes they were at it again and a sentry with a loaded rifle had to be put over Henry, while Alick was sent out of the lines. Henry, crying with rage and sobriety, begged the sentry to shoot him right through the heart, otherwise nothing would stop him from killing Alick at the first opportunity.

By nightfall they were firm friends again. Handling native transport drivers is one of the things they don't teach in the books.

July 28th, 1900. Caledon Valley, South Africa — Day of Prinsloo's surrender. The men we caught were like sheep without a shepherd. They had moved up the valley, hoping to get out at Naauwpoort Nek, and when we blocked them they fell into a disorganised rabble. Each commandant took his own course. They had forced their guns and waggons up rocks and down fathomless abysses, along sidelings and across gullies till they could not extricate themselves. They had thousands of cattle and sheep with them, and the winding road — if road you could call it — for miles up the valley was one long bewildering string of ex-waggons, Cape carts, cattle, sheep, horses, armed men, women, children and kaffirs. They couldn't get off the road. They could go neither backward nor forward without our permission. They could have left their waggons and gone over the mountains on horseback, but, as Roux, the fighting parson, put it, the Boers love their waggons more than their fatherland.

All the first day the fighting men trooped in, and they brought a fair number of Cape carts with them; in fact, we were surprised to see that each commando had as many private carts as one of our crack cavalry regiments. The next day we found out that, on the previous day we hadn't, comparatively speaking, seen any carts at all.

On the second day we saw miles and miles of carts — driven by fat old Rip Van Winkles, with white hair streaming down their backs; driven by dandified young Boers with peaked braids and tailor-made clothes; driven by grinning kaffirs: some drawn by horses, some by mules, and some by oxen. Hour after hour, they streamed in, till we began to think that the Boers must be driving them through our camp round the hill and back again, like a pantomime army in a theatre.

I had an interview with the fighting parson, Roux. He blamed Prinsloo for surrendering. Said that, at the very time the fight was going on, an election was being held to decide whether he or Prinsloo should be commandant!

Well, we did some silly things ourselves, but nothing quite as bad as that.

from *Happy Dispatches*

Song of the Pen

Not for the love of women toil we, we of the craft,
    Not for the people's praise.
Only because our Goddess made us her own, and laughed,
    Claiming us all our days.

Claiming our best endeavour, body and heart and brain,
    Given with no reserve.
Niggard is she towards us, granting us little gain,
    Still we are proud to serve.

Not unto us is given choice of the tasks we try —
    Gathering grain or chaff.
One of her favoured servants toils at an epic high,
    One — that a child may laugh.

Yet if we serve her truly in our appointed place,
    Freely she doth accord
Unto her faithful servants always this saving grace;
    Work is its own reward!

Australia's Pilgrim Fathers

So many people are on the lookout for someplace where they can make some money or can get a return on their money — if they have any — I thought that tonight I would say something about a place that is not so very far away and which seems to me to have great possibilities. I refer to the New Hebrides Islands which are due east of Townsville and I should say about four days' steam from there, and about six days from Sydney.

Now, you've all heard about our pioneer families who came out to this rough unsettled country and faced all the hardships and made a go of it, and you've heard about the American Pilgrim Fathers who did the same thing.

Well, about thirty years ago, I went down to the New Hebrides with a shipload of Australian Pilgrim Fathers who were going to settle there, and I'll tell you what I saw there and what happened to the Pilgrim Fathers. It was funny in parts and at the same time a bit of a tragedy.

I went down for the *Sydney Morning Herald* to chronicle the doings of these adventurers and to describe the country so that other people might follow if they thought it good enough.

And first of all let us consider the motives which prompted these men to hazard their lives — we cannot say their fortunes, for they had no fortunes — in an expedition to such an unhealthy and inhospitable country. Were there no attractions sufficient to keep them in Australia? Unrest! That is the key word of the puzzle.

In the early days of Australia, there had always been big chances for small men. According to José's *History of Australia* the first diggers on Ballarat were taking thirty and forty pounds a day from their claims for weeks at a time. The early selectors who got in on good blocks of country found the ball of fortune at their feet but in 1902 life in Australia had settled down, not exactly to what Swinburne calls a "time of famished hours" but at any rate to a time of very hard work with very little return. Small wonder it is, then, that men were found ready to jump at any chance of making what they called a big rise in a little time.

We have seen the same sort of exodus to New Guinea in the last few years. This unrest, then, accounted for the personnel of the pioneer company and the necessary capital provided in the following way. The credit for all these pioneering ventures must be divided equally between the men who are ready to go out and risk their lives, and the men (or the firms) who are prepared to risk their money in these hazardous undertakings: and it so happened that we had in Australia a firm which specialised in this sort of thing.

Ever since its foundation, the firm of Burns, Philp and Co. had been putting their money behind pioneers away up on the Queensland rivers where the settlers were liable to be scuppered by blacks at any time: they had financed storekeepers in little bush towns away out in the ranges where these storekeepers, again, found what are called grubstakes for penniless prospectors and miners.

The firm had traded to the Islands in the days when no boat's crew dare land unless the bow man had a loaded rifle across his knees; and they ran small steamships to places where there were no wharves and the boat just tied up alongside the bank to discharge or take in her cargo. They were always looking ahead, always hoping that some seed, thus sown, might fertilise and grow into a really big trade: and sometimes they got their money back with fifty per cent profit, and sometimes they lost the lot. The late Colonel Sir James Burns was the Commander-in-Chief of these operations, a man of vision with a great grip of finance and a capacity for getting good work out of very rough characters. If his lines had been cast in other places, if he had had to deal with diamonds instead of with copra and bananas, he might have been another Cecil Rhodes.

Sir James explained the position to me. He said that the Islands belonged to the English and French governments jointly, but the Islands had never gone ahead because the two Governments could not agree on issuing titles to the land. The trouble was that in the very early days the English and French traders and the English and French skippers of ships would go along the coast and every time a native chief came off in a canoe, they would give him a few sticks of tobacco and a bottle of rum and get him to make his mark to a paper selling them a mile of frontage to the beach by ten miles deep, and they would go ashore and peg out the frontage. Next week another trader, perhaps a Frenchman this time, would come along and he would buy the same frontage from the same native at the same price. If they didn't get the chief, any other native would do just as well, and the natives didn't mind how many bits of paper they signed so long as they got the rum and tobacco. The result was that the ownership of land was just in a state of absolute chaos and the governments were so jealous of each other that they would not establish a tribunal to settle the titles. So far as I know, they have not settled it yet.

Burns, Philp and Co. had a better claim than other people, for they had bought out the original exploration company, usually known as the Scotch Company. This Scotch Company were the original pioneers there in the very early days, and they acquired about thirty thousand acres of land, meaning to exploit it; but it exploited them, so they were glad to sell out to Burns, Philp and Co.

Sir James Burns thought that when a tribunal was appointed to settle the titles, it would give the land to whoever was in possession. So he decided to send in a shipload of Australians to occupy the lands to which Burns, Philp laid claim. He paid all expenses and was willing to give the settlers the land free of charge and to finance them and give them trade goods and help them in every way. He expected, of course, to benefit by trading with these people when they got established.

"Do you know," Sir James said to me, "that those Islands are as rich as Java and that Java carries the same population per square mile as England and yet

Java is so rich that it exports millions of pounds of foodstuffs every year? There is a great future for those Islands and we are prepared to send men down and give them the land for nothing and to advance them all they want to keep them going till they see whether they can make a go of it. If it is a success, then we'll get our money back in the trade. If it is not a success, then we'll lose our money, as we have often lost it before."

Well, the Pilgrim Fathers were a pretty genuine lot, farmers, miners, prospectors, maize growers and a few adventurers that had never been on the land in their lives, but were willing to try anything once. Some of them were pretty old but they were the sort that didn't know they were old.

The ship was taking goods down to the traders and if I described her as a floating grocer's shop and hardware store I'd be about right. There were a lot of Scotch missionaries on board and one of them was very seasick. When he recovered I asked him how he got on, and he said, "Man, ah thought ah'd swallowed a churrn". It had churned his inside up pretty well.

These Scotch missionaries were mostly doctors of medicine and they were maintaining a very uphill fight trying to save the natives. They opposed giving the natives any liquor and they were able to prevent the English settlers giving them liquor, but the French gave their settlers permission to give them wine, and of course a native would sooner work for a Frenchman where he could get a drink, than for an Englishman, where he could not.

On their way down, the settlers called at Norfolk Island.

The settlers could hardly believe in Norfolk Island, such a sleepy, take-it-easy sort of place. Their cicerone was a dentist from Sydney who let his imagination run loose.

Showing them some scars on his arm, he said, "How do you think I got those?" Nobody had any suggestion to offer. "I got those," he said, "in the first couple of years I was here, sticking a knife into myself to see if I was alive or dead. What do you think makes the horses here have such long upper lips?"

Again nobody would come at it.

"There's so much grass here," he said, "that the horses get tired of eating it and they use those long upper lips to pull down bananas off the trees. I saw a thing called a tapir in a zoo once, and I think these horses have some tapir blood in them. When these Islanders go for a ride they carry about two fathom of sounding line round the horse's neck to moor him when they get off him: and when they get aboard of him again they hit him under the flanks with the slack of the sounding line. That's the signal for full speed ahead. And don't they travel? Not half! The Island isn't big enough to knock a horse up, and they go full split all the time. You'd think the whole Island was on fire."

They loafed about the Island all day, drinking in the sunlight and the scented air, heavy with the fragrance of orange blossoms. From the top of a hill they could see a panorama of farms and little cottages sleeping in the sun, while occasionally an Islander on a horse dashed across the landscape as though the police were after him.

Before we left Norfolk Island there was a fracas between the Islanders and the ship. The Islanders, unspoilt children of Nature, still had an eye to the main chance, and sharp at sundown they went ashore and pulled their boats up for the night. This they did so that the ship would have to wait a night in harbour and pay extra port dues and extra labour for taking the final ton of cargo out of the ship. They left the customs officer on board so that the ship could not get away. Then they went home and sat tight. The captain blew the whistle and waved flag signals for half an hour and then he pulled up the anchor and went away, customs officer and all. This customs officer was one Mart Adams, a direct descendant of one of the original *Bounty* mutineers with a touch of Tahitian in his make-up. He told us that he had not been off Norfolk Island for fifteen years and his only trouble seemed to be that he had the key of the Methodist Church in his pocket, and what were the Methodists to do while he was away? Soon his Island home was far beyond the wave, but he did not seem to worry. Then we ran into a cyclone and tons of water came aboard. A power launch on deck got adrift and went banging around; a penful of swine, described by Adams as a package of pigs, drifted about the deck with the pigs screaming and trying to stand on each other's shoulders; a dog, a monkey, and a cockatoo belonging to the settlers added their protests; and through it all, the old seafaring blood in Mart Adams asserted itself and he plunged barefooted into the smother of water, made lines fast, picked up loose pigs and threw them into the whale boat, and generally covered himself with glory.

"'Tis naught but a capful o' wind," said Mart. "There be girt seas off Norfolk."

I asked the captain where Mart had learnt his seamanship.

"Never learnt it," he said. "He was born knowing it. He never was in anything bigger than a whale boat but he and his mates will go out in an open boat and kill a whale with old-fashioned harpoons, and you've got to keep your feet and your hands in the right place when the whale line is running overboard. That's the reason he doesn't talk. There's only one man talks in a whale boat from the time they strike him till they get him in.'

When we landed at Aneityum, the first of the Hebrides, and saw the promised land, it gave the pilgrims a bit of a shock. Pretty well all these South Sea Islands are the same. There are always some mountains in the centre of the island, some of them looked about four thousand feet to me, and between the mountains and the sea there is the coast land, as rich as possible, all volcanic soil, with a tremendous rainfall.

But the coast land is most densely timbered, great lowering trees with their saplings, and creepers, and ferns, and climbing vines, that make a jungle you can't walk into. This paralysed the pilgrims, who said, "Is *that* what we've got to clear? Why, they told us it would cost ten bob an acre, and it will cost four quid." It took Lucas of Burns, Philp and Co. all his time explaining to the pilgrims that they would have native labour and that they cleared this stuff by cutting the bigger trees half through. The trees are all interlaced with vines and when a wind comes they all go down together and they burn right off as soon as they dry.

We saw some land they were clearing and as fast as they burned the stuff off they planted maize in the ashes and got a crop straight away. They reckoned they got three and sometimes four certain crops of maize a year. I asked one old dairy farmer from Camden, "Is this soil rich enough for you?" He said, "Yes, if a man planted a pumpkin vine here he'd have to run for his life." And I said, "Why?" "Well", he said, "it might grow up and choke him before he could get to the fence."

Then we visited a mission station and there was a shorthorn bull there that knocked the pilgrims cold. They reckoned they had never seen a bull like him. It turned out that one of the greatest Scotch shorthorn breeders in the world, a man named Cruickshank, was a great supporter of the mission and he used to send them out a yearling bull every now and again, and this was one of them. Our stock expert among the pilgrims said, "That's a bull a man could sit and look at all day."

The missionaries had some geese there that a great goose breeder in Scotland had sent them, and our poultry expert said, "Them ain't geese! They've got 'em crossed with an emu or something." Of course it was very hot and muggy and I said to one pilgrim, "How would this hot damp climate suit you?" "Oh", he said, "I've been timber getting on the Johnstone River in Queensland where we had to carry our matches wrapped in wadding in a pickle bottle lest they'd get too damp to strike. I can stand this all right."

The natives on the Islands were quite a problem. The coastal tribes, known as "man salt water" had been civilised to the extent that they were cured of cannibalism but the inland tribes, known as "man-a-bush", were like Mark Twain's Indians; they would eat anything they could bite and they were liable to come down any day or night and wipe out the coastal tribes, settlers, traders, missionaries or anybody else. Raids and battles were frequent and up to the time of the coming of the white men the inland tribes, being fierce and stronger, had had all the best things: but the early traders supplied the coastal tribes with old Martini muskets which they always carried loaded and at full cock. True, they always shut their eyes when they fired and they could be backed to miss a barn at twenty yards; but the possession of these weapons gave them a superiority complex and on the day of the arrival of the Pilgrim Fathers the coastal natives hooted at any idea of doing any work discharging the ship.

"All boy go fight man-a-bush," they said and, sure enough, they had challenged the inland natives to come down to a certain creek which represented what we afterwards got to call "no man's land" in a somewhat bigger war.

A few settlers had been in the South African war and they pushed on up to the front line where one could not see twenty yards in any direction because of the jungle. They hadn't been there five minutes when the stretcher bearers brought in a dead man, his skull crushed in by a waddy: and the leader of the settlers, who had been a sergeant-major in his time, took his detachment back to the base at the double. This was the introduction of the Australian Pilgrim Fathers to their new country.

How then did the Pilgrim Fathers get on? They found the British missionaries on the Islands were all Scotch: hard, black Scotch with short teeth; combative Scotch, fighting the black man's battle all the time. Most of them held medical degrees as well as their degrees in Divinity; and the healing of the flesh took up the greater part of their time. Epidemics of measles, epidemics of influenza, swept the Islands from time to time, and the missionaries had to deal with patients who were grown men and women with the minds of wayward children. The Pilgrim Fathers who went over to America in the *Mayflower* had the same experience, for we read that an epidemic swept off nine-tenths of the Indians who inhabited the region. The New Hebrides missionaries had an uphill fight, but these Scotch never let go their grip. They physicked and drenched and operated and preached, day in and day out, in a climate where their own children sometimes developed malaria before they were a couple of months old. It was the same with the French missionaries who concentrated on trying to save the children.

A typical house occupied by a missionary was a long, rambling, wooden structure, much in the style of a station homestead. A garden in front with roses and crotons, fenced with wire netting. At the back was a yam house and a fowl house with walls of coral and roofed with thatch.

The yard was all gravelled with coral, the paths were all marked out with coral, and were bordered with slabs of coral. This missionary had his own room where he saw his (unfortunately) too numerous patients. Sometimes a man-a-bush native, a wild man from the mountains, would hang around the house looking in at the windows, equally fascinated and terrified, speaking to nobody and with nobody speaking to him. The missionaries' children learnt the language from their nurses faster than their fathers could learn it from books; and after a time one of the children asked the native what he wanted. Then he translated between his father and the native, and the child of five could be seen acting as interpreter between two grown men.

How fared it, then, between the French and the Australian settlers? Was there hostility, mutual misunderstanding, open conflict? As wild animals of warring species will live amicably together when marooned on an Island in times of flood; as soldiers on active service will exchange tobacco and gifts with the enemy when a temporary truce is declared; so did the French and Australian settlers, linked by a bond of danger and hardship, give each other whatever help they could. One would think that the mercurial Gaul, child of the cafés and the boulevards, would hardly be at his best when confronted by Nature in the rough; but the nation, which, under Napoleon Bonaparte, defied all Europe, has an ingrained strain of toughness, only to be discovered by test and trial.

We went ashore at a boat landing where the coral had been neatly raked up on both sides, a sort of concession to the French regard for appearances. The Frenchman's house, however, lacked somewhat of luxury. It was just a two-roomed shack, built of saplings driven into the ground, with a roof of thatch; much the sort of affair that is built for a hen-house in Australia. Here in this unlikely milieu we found the Frenchman and his wife supervising the work of a lot of savages who were winnowing maize with a primitive machine, while two rifles, loaded and cocked, leaned against the wall. The man was a broad-chested, powerful little fellow, a sort of Jean Valjean. His wife, dressed in a cotton dress, with blucher boots and no stockings, had only landed from Paris a few days previously but seemed quite cheerful and competent in her dreadful surroundings. The inner room was roughly partitioned off by saplings and bags, and the floor was of earth.

Our party of about six were treated to coffee — taking turns to drink out of the two cups — and a bottle of very good light wine was shared among us. This brought the remark from one of the settlers: "If they do all this for us, what would they do for their own people?" The Frenchman said that he hoped to do quite well, as maize was at a pound a bag in France, and the crop never failed. His main concern seemed to be that he had not yet got a name for his house. Someone suggested *"Bois de Boulogne"*. Waving his hand at the dense jungle, he said, "I have the trees already, but not the avenues."

Thus we get a glimpse of the genuine pioneering; later on the settlers visited the home of a French planter who had made good. Him they found to be a genuine *boulevardier*, except that his costume consisted solely of a suit of pyjamas and a sola topee. It was hard to believe that this ebullient humorist, whose outlook on life was that of a mischievous schoolboy, had lived for years in a sapling shack, like that of the young French couple; had slept every night with a rifle within reach of his hand; and had never gone out by himself alone at night lest he should be ambushed and killed. But the lean years had been succeeded by the years of plenty, and who can say that his prosperity was undeserved? He took the settlers to a ten-roomed house, with cool deep verandahs, sheltered by climbing roses; he sat them down in lounge chairs before an assortment of liquors undreamed of in their philosophy; and at intervals he roared magnificent French marching songs or played, impartially, French and English records on a gramophone.

Figure now to yourselves the effect of this demonstration on the pilgrims. Gone was any inferiority complex. Anything that could be done by a middle-aged Frenchman with a slightly protuberant outline could surely be done by these hard-handed men who had milked cows and shorn sheep and watched over travelling mobs of cattle on the dry stages of the outback. They decided to finish the inspection of their own land next day and then to draw lots for the choice of blocks. "I never knew that Frenchies were like that," said one man. "I always thought that they lived on cigarettes and absinthe and that hard work was a stranger to them. Fancy sixty bushels of maize to the acre — that's fifteen bags at five bob a bag and three crops a year; that's eleven pounds five a year per acre from maize and this Frenchman says it doesn't interfere with the coconuts for two years. It'll do us!"

The settlers visited a coconut plantation owned by a Frenchman named

Chevilliard at Vila. He had fifty thousand coconut trees planted, forty to the acre, and each tree in those days returned a shilling a year. That was £2500 a year from coconuts, and he had a lot of banana and maize land and he was making £10 a year per acre out of the maize and it could be planted with the coconuts for the first two years. Of course this bucked our pilgrims up a lot, and they were talking about the sort of maize they'd plant, Early Hogan and so on. In fact we christened one of them Early Hogan, he was so shook on it. Then we went to a coffee plantation owned by a New South Wales man, a Mr Roche, a relation of the Castle Roche family at Cavan near Yass. Their coffee was growing all right, in fact everything would grow, but it had only just started so I don't know how they got on.

Then at an Island called Erromanga there was a Scotch missionary named Robertson who came from Balmain, and on this Island they had the most beautiful oranges. They said Captain Cook had planted the seeds originally.

There was a big bare plateau on this Island, and believe it or not — as that Yankee fellow said the other day — they had a mob of merino sheep there doing quite well.

The scene now shifts to the inspection of blocks. Zero hour for the march was at four o'clock in the morning. Accompanied by an escort of natives (and of course their dogs, for whoever saw a native of any sort without a dog?) they plunged into the forest primeval. There was dense jungle everywhere, jungle so dense that they could only go through it in single file along old native paths. They moved in the shadow of darkness like pygmies in a forest, getting only occasional glimpses of the sun. Here and there a few crumbling coral walls and ruined huts showed where the coastal natives had lived until an epidemic had wiped them out utterly. They were taking over a kingdom of the departed; and when the dogs flushed a wild boar from a ruined garden, it recalled the lines of Omar Khayyam:

> They say the lion and the lizard keep
> The halls where Jamsheyd gloried and drank deep.

Jamsheyd had gloried and passed on, leaving as monument only a few scattered heaps of coral, already overgrown by jungle, but the ghost of Jamsheyd troubled the settlers not at all. Rather they looked at the fat land, black, greasy, volcanic and slippery, full of the scent of decaying vegetable matter. For centuries, Nature had been top-dressing this land with soil thrown out by the volcanoes, and had overlaid it with a mulch of dead leaf and rotting fruit. She had jungle as guardian over it, but the jungle had now no terrors for these hard-handed men of the axe. They had seen what could be done with jungle.

Lots were drawn for the various blocks, some with assured titles, others more or less in doubt (as the original sellers of the land had disappeared or recognised no law). Some blocks, too, were claimed by the French, but there was plenty of land for everybody and the settlers entered into occupation with few misgivings. What, then, was the outcome of the expedition? Here our diarist may provide us with a sketch of the pilgrims at this stage of their progress. "On leaving the Frenchman's plantation," he says, "they saw the future through a mist of French liqueurs. They were prepared to live on bananas, breadfruit, fish and the flesh of wild pigs, until their returns came in. One man suggested that he would sell the rights of shooting wild pigs on his estate to sportsmen from Sydney. Meanwhile the local missionary and his wife looked after them, letting them have a native to cook for them and plenty of labour to carry their packages and to put them across in canoes to their land on the other side of the bay. This missionary and his wife were the most hospitable and kindest-hearted little pair of Scotch people in the world. The French missionaries, too, have offered to do all that they can for them; and if this expedition fails it will not be for want of help from the French and the missionaries."

Why, then, did the expedition fail? For fail it did, in its principal object of starting a new Eldorado for English and Australian settlers. Of all the difficulties that menaced the undertaking in its early stages, not one proved insurmountable; not one proved even formidable. Disaster came from an utterly unexpected quarter.

Years were spent in preliminary work — clearing, burning off and planting. Then, as a cyclone tears through the forest, leaving destruction in its wake, so did the Depression smash down the strongest financial fortresses and up-root the oldest established businesses. It is said that a steam hammer can be used to crack a walnut; but it is a great waste of power to use a steam hammer for such a purpose; and it did seem a waste of power for the great Depression cyclone to demolish such puny objects as these few settlers toiling away in an obscure South Sea Island; their very insignificance might have saved them, but they were not overlooked and they suffered in common with the rest of humanity. Nations, for their own safety, set frantically to work to erect tariff barriers; demand died out; and the settlers were left sitting with their copra and their maize, which nobody seemed to want! Some of the settlers came home; others went in for trading or *bêche-de-mer* fishing; others are still there, hoping that the pendulum will swing back again; but they are old men now and if any great reward should ever come to this venture, it will come to the younger generation.

I will just finish by telling you of one Pilgrim Father in whom I took great interest. He was a small boy of about thirteen that had run away from his home in the Glebe to join this expedition. He stowed away, and when he was found they put him on to help the stewards. He was dreadfully sick, but he never shirked his work and one day he was coming along the deck carrying a big open tray of stew for the messroom table. The ship gave a roll and down he went, flop! into the stew. Well, we on the bridge all burst out laughing, but he never whimpered. He struggled to his feet and he looked at us with his face all smothered in stew and he said, "Well, I have done silly things in my time" — he was about thirteen — "I have done some silly things in my time, but this caps the lot. I thought a man'd have some adventures on a trip like this, and all I get is to be scalded with stew!"

The captain wouldn't let him land in the Islands, and made him come home again, so he had to give up any idea of becoming a pioneer or a Pilgrim Father, but he was the right sort and while Australia can turn them out like that we won't come to much harm.

Song of the Artesian Water

Now the stock have started dying, for the Lord has sent a drought;
But we're sick of prayers and Providence — we're going to do without;
With the derricks up above us and the solid earth below,
We are waiting at the lever for the word to let her to.
   Sinking down, deeper down,
   Oh, we'll sink it deeper down:
As the drill is plugging downward at a thousand feet of level,
If the Lord won't send us water, oh, we'll get it from the devil;
   Yes, we'll get it from the devil deeper down.

Now, our engine's built in Glasgow by a very canny Scot,
And he marked it twenty horsepower, but he don't know what is what:
When Canadian Bill is firing with the sun-dried gidgee logs,
She can equal thirty horses and a score or so of dogs.
   Sinking down, deeper down,
   Oh, we're going deeper down:
If we fail to get the water then it's ruin to the squatter,
For the drought is on the station and the weather's growing hotter,
   But we're bound to get the water deeper down.

But the shaft has started caving and the sinking's very slow,
And the yellow rods are bending in the water down below,
And the tubes are always jamming and they can't be made to shift
Till we nearly burst the engine with a forty horsepower lift.
   Sinking down, deeper down,
   Oh, we're going deeper down
Though the shaft is always caving, and the tubes are always jamming,
Yet we'll fight our way to water while the stubborn drill is ramming —
   While the stubborn drill is ramming deeper down.

But there's no artesian water, though we've passed three thousand feet,
And the contract price is growing and the boss is nearly beat.

But it must be down beneath us, and it's down we've got to go,
Though she's bumping on the solid rock four thousand feet below.
  Sinking down, deeper down,
  Oh, we're going deeper down:
And it's time they heard us knocking on the roof of Satan's dwellin';
But we'll get artesian water if we cave the roof of Hell in —
  Oh! we'll get artesian water deeper down.

But it's hark! the whistle's blowing with a wild, exultant blast,
And the boys are madly cheering, for they've struck the flow at last,
And it's rushing up the tubing from four thousand feet below
Till it spouts above the casing in a million-gallon flow.
  And it's down, deeper down —
  Oh, it comes from deeper down;
It is flowing, ever flowing, in a free, unstinted measure
From the silent hidden places where the old earth hides her treasure —
  Where the old earth hides her treasure deeper down.

And it's clear away the timber, and it's let the water run:
How it glimmers in the shadow, how it flashes in the sun!
By the silent belts of timber, by the miles of blazing plain
It is bringing hope and comfort to the thirsty land again.
  Flowing down, further down;
  It is flowing further down
To the tortured thirsty cattle, bringing gladness in its going;
Through the droughty days of summer it is flowing, ever flowing —
  It is flowing, ever flowing, further down.

Golden Water

Diamonds in South Africa, irrigation in Egypt, oil in America, and bore water in Australia — these are the things which help to make the world go round, more important than wars and tumults. When the early settlers met their first Queensland droughts out on the dry country, there did not seem to be much hope for the interior of Queensland: and then it turned out that Nature had been storing water underground so that man might drill down and get it.

I cannot claim to have seen the beginnings of bore water in Australia — there were bores before me, and since: but I was fairly early on the scene, in the days when they were just beginning to find out something about bores.

Longreach and Winton, which nowadays are cities of the plains, were four-in-hand towns in those days. The districts round Longreach and Winton were inhabited by squatter kings who made royal progresses to each other's stations, driving four horses in harness with four spare horses, driven loose by a black boy, following up to be used as a change halfway through the journey.

There was a lot of Melbourne money in those parts. Chirnside and Riley were at Vindex, Knox at Evesham, the Ramsays at Oondooroo, Bells, Fairbairns, *et hoc genus omne* at other places.

They could be excused if their prospects went to their heads, for such bores as had been put down were yielding freely and each squatter king saw himself an emperor in the near future. Trifles of expenditure were disdained, and such things as horses and traps were freely lent and sometimes got astray. In the big American railroad systems, a whole string of trucks would sometimes get on to other lines and be missing for months: similarly, a squatter king would sometimes be heard asking a friend, "Bill, haven't you got eight horses and a trap and a black boy of mine over at your place?"

"No, I lent 'em to one of Jowett's buyers, going out to Penola."

"Oh, well, I suppose they'll turn up sometime."

At the time of my visit there was grass everywhere, beautiful blue grass and Mitchell grass, with the sheep all fat and the buyers all busy. Before the bores came, Chirnside at Vindex had had to cut the throats of five thousand sheep, to try to save the remainder. Now that the bore had come in, he was sitting in a cloud of hope and glory. Bore contractors and divining rod experts were everywhere, looking for likely places, and thus it was that I met my first expert. He was a large man with a pronounced American accent. He disdained the divining rod and it seemed to be just a natural gift with him to find water. For a large fee he would drive over the paddocks, looking to the right and to the left but saying nothing; until at last he would hold up his hand and say, "Put the bore down here", and he always got water. After a somewhat convivial evening I asked how he did it. Swearing me to secrecy he said,

"They think I'm an American water borer, but I'm not. I'm a Canadian oil borer. I don't know the first thing about water but my guess seems to be as good as anybody's so what's the odds so long as they're all happy!"

The next expert was a Government man sent out to test the flow of the bores which he did by screwing a recording machine onto the top of the piping and checking the result for a while. There were two schools of thought in Queensland, one lot holding that the water was the result of an underground stream fed by tropical rains in the north: the others held that the water was stored from past ages in underground reservoirs and would give out in time. I asked this expert which school he favoured and he said that he played for safety.

"Nobody knows for certain," he said, "so I always agree with the Minister in power. A man mustn't let his opinions do him out of his bread and butter."

So they went at it in true light-hearted Queensland style, carting out boring plants; and alongside a belt of gidyea timber one would see the derricks and hear the thud and rattle of the machinery. Nature seemed to have foreseen this business, for the gidyea wood made superb fuel for the engine, burning away to a white feather-like ash and after a plant had been at work for a while one could see in the distance a miniature mountain of this white ash gleaming in the sunshine.

Sometimes they broke one of the boring tools a couple of thousand feet underground and would spend months in fishing for it with a grappler.

Before the bores came in, Queensland depended entirely on rainfall and its weather destinies were ruled by an erratic genius named Clement Wragge. Any Queenslander would back Wragge as a weather prophet against the best talent in the southern states and he very seldom let them down: but he had a queer streak of showmanship in him and was fond of giving fantastic names to the cyclones and storms which he predicted. On one occasion a wire arrived at Winton which read as follows: "Terrific cyclone approaching, everyone should keep under shelter for two days. I have named it the Great Bustyuptikus."

This was exactly the sort of name which Wragge would give to a cyclone, so nobody suspected anything and the inhabitants of Winton shut themselves indoors and drank steadily for two days. At the end of the second day they ventured to put their heads out and found that Winton stood exactly where it did: the pepper trees about the town had not lost a leaf: the coolibahs down by the water still spread their limbs to the sky: and it turned out that some miscreant from Longreach, being on holiday in Brisbane had set himself to take a rise out of the town of Winton. Men loomed large on the out trail in those days and their jokes were Homeric. Even Wragge himself, meteorologist, scientist, and showman was not averse from a little "show-off". Long before anyone thought of snow sports at Kosciusko, he built a sort of cabin on the top of the mountain, stored it with food, and sent a nephew of his to live on the top of the mountain through winter, with strict orders not to shave. When the winter was over Wragge's nephew came down looking like a cross between a walrus and a hairy rhino, and Wragge made him come and stand on the platform while he (Wragge) delivered a lecture on weather forecasting — a lecture which nobody understood but which gave the impression that these weather forecasters earned their salaries. "Look at Wragge's nephew!"

Another result of the bore water was that it started all sorts and conditions of small men off to Queensland to take up country. Clerks and bookkeepers threw up their jobs and made for the land of the golden water — just a few years earlier, similar men had made for the Golden Mile in West Australia. I happened to travel up with one of the first of them — a young Victorian who meant to take up country on Oondooroo. This place was somewhere about a million acres, so there was plenty of room for him: and in a very straightforward way he went and told Mr M. F. Ramsay of his intention. The Ramsays had come out with a great deal of capital and one of them had bowled for the Gentlemen of England, so the young fellow got a friendly reception.

"It's all right, young fellow," said Ramsay, "don't worry about taking a bit of our country. We've been very nearly broke three times on this place and if you can show us how to make money off 1000 acres while we can't make it off a million, we'll give you a good salary to manage Oondooroo for the rest of your life."

On a subsequent Queensland trip, I met E. T. Theodore who was then Premier of the state. Of Roumanian descent, he had had the advantage of a good education and cultured surroundings in his early years, but had run away to the mines and had worked with a drill on the deep levels of Charters Towers. In his wanderings he had learnt a lot about Australia and it was interesting to learn his views on the bore water development.

"Queensland's a queer place," he said. "They all want me to let the small men buy freeholds out in the dry west, now that the water has come in. But I don't believe in it. They'll only run themselves into debt buying land, and they'll get wiped out like flies in the first big drought. There'll never be a foot of freehold sold out there while I'm Premier. Let 'em do like people do in Java, take long leases, and save their money for working expenses and hard times." Which may have been wisdom or it may not: but at any rate it was interesting to meet a man who had control of such a vast asset and to see how he proposed to handle it.

I do not know that I have properly conveyed the feeling of excitability which possessed everybody in the early days of the bore water: people seemed to be looking out on to limitless horizons and except (very occasionally) in a mining camp I can remember nothing like it. The shearers staged a strike by way of expressing themselves, and MacPherson's woolshed at Dagworth was burnt down and a man was picked up dead. This engendered no malice and I have seen the MacPhersons handing out champagne through a pub window to these very shearers. And here a personal reminiscence may be worth recording. While resting for lunch, or while changing horses on our four-in-hand journeys, Miss MacPherson, afterwards wife of the financial magnate, J. M'Call MacCowan, used to play a little Scottish tune on a zither and I put words to the tune and called it "Waltzing Matilda". Not a very great literary achievement, perhaps, but it has been sung in many parts of the world. It was the effect of the bore water.

With the Cattle

The drought is down on field and flock,
    The river bed is dry;
And we shift the starving stock
    Before the cattle die.
We muster up with weary hearts
    At breaking of the day,
And turn our heads to foreign parts,
    To take the stock away.
        And it's hunt 'em up and dog 'em,
        And it's get the whip and flog 'em,
For it's weary work is droving when they're dying every day;
        By stock routes bare and eaten,
        On dusty roads and beaten,
With half a chance to save their lives we take the stock away.

We cannot use the whip for shame
    On beasts that crawl along;
We have to drop the weak and lame,
    And try to save the strong;
The wrath of God is on the track,
    The drought fiend holds his sway,
With blows and cries and stockwhip crack
    We take the stock away.
        As they fall we leave them lying,
        With the crows to watch them dying,
Grim sextons of the Overland that fasten on their prey;
        By the fiery dust storm drifting,
        And the mocking mirage shifting,
In heat and drought and hopeless pain we take the stock away.

In dull despair the days go by
    With never hope of change,
But every stage we draw more nigh
    Towards the mountain range;
And some may live to climb the pass,
    And reach the great plateau,
And revel in the mountain grass,
    By streamlets fed with snow.
        As the mountain wind is blowing
        It starts the cattle lowing,
And calling to each other down the dusty long array;
        And there speaks a grizzled drover:
        "Well, thank God, the worst is over,
The creatures smell the mountain grass that's twenty miles away."

They press towards the mountain grass,
    They look with eager eyes
Along the rugged stony pass,
    That slopes towards the skies;
Their feet may bleed from rocks and stones,
    But though the blood-drop starts,
They struggle on with stifled groans,
    For hope is in their hearts.
        And the cattle that are leading,
        Though their feet are worn and bleeding,
Are breaking to a kind of run — pull up, and let them go!
        For the mountain wind is blowing,
        And the mountain grass is growing,
They settle down by running streams ice-cold with melted snow.

The days are done of heat and drought
    Upon the stricken plain;
The wind has shifted right about,
    And brought the welcome rain;
The river runs with sullen roar,
    All flecked with yellow foam,
And we must take the road once more,
    To bring the cattle home.
        And it's "Lads! we'll raise a chorus,
        There's a pleasant trip before us."
And the horses bound beneath us as we start them down the track;
        And the drovers canter, singing,
        Through the sweet green grasses springing,
Towards the far-off mountain land, to bring the cattle back.

And dashing down the rugged range
We hear the stockwhip crack,
Good faith, it is a welcome change
To bring such cattle back.

With the Cattle, p. 177

When they first came on the place, they were so wild that the sight
of a man would set them galloping in all directions, . . .

In the Cattle Country, p. 184

Are these the beasts we brought away
   That move so lively now?
They scatter off like flying spray
   Across the mountain's brow;
And dashing down the rugged range
   We hear the stockwhip crack,
Good faith, it is a welcome change
   To bring such cattle back.
      And it's "Steady down the lead there!"
      And it's "Let 'em stop and feed there!"
For they're wild as mountain eagles and their sides are all afoam;
      But they're settling down already,
      And they'll travel nice and steady,
With cheery call and jest and song we fetch the cattle home.

We have to watch them close at night
   For fear they'll make a rush,
And break away in headlong flight
   Across the open bush;
And by the campfire's cheery blaze,
   With mellow voice and strong,
We hear the lonely watchman raise
   The Overlander's song:
      "Oh! it's when we're done with roving,
      With the camping and the droving,
It's homeward down the Bland we'll go, and never more we'll roam;"
      While the stars shine out above us,
      Like the eyes of those who love us —
The eyes of those who watch and wait to greet the cattle home.

The plains are all awave with grass,
   The skies are deepest blue;
And leisurely the cattle pass
   And feed the long day through;
But when we sight the station gate,
   We make the stockwhips crack,
A welcome sound to those who wait
   To greet the cattle back:
      And through the twilight falling
      We hear their voices calling,
As the cattle splash across the ford and churn it into foam;
      And the children run to meet us,
      And our wives and sweethearts greet us,
Their heroes from the Overland who brought the cattle home.

Song of the Wheat

We have sung the song of the droving days,
   Of the march of the travelling sheep;
By silent stages and lonely ways
   Thin, white battalions creep.
But the man who now by the land would thrive
   Must his spurs to a ploughshare beat.
Is there ever a man in the world alive
   To sing the song of the Wheat!

It's west by south of the Great Divide
   The grim grey plains run out,
Where the old flock masters lived and died
   In a ceaseless fight with drought.
Weary with waiting and hope deferred
   They were ready to own defeat,
Till at last they heard the master-word
   And the master-word was Wheat.

Yarran and Myall and Box and Pine —
   'Twas axe and fire for all;
They scarce could tarry to blaze the line
   Or wait for the trees to fall,
Ere the team was yoked and the gates flung wide,
   And the dust of the horses' feet
Rose up like a pillar of smoke to guide
   The wonderful march of Wheat.

Furrow by furrow, and fold by fold,
   The soil is turned on the plain;
Better than silver and better than gold
   Is the surface-mine of the grain.
Better than cattle and better than sheep
   In the fight with the drought and heat.
For a streak of stubbornness wide and deep
   Lies hid in a grain of Wheat.

When the stock is swept by the hand of fate,
   Deep down in his bed of clay
The brave brown Wheat will lie and wait
   For the resurrection day:
Lie hid while the whole world thinks him dead;

But the spring rain, soft and sweet,
Will over the steaming paddocks spread
　　The first green flush of the Wheat.

Green and amber and gold it grows
　　When the sun sinks late in the west
And the breeze sweeps over the rippling rows
　　Where the quail and the skylark nest.
Mountain or river or shining star,
　　There's never a sight can beat —
Away to the skyline stretching far —
　　A sea of the ripening Wheat.

When the burning harvest sun sinks low,
　　And the shadows stretch on the plain,
The roaring strippers come and go
　　Like ships on a sea of grain;
Till the lurching, groaning waggons bear
　　Their tale of the load complete.
Of the world's great work he has done his share
　　Who has gathered a crop of wheat.

Princes and Potentates and Czars,
　　They travel in regal state,
But old King Wheat has a thousand cars
　　For his trip to the water-gate;
And his thousand steamships breast the tide
　　And plough thro' the wind and sleet
To the lands where the teeming millions bide
　　That say, "Thank God for Wheat!"

The Weather Prophet

" 'Ow can it rain," the old man said, "with things the way they are?
You've got to learn off ant and bee, and jackass and galah;
And no man never saw it rain, for fifty years at least,
Not when the blessed parakeets are flyin' to the east!"

The weeks went by, the squatter wrote to tell his bank the news.
"It's still as dry as dust," he said, "I'm feeding all the ewes;
The overdraft would sink a ship, but make your mind at rest,
It's all right now, the parakeets are flyin' to the west".

Weary Will

The strongest creature for his size
    But least equipped for combat
That dwells beneath Australian skies
    Is Weary Will the Wombat.

He digs his homestead underground,
    He's neither shrewd nor clever;
For kangaroos can leap and bound
    But wombats dig for ever.

The boundary rider's netting fence
    Excites his irritation;
It is to his untutored sense
    His pet abomination.

And when to pass it he desires,
    Upon his task he'll centre
And dig a hole beneath the wires
    Through which the dingoes enter.

And when to block the hole they strain
    With logs and stones and rubble,
Bill Wombat digs it out again
    Without the slightest trouble.

The boundary rider bows to fate,
  Admits he's made a blunder,
And rigs a little swinging gate
  To let Bill Wombat under.

So most contentedly he goes
  Between his haunt and burrow:
He does the only thing he knows,
  And does it very thorough.

In the Cattle Country

We were going for a day in the cattle country, and also to vary it with a dash after dingoes. Nowadays there are not many cattle stations left in New South Wales, and there are fewer still where there are any dingoes; but there are still some bits of ragged country left where, even from the train, one can see the wary dingo slinking through the scrub and the wallaby skipping among the rocks.

The trouble began at the homestead over the horses. Being drought time, one naturally thought that the horses would be poor and weak, and hardly able to gallop: instead of which they were all fed on maize and were fat and jumping out of their skins with animal spirits. The horse that I rode was a big bay with hair on his back and clipped underneath. He was introduced as a grandson of Musket, and the head stockman was enthusiastic about him.

"Man and boy," he said, "I've been ridin' horses for five and forty years, and this is the best horse I've ever ridden. There's no day too long for him. He can win a shearers' race, he can cut out cattle, and he can go through scrub like a wallaby."

"I suppose he won't hit me against a tree in the scrub, will he?"

"Oh, won't he just! He ain't afraid of a tree. He don't care where he goes."

"Does he pull much?"

"Well, if he gets woke-up like, he's a very hard horse to hold. We mostly ride him in a curb bit, but we put the snaffle on him for you. It was you wrote about the "Man from Snowy River", wasn't it? Yes, well you ought to be able to ride him right enough."

This was a gay prospect for a man who had not ridden in scrub for ten years, and was never very expert at it at the best of times. Anyhow, I put a good face on it, and the grandson of Musket was brought forth ready saddled and bridled.

It was indeed a treat to ride such a horse — a great raking sixteen-hand bay with black points, with enormous barrel and ribs, broad hips, and a shoulder laid right back till there seemed at least the length of an ordinary horse in front of the saddle. He was one of the examples of the old type of stockhorse — a horse with quality enough to run a race, strength enough to pull a cart, and pluck enough to die galloping.

The head stockman did not come with us. He sent a sunburnt substitute who was well mounted, and who was the master of the dingo hounds, that is to say, he had with him a kangaroo slut, so narrow and wasp-waisted that she looked like an embodiment of hunger and speed, and a fierce-looking brown staghound, with a rough coat, and three sore feet, on which he limped alternately. But the genius of the party was Barney, the cattle dog, an aged dingo-looking reprobate into whose face all the wisdom of centuries was crowded. It was understood that Barney would follow nothing but dingoes. Emus might frolic around him in flocks, kangaroos might leap affrighted from under his very nose, but nothing would turn Barney off a dingo.

The sunburnt stockman advised me, if I fell off or got lost, to sit still and not move about, as they were sure to find me again some time or other; and with this comforting advice we started. The young squatter who went with us was riding a station mare, well-bred, and a good mare in scrub, but running to weediness. The grandson of Musket strode out sleepily as a carthorse, lounging along as placidly as an old cow. The other two stockhorses fretted and fidgeted at their bits, but not so this veteran. He was waiting for the climax — the great critical moment when he would set the seal on his reputation by knocking me off against a tree and catching the dingo himself.

We rode through scrub and stringybark, over country consisting mostly of loose rocks up on end, and covered carefully from view by hop scrub, thickets of wattle, and the limbs of fallen trees. Sometimes we scrambled up hills, clinging round the horses' necks for fear we should slip over the tail. Other times we slid down mountains with the stones clattering round us, the horses blundering from rock to rock, and grazing our shins against the trees as they walked. We rode for hours without seeing any dingoes, or any cattle for that matter. Just mile after mile of worthless scrub and rock and wilderness: I was beginning to lose interest in the thing, and to believe that the dingoes were a myth, and to hope that after all the grandson of Musket wouldn't have the chance to destroy me against a tree, when all of a sudden, just as we were scrambling down the wickedest piece of rock and scrub in the world, the sunburnt stockman yelled out, "Hool 'im, hool 'im, hool 'im!" The sagacious Barney began to utter loud yelps of excitement; the greyhound and staghound flashed like arrows into the scrub; and the grandson of Musket took the bit in his teeth and tore through the timber, going as if he were on a racecourse, while the crash, crash, crash of the small scrub and fallen timber was punctuated by hairbreadth escapes — say twenty every second — from trees and saplings and overhanging branches. I never saw the dingo. I don't think anyone else did. We tore madly down the side of a range, arrived by some miracle at the foot of it, and there found ourselves face to face with a bottomless dry gully over which the grandson of Musket strode as if it were a crack in the earth; and then up, like rock wallabies, over the rocks and fallen stones on the opposite slope.

We had ridden about a mile. The two hounds had been out of sight from the very start. The feathery tail and the loud yelp of the sagacious Barney had been our guiding star — our oriflamme as it were — and now even Barney had disappeared. His yelping had suddenly ceased.

We managed to pull the horses up, and then everyone began to make excuses.

The sunburnt stockman started. "I was follerin' the kangaroo slut," he said, "and I see you two fellows makin' over here towards the left like, and I thought, of course, you must be on to the dingo, so I come over after you. That's how I come to lose the dorgs."

The young squatter followed suit. "I was following Ranji" [the deerhound] "but when I heard old Barney yelping I made across after him. And that bad clump of wattle delayed me a lot, and that's how I came to lose 'em."

Then they looked at me as if it was time for me to put in my explanation.

"How did you come to lose 'em?"

"Well," I said, "when I started of course I made sure of catching a dingo straight off, but I shaved the bark off so many saplings and knocked the limbs off so many trees with my head that my attention sort of wandered from the dogs. I wasn't following the dogs at all, it took me all my time to navigate this horse. That's how I came to lose the dogs."

The sunburnt stockman shook his head despondingly. "It's a pity," he said, "they're sure to catch him, in fact they've got him cot by now."

"Do you really think so?"

"Oh, certain," he said with a superior smile, "quite certain. They never miss a dorg, once they start him. Now, if we'd only kep' up with 'em, I'll bet you," he went on slowly and impressively, "if we'd only kep' up with em', I'll bet you we would have found them now killin' him. After as good a run as a man could want! It's a great pity!"

It was indeed sad. Visions arose of the sagacious Barney and the shadow-like kangaroo slut engaged in the combat to the death with the dingo, who was dying silently, fighting to the last. I thought sadly of all I was missing, for I had come all the way from Sydney to see a dingo killed, and now he was actually being killed, and I hadn't been able to keep up.

Here I happened to look over my shoulder and saw the sagacious Barney trying to dig a lizard out from under a fallen log, while the two hounds watched him with an air of grave interest.

"There they are," said I, "there's the dogs now."

The stockman wasn't a bit taken aback. "So they are," he said. "They must have come on-sighted. This time last year they missed a dingo just about the same way — just about here it was, too. It's only an accident like when they miss one, I tell you."

We had many another dash after Barney and his dingoes, and they all ended in the same way. The dogs dashed yelping out of sight, the horses tore through the scrub, the sunburnt stockman screamed encouragement from the rear, and the grandson of Musket swept through the timber over rocks and fallen logs, with the swoop of some great bird. After half a mile or so we would find ourselves left in the vast silence of the Australian bush, no dog nor dingo in sight; then we put in the time till the dogs came back, explaining to each other how it was that we had failed to keep up with them.

We didn't catch any dingoes. I saw one once in the distance and Barney was taken up and put on the scent; it was an anxious moment for me, because if Barney failed to howl and run on the scent, then that would have proved that I was a liar, and had not seen a dingo. Luckily for me Barney went nearly into hysterics when he came on the scent, and we had a glorious dash for a while; shortly after, we came on a dead yearling calf which the dingoes had killed. They had eaten the carcase almost out of the skin, leaving the empty skin like a discarded glove. The sunburnt stockman said that when they want to kill a calf they snap and bite at the heels of the mob till they start them racing, and as soon as a weak one falls to the rear, they snap at its hocks till they hamstring it; then they bite it to death.

The squatter produced a little bottle of strychnine and put some into the body of the calf. While he was doing this the sagacious Barney and the two hounds returned from their fruitless chase. Barney snuffed round the carcase for a while, then threw up his head and set off across the range at a business-like trot.

"Look at him," said the stockman. "He's on to 'em! He's trailin' 'em! There's been a lot round that calf, and he'll be on to 'em in a minute! Be ready now! Be ready! That's the way he always goes when he's trailin' 'em!"

My heart beat high with excitement. I gripped the grandson of Musket by the head and peered through the dense timber to see if I could risk a hundred yards of safe going, so that I might see a little of the hunt before I was killed. I expected a summons to death at any moment.

With intense excitement we watched Barney pause on the top of the rocks and snuff the air, irresolute; then he trotted on for some distance and wagged his tail, evidently having found what he wanted. There was a pool of water there and he lay down in it; he had not been after dingoes at all; having slaked his thirst, he trotted back and began to eat the poisoned calf. I suggested that in reward for having sold us like that, he should be allowed to eat as much of it as he wanted, but his owner explained that there had been dingoes drinking at the waterhole and Barney had gone there to see if any were planted near there. No matter what happened, you couldn't shake his faith in Barney.

After this contretemps we lost interest in the dingoes and went to look for cattle. We found a few poor starving relics, eating the scrub which was cut down for them from day to day. When they first came on the place, they were so wild that the sight of a man would set them galloping in all directions, and now, as soon as they heard an axe they would come crowding down to it.

Cattle are going to be worth phenomenal money after the drought. Judging by what we saw in the bush, next year's export of frozen meat will be mostly frozen bone dust.

The hounds caught a few kangaroos during the day, and the shades of night saw us returning to the station with horses, dogs, and men all pretty tired, and no result in the shape of dingoes. But that wasn't Barney's fault. As his owner said, "If we'd only have been able to have kept up, he would have got a lot of 'em."

Old Pardon, the Son of Reprieve

You never heard tell of the story?
   Well, now, I can hardly believe!
Never heard of the honour and glory
   Of Pardon, the son of Reprieve?
But maybe you're only a Johnnie
   And don't know a horse from a hoe?
Well, well, don't get angry, my sonny,
   But, really, a young 'un should know.

They bred him out back on the "Never",
   His mother was Mameluke breed.
To the front — and then stay there — was ever
   The root of the Mameluke creed.
He seemed to inherit their wiry
   Strong frames — and their pluck to receive —
As hard as a flint and as fiery
   Was Pardon, the son of Reprieve.

We ran him at many a meeting
   At crossing and gully and town,
And nothing could give him a beating —
   At least when our money was down.
For weight wouldn't stop him, nor distance,
   Nor odds, though the others were fast,
He'd race with a dogged persistence,
   And wear them all down at the last.

At the Turon the Yattendon filly
   Led by lengths at the mile and a half,
And we all began to look silly,
   While *her* crowd were starting to laugh;
But the old horse came faster and faster,
   His pluck told its tale, and his strength,
He gained on her, caught her, and passed her,
   And won it, hands down, by a length.

And then we swooped down on Menindie
   To run for the President's Cup —
Oh! that's a sweet township — a shindy
   To them is board, lodging, and sup.
Eye-openers they are, and their system
   Is never to suffer defeat;
It's "win, tie, or wrangle" — to best 'em
   You must lose 'em, or else it's "dead heat".

We strolled down the township and found 'em
   At drinking and gaming and play;
If sorrows they had, why they drowned 'em,
   And betting was soon under way.
Their horses were good 'uns and fit 'uns,
   There was plenty of cash in the town;
They backed their own horses like Britons,
   And Lord! how *we* rattled it down!

With gladness we thought of the morrow,
   We counted our wagers with glee,
A simile homely to borrow —
   "There was plenty of milk in our tea".
You see we were green; and we never
   Had even a thought of foul play,
Though we well might have known that the clever
   Division would "put us away".

Experience *"docet"*, they tell us,
   At least so I've frequently heard,
But, "dosing" or "stuffing", those fellows
   Were up to each move on the board;
They got to his stall — it is sinful
   To think what such villains would do —
And they gave him a regular skinful
   Of barley — green barley — to chew.

He munched it all night, and we found him
    Next morning as full as a hog —
The girths wouldn't nearly meet round him;
    He looked like an overfed frog.
We saw we were done like a dinner —
    The odds were a thousand to one
Against Pardon turning up winner,
    'Twas cruel to ask him to run.

We got to the course with our troubles,
    A crestfallen couple were we;
And we heard the "books" calling the doubles —
    A roar like the surf of the sea;
And over the tumult and louder
    Rang, "Any price Pardon, I lay!"
Says Jimmy, "The children of Judah
    Are out on the warpath to-day."

Three miles in three heats: Ah, my sonny
    The horses in those days were stout,
They had to run well to win money;
    I don't see such horses about.
Your six-furlong vermin that scamper
    Half a mile with their featherweight up;
They wouldn't earn much of their damper
    In a race like the President's Cup.

The first heat was soon set a-going;
    The Dancer went off to the front;
The Don on his quarters was showing,
    With Pardon right out of the hunt.
He rolled and he weltered and wallowed —
    You'd kick your hat faster, I'll bet;
They finished all bunched, and he followed
    All lathered and dripping with sweat.

But troubles came thicker upon us,
    For while we were rubbing him dry
The stewards came over to warn us:
    "We hear you are running a bye!
If Pardon don't spiel like tarnation
    And win the next heat — if he can —
He'll earn a disqualification;
    Just think over *that*, now, my man!"

Our money all gone and our credit,
    Our horse couldn't gallop a yard;
And then people thought that *we* did it!
    It really was terribly hard.
We were objects of mirth and derision
    To folk in the lawn and the stand,
And the yells of the clever division
    Of "Any price, Pardon!" were grand.

We still had a chance for the money,
    Two heats still remained to be run;
If both fell to us — why, my sonny,
    The clever division were done.
And Pardon was better, we reckoned,
    His sickness was passing away,
So he went to the post for the second
    And principal heat of the day.

They're off and away with a rattle,
    Like dogs from the leashes let slip,
And right at the back of the battle
    He followed them under the whip.
They gained ten good lengths on him quickly,
    He dropped right away from the pack;
I tell you it made me feel sickly
    To see the blue jacket fall back.

Our very last hope had departed —
    We thought the old fellow was done,
When all of a sudden he started
    To go like a shot from a gun.
His chances seemed slight to embolden
    Our hearts; but, with teeth firmly set,
We thought, "Now or never! The old 'un
    May reckon with some of 'em yet."

Then loud rose the warcry for Pardon;
    He swept like the wind down the dip,
And over the rise by the garden,
    The jockey was done with the whip;
The field were at sixes and sevens —
    The pace at the first had been fast —
And hope seemed to drop from the heavens,
    For Pardon was coming at last.

And how he did come! It was splendid;
   He gained on them yards every bound,
Stretching out like a greyhound extended,
   His girth laid right down on the ground.
A shimmer of silk in the cedars
   As into the running they wheeled,
And out flashed the whips on the leaders,
   For Pardon had collared the field.

Then right through the ruck he came sailing —
   I knew that the battle was won —
The son of Haphazard was failing,
   The Yattendon filly was done;
He cut down the Don and the Dancer,
   He raced clean away from the mare —
He's in front! Catch him now if you can, sir!
   And up went my hat in the air!

Then loud from the lawn and the garden
   Rose offers of "Ten to one *on!*"
"Who'll bet on the field? I back Pardon!"
   No use; all the money was gone.
He came for the third heat light-hearted,
   A-jumping and dancing about;
The others were done ere they started
   Crestfallen, and tired, and worn out.

He won it, and ran it much faster
   Than even the first, I believe
Oh, he was the daddy, the master,
   Was Pardon, the son of Reprieve.
He showed 'em the method to travel —
   The boy sat as still as a stone —
They never could see him for gravel;
   He came in hard-held, and alone.

But he's old — and his eyes are grown hollow;
   Like me, with my thatch of the snow;
When he dies, then I hope I may follow,
   And go where the racehorses go,
I don't want no harping nor singing —
   Such things with my style don't agree;
Where the hoofs of the horses are ringing
   There's music sufficient for me.

And surely the thoroughbred horses
　　Will rise up again and begin
Fresh races on faraway courses
　　And p'raps they might let me slip in.
It would look rather well the race card on
　　'Mongst cherubs and seraphs and things,
"Angel Harrison's black gelding Pardon,
　　Blue halo, white body and wings".

And if they have racing hereafter,
　　(And who is to say they will not?)
When the cheers and the shouting and laughter
　　Proclaim that the battle grows hot;
As they come down the racecourse a-steering,
　　He'll rush to the front, I believe;
And you'll hear the great multitude cheering
　　For Pardon, the son of Reprieve.

Our New Horse

The boys had come back from the races
　　All silent and down on their luck;
They'd backed 'em, straight out and for places,
　　But never a winner they struck.
They lost their good money on Slogan,
　　And fell most uncommonly flat,
When Partner, the pride of the Bogan,
　　Was beaten by Aristocrat.

And one said, "I move that instanter
　　We sell out our horses and quit,
The brutes ought to win in a canter,
　　Such trials they do when they're fit.
The last one they ran was a snorter —
　　A gallop to gladden one's heart —
Two-twelve for a mile and a quarter,
　　And finished as straight as a dart.

"And then when I think that they're ready
  To win me a nice little swag,
They are licked like the veriest neddy —
  They're licked from the fall of the flag.
The mare held her own to the stable,
  She died out to nothing at that,
And Partner he never seemed able
  To pace it with Aristocrat.

"And times have been bad, and the seasons
  Don't promise to be of the best;
In short, boys, there's plenty of reasons
  For giving the racing a rest.
The mare can be kept on the station —
  Her breeding is good as can be —
But Partner, his next destination
  Is rather a trouble to me.

"We can't sell him here, for they know him
  As well as the clerk of the course;
He's raced and won races till, blow him,
  He's done as a handicap horse.
A jady, uncertain performer,
  They weight him right out of the hunt,
And clap it on warmer and warmer
  Whenever he gets near the front.

"It's no use to paint him or dot him
  Or put any 'fake' on his brand,
For bushmen are smart, and they'd spot him
  In any saleyard in the land.
The folk about here could all tell him,
  Could swear to each separate hair;
Let us send him to Sydney and sell him,
  There's plenty of Jugginses there.

"We'll call him a maiden, and treat 'em
  To trials will open their eyes,
We'll run their best horses and beat 'em,
  And then won't they think him a prize.
I pity the fellow that buys him,
  He'll find in a very short space,
No matter how highly he tries him,
  The beggar won't *race* in a race."

Next week, under "Seller and Buyer",
   Appeared in the *Daily Gazette*:
"A racehorse for sale, and a flyer;
   Has never been started as yet;
A trial will show what his pace is;
   The buyer can get him in light,
And win all the handicap races.
   Apply here before Wednesday night."

He sold for a hundred and thirty,
   Because of a gallop he had
One morning with Bluefish and Bertie,
   And donkey-licked both of 'em bad.
And when the old horse had departed,
   The life on the station grew tame;
The racetrack was dull and deserted,
   The boys had gone back on the game.

The winter rolled by, and the station
   Was green with the garland of spring,
A spirit of glad exultation
   Awoke in each animate thing.
And all the old love, the old longing,
   Broke out in the breasts of the boys,
The visions of racing came thronging
   With all its delirious joys.

The rushing of floods in their courses,
   The rattle of rain on the roofs
Recalled the fierce rush of the horses,
   The thunder of galloping hoofs.
And soon one broke out: "I can suffer
   No longer the life of a slug,
The man that don't race is a duffer,
   Let's have one more run for the mug.

"Why, *everything* races, no matter
   Whatever its method may be:
The waterfowl hold a regatta;
   The possums run heats up a tree;
The emus are constantly sprinting
   A handicap out on the plain;
It seems like all nature was hinting,
   'Tis time to be at it again.

The boys had come back from the races
All silent and down on their luck;
They'd backed 'em, straight out and for places,
But never a winner they struck.

Our New Horse, p. 190

'Twas a big black horse, that I had not seen
  In the part of the race I'd ridden;
And his coat was cool and his rider clean,
And I thought that perhaps I had not been
  The only one that had hidden.

The Old Timer's Steeplechase, p. 201

"The cockatoo parrots are talking
    Of races to faraway lands;
The native companions are walking
    A go-as-you-please on the sands;
The little foals gallop for pastime;
    The wallabies race down the gap;
Let's try it once more for the last time,
    Bring out the old jacket and cap.

"And now for a horse; we might try one
    Of those that are bred on the place,
But I think it better to buy one,
    A horse that has proved he can race.
Let us send down to Sydney to Skinner,
    A thorough good judge who can ride,
And ask him to buy us a spinner
    To clean out the whole countryside."

They wrote him a letter as follows:
    "We want you to buy us a horse;
He must have the speed to catch swallows,
    And stamina with it of course.
The price ain't a thing that'll grieve us,
    It's getting a bad 'un annoys
The undersigned blokes, and believe us,
    We're yours to a cinder, 'The boys'."

He answered: "I've bought you a hummer,
    A horse that has never been raced;
I saw him run over the Drummer,
    He held him outclassed and outpaced.
His breeding's not known, but they state he
    Is born of a thoroughbred strain,
I paid them a hundred and eighty,
    And started the horse in the train."

They met him — alas, that these verses
    Aren't up to the subject's demands —
Can't set forth their eloquent curses,
    For Partner was back on their hands.
They went in to meet him in gladness,
    They opened his box with delight —
A silent procession of sadness
    They crept to the station at night.

And life has grown dull on the station,
  The boys are all silent and slow;
Their work is a daily vexation,
  And sport is unknown to them now.
Whenever they think how they stranded,
  They squeal just like guinea-pigs squeal;
They bit their own hook, and were landed
  With fifty pounds' loss on the deal.

Punters and Professional Backers

"When you don't draw anything, don't bet." Partially defaced
inscription on the tomb of Aotun II, who is supposed to have
discovered the ten lost tribes.

Punters are backers run mad. Our investigations into bookmakers' odds have shown us that, on the usual run of races, a backer of horses has on figures a somewhat worse chance than a backer of the numbers at Monte Carlo: and the heavy backer of horses has another set of expenses against him. He has to pay out such a lot of money for information, presents to harriers, presents to jockeys and share of the spoil to owners that the odds against him are enormously increased. For example, if a man takes a wager of £1500 to £200 on a race, he may stand quite a reasonable chance, on figures and probabilities, of receiving some money. A thousand pounds to two hundred may be quite fair odds, even allowing a margin for bookmakers' profits. Should he win, however, out of his £1500 he has to give the winning jockey a present of £50, the trainer possibly another £50; the owner of the horse, if he has been consulted at all, expects at least another £50. Then the odds he gets are really £850 to £200 and the difference is just what ruins the "punter". He cannot keep on taking these short odds with any prospect of success. This is the reason why thousands of men can keep on for years betting in a small way for amusement and do themselves no great harm, while the "big punter" invariably comes to grief. The punter must not be compared with the professional backer. This latter individual does not need to give anything away for information, as he is a better judge of racing than any owner, jockey, trainer or whisperer, and can hold his own with the ring by reason of his coolness and judgment. The usual *modus operandi* for a punter is to attach himself to some stable and back their horses heavily when they are supposed to have extra good chances. An owner racing for a living will ask a punter to "take his horse on", that is to say, to back it heavily and give the owner a share out of the winnings. The owner pulls his horse a few times (we are now speaking of the sordid non-sporting side of racing) and when it is in a race with a lightweight, he invites the punter to come in and do the betting. It might be thought that these "coups" could be brought off fairly often, and that a punter might do very well at the business. But the trouble is that there are so many at it. In the very race for which the horse has been "got ready", there are probably three or four other horses that have been similarly working for a "coup". And when the punter steps in and backs his choice heavily, the ring often offer tempting prices against the others and their owners "put a punter in too", and it becomes a battle royal among them. Only one can win, so the punters or the others lose their money. Punters, too, get too much information. They are for ever being told tales, all the more fascinating because of their mystery, about horses that have done wonderful gallops or won phenomenal trials and the punter acts on this select inside information, with poor results.

There are two reasons why these mysterious certainties seldom come off. The first is that if a horse has really done anything phenomenal in private the secret is sure to leak out, and the punter has to take a short price with the rest of the public: secondly, jockeys and trainers are always apt to overrate the horses they are interested in, and they unintentionally mislead the "punter". The trainer and rider of a horse may honestly hold the opinion that it "can't possibly get beaten": but it does get beaten all the same. A trainer's opinion about another trainer's horses is always more worth following than his opinion about his own. The turf "expert" nearly always tells us how the boss makes a fortune by heavily backing some animal that has been kept a dark deadly secret, and which goes out at a hundred to one and romps home last: but the punter in real life knows, or at any rate learns sooner or later, that it is very rare indeed for any horse with a really good chance to be at a fortune price in the betting. When fortune-priced horses do win, it is generally a bigger surprise to their owners and immediate connections than to anyone else: and a backer who thinks of backing a rank outsider should always pause and ask himself, "Am I the only good judge of racing here?" Neither by following favourites nor by supporting rank outsiders can the heavy bettor ever hope to beat the bookmakers for long. An official of a big betting club once confided to the writer, "I have never seen a man come into this club and start betting heavily that he did not leave it without boots. Men talk about breaking the ring. When a man starts that game, all that the bookmakers ask themselves is, 'How long will he last?' I have seen a man come into this club with £1000 for every day in the year — he had £365,000 — and he started betting in a big way and in three years he was ruined. The ring did not get it all, don't think that, but the turf got it. Whenever he did win, he had to give away a lot of his money. As a matter of fact he pretty well settled one or two of the bookmakers, but the others beat him."

The worst of heavy betting is that it becomes a craze, just like drinking or taking drugs. A victim to this disease — if that is what we must call it — may see his money going away before his eyes and may make fifty resolutions to give up betting, but he cannot give it up, and one or two winning days will start him at it again as keenly as ever. Then comes the inevitable crash, and the inevitable stories that another man has been "swindled out of his money" on the turf. As a matter of fact there is not such a great deal of swindling. A bookmaker of any standing does not care to put himself in the power of an unscrupulous jockey by bribing him to pull a horse. He does not need to do it while he can get the public to take three to one in a field of twenty. Jockeys' rings occasionally manifest themselves, but here, too, the difficulty of keeping things quiet and keeping all the gang and their following satisfied soon brings this to a crisis. Men who are not honest to their employers are not likely to be honest to each other: and, to use turf slang for once in a way, when you hear of things being "done on the cross", you soon hear of their being done on the "double cross"; in other words, the swindlers soon take to swindling each other; and the "punter" who tries to arrange the result of races by conspiring with the jockeys will come to grief even more quickly than the straight-going man. The man who goes on the turf and tries to be "clever" will be surprised to find how many there are that can beat him at his own game, as the following strictly true story may help to illustrate.

A big country man came once to an Australian metropolis with a racehorse. "The 'orse was a good 'orse", as the man says in the play, and the country man was brimming over with money and self-confidence. What he was short of was honesty. He trained the horse himself, but he could not ride it himself: that was where his difficulties began. After much thought he went to a trainer who had a widespread and well-deserved reputation for working successful "coups" and put the matter to him bluntly. He wanted the trainer's apprentice to ride his horse and to pull the animal. Until such time as the handicapper let it into a race with a lightweight, the bookmakers were prepared to bet heavily against it. Of course he did not make any such laboured explanation to the trainer. He simply said, "Will you lend me your boy to ride my horse Braneater a few times? When it's all right you can have a bit on, and I'll treat the boy well."

The trainer said, "All right."

The country man said, "I suppose the boy will do what I tell him."

By way of guaranteeing good faith, the trainer called the boy up. "Ernie", he said, "you're to ride Mr Wayback's horse and you're to do whatever he tells you."

The boy said, "All right."

End of Act I.

The second act discloses a racecourse. Mr Wayback's horse Braneater a competitor. No money for it in the ring and the bookmakers call out, "Seven to one Braneater!" Mr Wayback slips into the ring ostentatiously and puts £25 on with the loudest of the bookmakers. News spreads through the ring like ripples through a pool that Wayback's horse is having a try and the bookmakers call out, "Five to one on Braneater!" Race is run and Ernie rides a most artistic losing race on Braneater. Two hard-heads discuss the race and one says, "I believe Braneater was pulled." The other says, "Couldn't ha' been. I myself saw the bloke do a pony on him with Crackitt."

Trainer interviews boy. "How did that horse run with you, Ernie?"

"Could have won as he liked. I had to get blocked every three lengths or I'd have won." Mr Wayback enters and gives boy £1 for having ridden to orders.

End of Act II.

Act III opens with the trainer in a thinking part. He thinks aloud. "Every time my boy runs a losing race on that horse, he runs a big risk of disqualification. When the horse is ready to win, that large bushman will probably have some other rider up, so as to have a good excuse for the change of form. Even if he keeps my boy on, what will I get out of it? A few pounds. Can I do any better for myself? If I am in anything like my old form, I can." Is left thinking furiously.

Act IV, Scene I: another race meeting. Braneater a competitor. Bookmakers offer seven to one. Trainer sends a confederate to the ring and puts £200 on Braneater. Public lay various and sundry sums of money on it. Bookmakers call "Six to four Braneater!" Enter Mr Wayback, very indignant. "Someone has got in ahead of me and backed my horse. I'll teach them a lesson. Don't you try a yard with him today, Ernie."

Ernie says, "All right." Exit Mr Wayback.

Trainer takes jockey aside and whispers impressively. "You must do your best today, Ernie. It don't do to be pullin' horses for everybody. It's not honest. You understand me now. You jump him out as quick as you can, and move along all the way, and it don't matter if you win by half a mile. Honesty is the best policy, Ernie."

Ernie says, "All right."

The race gets a start, but it is nothing to the start Mr Wayback gets when he sees Ernie racing away from his field with a four lengths lead, with Braneater going like a locomotive. The horse wins by ten lengths pulling up. Mr Wayback seeks Ernie for explanations, but cannot find him. Trainer sympathises with Mr Wayback and says the boy must have been bribed by some unscrupulous person to win the race. Scene ends with trainer and Mr Wayback having a drink together, and the trainer's confederate collecting £1,400 from the bookmakers. Curtain.

The reader must not suppose that all racing is run on this sort of scoundrelly basis. A good punter — one who bets freely and pays liberally for information — can get fair treatment. It is the would-be smart man who comes to grief, and who is the loudest in his denunciations of turf roguery. Occasionally a turf Machiavelli arises who can work swindles and can command loyalty from his subordinates, and a few such men have won large sums of money at different periods of turf history. But these men are usually in the class of "professional backers" rather than "punters" and are so few in number that they are really exceptions that prove the rule. Backers come and go, punters win fortunes at one meeting and are asking for time after the next, but the man with the book and pencil is still on top. "Six to four on the field" — no judgment, no information; no run of luck, can stand against that for any length of time. With the totalisator it is just the same. The ten per cent that the machine takes must beat the punter in the long run. It must always be remembered that the starting prices recorded in a newspaper on a day's racing when bookmakers operate do not really represent the prices that the early backers and stable followers get: usually the stable money is got on at a good deal longer price than the starting price quoted in the paper. But the totalisator has only the one price for owners and strangers, early bettors and latecomers alike. The machine never takes any chances, never puts its own money against what looks like a paper certainty: the ring do sometimes face an almost certain loss, and so give backers a chance to carry away a bit of money for a while. Looking at the two systems of betting from the owners' and heavy bettors' point of view, the ring is possibly the better of the two, but it is a choice of evils, anyhow.

While he lasts, the punter is the observed of all observers. It is said that all the world loves a lover: well, all the turf world loves a punter. All the small fry of horse backers watch with intense interest the career of the daring speculator who goes out to battle with the books, even as David went out against Goliath of Gath. All that the trainers know, all the acquired wisdom of the knowledge boxes and the tactical skill of the hard-heads, all these are at his disposal if he is a likeable fellow. Other punters and backers will give him a hint when they know of anything good. Alas, it always ends the same way. He may rush in on the spurs and even drag a few of the enemy down with him, but after the disturbance the bookmakers close up their phalanx again and the punter is as if he had never existed. Another always steps into the fighting line, and so the game goes on. The heavy punters never last long but the seasoned racegoers last for years. One old jockey revisiting a race-course after an absence of fifteen years said, "I see all the same old faces that I used to see when I was riding. There's old Bill Saunders, and Jack Whatshisname, and Charley Whosthis still going strong. They say the good die young. I suppose that's why all these old fellows have lasted so long."

from *Racehorses and Racing*

The Old Timer's Steeplechase

The sheep were shorn and the wool went down
   At the time of our local racing:
And I'd earned a spell — I was burnt and brown —
So I rolled my swag for a trip to town
   And a look at the steeplechasing.

'Twas rough and ready — an uncleared course
   As rough as the blacks had found it;
With barbed wire fences, topped with gorse,
And a water jump that would drown a horse,
   And the steeple three times round it.

There was never a fence the tracks to guard —
   Some straggling posts defined 'em:
And the day was hot, and the drinking hard,
Till none of the stewards could see a yard
   Before nor yet behind 'em!

But the bell was rung and the nags were out,
   Excepting an old outsider
Whose trainer started an awful rout,
For his boy had gone on a drinking bout
   And left him without a rider.

"Is there not one man in the crowd," he cried,
   "In the whole of the crowd so clever,
Is there not one man that will take a ride
On the old white horse from the northern side
   That was bred on the Mooki River?"

'Twas an old white horse that they called The Cow,
   And a cow would look well beside him;
But I was pluckier then than now
(And I wanted excitement anyhow),
   So at last I agreed to ride him.

And the trainer said, "Well, he's dreadful slow,
   And he hasn't a chance whatever;
But I'm stony broke, so it's time to show
A trick or two that the trainers know
   Who train by the Mooki River.

"The first time round at the further side,
  With the trees and the scrub about you,
Just pull behind them and run out wide
And then dodge into the scrub and hide,
  And let them go round without you.

"At the third time round, for the final spin
  With the pace, and the dust to blind 'em,
They'll never notice if you chip in
For the last half-mile — you'll be sure to win,
  And they'll think you raced behind 'em.

"At the water jump you may have to swim —
  He hasn't a hope to clear it —
Unless he skims like the swallows skim
At full speed over, but not for him!
  He'll never go next or near it.

"But don't you worry — just plunge across,
  For he swims like a well-trained setter.
Then hide away in the scrub and gorse
The rest will be far ahead of course —
  The further ahead the better.

"You must rush the jumps in the last half-round
  For fear that he might refuse 'em;
He'll try to baulk with you, I'll be bound,
Take whip and spurs on the mean old hound,
  And don't be afraid to use 'em.

"At the final round, when the field are slow
  And you are quite fresh to meet 'em,
Sit down, and hustle him all you know
With the whip and spurs, and he'll have to go —
  Remember, you've *got* to beat 'em!"

The flag went down and we seemed to fly,
  And we made the timbers shiver
Of the first big fence, as the stand flashed by,
And I caught the ring of the trainer's cry:
  "Go on! For the Mooki River!"

I jammed him in with a well-packed crush,
  And recklessly — out for slaughter —
Like a living wave over fence and brush

We swept and swung with a flying rush,
　　Till we came to the dreaded water.

Ha, ha! I laugh at it now to think
　　Of the way I contrived to work it.
Shut in amongst them, before you'd wink,
He found himself on the water's brink,
　　With never a chance to shirk it!

The thought of the horror he felt, beguiles
　　The heart of this grizzled rover!
He gave a snort you could hear for miles,
And a spring would have cleared the Channel Isles
　　And carried me safely over!

Then we neared the scrub, and I pulled him back
　　In the shade where the gum leaves quiver:
And I waited there in the shadows black
While the rest of the horses, round the track,
　　Went on like a rushing river!

At the second round, as the field swept by,
　　I saw that the pace was telling;
But on they thundered, and by and by
As they passed the stand I could hear the cry
　　Of the folk in the distance, yelling!

Then the last time round! And the hoofbeats rang!
　　And I said, "Well, it's now or never!"
And out on the heels of the throng I sprang,
And the spurs bit deep and the whipcord sang
　　As I rode! For the Mooki River!

We raced for home in a cloud of dust
　　And the curses rose in chorus.
'Twas flog, and hustle, and jump you must!
And The Cow ran well — but to my disgust
　　There was one got home before us.

'Twas a big black horse, that I had not seen
　　In the part of the race I'd ridden;
And his coat was cool and his rider clean,
And I thought that perhaps I had not been
　　The only one that had hidden.

And the trainer came with a visage blue
    With rage, when the race concluded:
Said he, "I thought you'd have pulled us through,
But the man on the black horse planted too,
    And nearer to home than you did!"

Alas to think that those times so gay
    Have vanished and passed forever!
You don't believe in the yarn you say?
Why, man! 'Twas a matter of every day
    When we raced on the Mooki River!

Constantine the Great

ARRIVAL AT "LIMESTONE"

The thoroughbred mares in their own exclusive paddock at Limestone stud were a very aristocratic lot, and as keen on their own dignity and precedence as a lot of patrician dowagers in a Court drawing-room: consequently, they were very much upset when a strange horse was turned in among them one bright December morning, without their permission being asked or their desires considered in any way whatever.

You must understand that these highly pedigreed ladies all figured in the pages of the *Stud Book*, which is the *Debrett's Peerage* of the Turf world, and they knew each other's pedigrees and relationships away back into the days of Charles I. Not a horse could win an important race in any part of the world and no mare could produce a Derby winner, but what such of the Limestone ladies as were related to the new celebrity became very proud and arrogant, and those who were not related became jealous — very jealous indeed.

Being a lot of highly bred dowagers, they were divided into as many cliques and coteries as the countesses and duchesses in a Mayfair drawing-room, and the credentials of any new arrival were very closely scanned before she was admitted to any of the more exclusive circles.

"That mare," a dowager countess would say, on considering the pedigree of a new arrival, "of course I shall call on her, but I really couldn't make a friend of her. My dear, do you know that her family haven't won a really big race for three generations?"

Besides an infinite number of smaller coteries, there were two clear-cut social sets among the mares — those born in England, and those born in

Australia.

The English mares did not actually patronise the others, but they just tolerated them, and on Derby Day the English mares got together and talked about Epsom and Newmarket till the other mares could hardly bear it: and a pert young Australian mare, after listening to as much of this conversation as she could stand, said, "The Epsom Derby! That's the race where they go up and down hills, isn't it, like our stockhorses go after cattle?" a remark that was passed over in a kind of pitying silence. But in spite of their bickering among themselves they presented a united front against all outsiders, and they looked upon any horse not in the *Stud Book* in much the same way as a duchess would look upon the bride of a costermonger.

And so, on this beautiful December day, a strange horse was actually being turned into their paddock, a big gaunt bay horse with hair on his fetlocks, a plain head and spur marks on his ribs: a horse that looked as though he ought to be carrying a general at the head of an army, so strong and resolute was his appearance, and so kind and intelligent was his eye; but the hair on his fetlocks, the spur marks on his ribs, and the plainness of his head decided the mares that he could not be a thoroughbred — perhaps something very near it, but not quite born in the purple. So they decided to ignore the intruder, and they cast calm supercilious glances at him as he strolled past them on his way to the river to get a drink.

The two men who had brought him to the paddock stood chatting by the rails. The mares knew one of them well enough, for the tall man with the heavy moustache and the slow soft way of speaking was Gordon Macallister, owner of the Limestone stud, and he was a personal friend of every mare in the paddock. He visited them nearly every day, he looked after them when they were sick and a word from him in praise of one of the foals was enough to make that foal's mother proud and joyful for a week.

The keen-eyed little man with the quick, staccato way of speaking was unknown to the mares and they put him down as not much class anyway; if they had known that he was Ike Heronshaw, the greatest trainer of the day, they would have been more impressed.

"Well, Ike," said Macallister, "this is the best I can do for you. No one goes through this paddock, and no one would dream of looking for him among my crack mares and foals. Why does his owner want him planted?"

"He's broke."

"Broke! I thought he had plenty of money?"

"So he did have. But he wanted more, so he bought half the wool in Australia and shipped it and struck a misere hand. He's got no ready money, y'understand, and his creditors are after him, and if they can get hold of this horse they'll sell him by order of the Court. But the market's risin' and if he can hold on for a few weeks he'll be all right again. That's why he wants this horse out of the road."

"I see. But I'm taking a risk putting him in with my mares and foals. I wouldn't dream of doing it for anybody but you. Is he quiet?"

"Quiet! You could bowl hedgehogs at his hind legs all day and he wouldn't kick at 'em. Your daughter could ride him, so then nobody would tumble to it that he is anything more than an ordinary hack. What I'm afraid of is that he might cripple himself if he gets galloping about with these foals."

"That's what you're afraid of, is it? Well, what about me, taking the risk of turning a stranger into this paddock? He might set the whole lot racing for their lives! If I'll chance my mares and foals, you've got to chance your horse. If I put him anywhere else, somebody's sure to see him and you'll have the bailiffs after him."

With that, the two men rode away to the homestead and the mares were left to size up the intruder.

Possibly the most aristocratic mare in the paddock was Lady Susan, a descendant of the great St Simon, and with so many other celebrated relatives that her position was almost unchallengeable. True, she was Australian-born, but her grandsire had won the English Derby and she herself had won the Australian Oaks, and what was more important, her foals had won two Derbies and a Melbourne Cup. The English mares might affect to despise Australian races, but any foal from Lady Susan was worth five thousand guineas as it stood on its delicate little hooves alongside her in the paddock. The English mares might talk about Epsom and Newmarket, but none of their foals averaged five thousand guineas, so there was no more to be said: all the mares waited for a lead from Lady Susan in most matters, but in regard to this new horse they thought they were on safe ground in criticising him.

The chorus was led off by Cat's Cradle, a young and pert Australian mare who was inclined to give herself airs because her full sister had won the last big race for two-year-old fillies by three lengths in very fast time. She was addicted to slang and after looking the newcomer over in a very supercilious way she gave a horse laugh, which is a kind of internal laugh that you can't see.

"Girls," she said, "what have we here? Pipe the marks of the harpoons on his ribs, and the whiskers on his fetlocks! I'll bet he's a winner — the winner of the Big Scrub Handicap with the first prize a bees' nest. After you've won the race, they show you the bees' nest in a tree, and you have to cut the tree down and rob the nest for yourself."

Meanwhile the English mares were muttering among themselves such remarks as "preposterous", "wouldn't be tolerated in England", "you never know what to expect in this extraordinary country", being faintly heard above the singing of Featherbrain, an English mare who was apt to be a bit hysterical, who screamed to her foal and set off up the paddock as hard as she could split, but finding that none of the others followed her, she returned in a shamefaced way to the mob. All this time old Lady Susan had said nothing until her foal, who was quite an important person, for he was expected to fetch at least six thousand guineas at auction, went up to her and said, "Mother, can I go and speak to the new horse? He seems so lonely, and none of the others will go near him."

"Yes," she said, "you can go. I seem to see a likeness in that horse to somebody I used to know. I think I must have raced against his mother at some time or other. You mustn't say anything rude to him about the hair on his fetlocks, for sometimes that comes to us from the old English horses that were in the pedigrees hundreds of years before the Arabs were ever brought into England. Just be civil to him, and if he tells you anything come back and tell me," — for even the greatest ladies are not above a little curiosity.

Without the slightest hesitation, Lady Susan's foal marched up to the newcomer and gave him the usual Australian salutation, "Good day. It looks very dry, doesn't it?"

The stranger, who appeared to be a rough and ready sort of person, said, "Yes, it's dry all right: and who may you be, young fellow?"

To which the foal, who had a great idea of his own importance though he was only a few months old, answered without any trepidation, "I'm Lady Susan's foal. Perhaps you've heard of my full brother Gaslight?"

"Gaslight!" said the stranger. "Why I ran against" — and here he stopped as though about to say too much. "I ran against a stone coming up, and bruised my heel a bit. But look here, young fellow, it doesn't matter what you are full brother to, the thing is, can you gallop yourself? The Judge don't place any horse first because he's full brother to something, you know."

"Oh, yes, I know that. But I can go a bit, and when the foals all get together for our gallop round the paddock this evening, you can see me travel. Did you ever do any racing yourself?"

"Oh yes, young fellow, I've raced a bit: not as much as some and more than others. The less you talk about what you can do in racing the better for you, you understand. The handicapper might hear you, and you'd never get the weight off. But I'll watch you go round this evening, and I might be able to give you a wrinkle or two that will do you some good when your time comes to go to the barrier."

That evening when the foals gathered for their customary sprint round the paddock, the stranger watched them for a while and then tossed up his head and set after them, going in surprising fashion, his great strides eating up the ground, while the foals with their little nostrils distended and their little hoofs rattling on the stony ridges strove valiantly for the lead. The Featherbrain mare got very excited and said, "Look, look, he'll kill the foals", to which Lady Susan, who had picked up some hard sayings in the training stables, replied, "Shut your head! The foals are all right."

You see, her foal was well in front and going like a champion.

After the gallop Lady Susan's foal strolled over to the stranger expecting to get all sorts of compliments, but the stranger was not of the gushing type. "Very fair," he said. "Very fair, but look here, youngster, when you first jump off, don't make too big a jump. It's all right with nothing on your back, but when you've got a jockey there, too big a jump will unbalance him. Just take half a stride as you move out of the barrier, and get the weight on your back under way. Then get down to it and deal it out to 'em all you know. Give my compliments to your mother and tell her I know all about her. Everybody on the Turf knows all about Lady Susan."

THE FIRE

That was the year of the big bushfire, the fire that swept up the river from a hundred miles south, burning all before it. It had been a great season, and the long grass and thistles on the flats were as dry as tinder, and the wind brought the fire along in great leaps, the burning cinders being carried by the wind from the dry trees to start fresh fires half a mile ahead. When the breeze brought the first scent of the burning gum leaves, and the clouds of smoke appeared over the distant hills, the mares gathered themselves and their foals together sniffing with pointed ears at the new terror — something of which none of them had had any experience.

It so happened that Macallister was away from the head station that day, and he only arrived in his car as night fell, bringing with him his daughter, Jean, a fourteen-year-old girl with just as much interest in the horses as Macallister himself. She had been riding ever since she could remember anything, ever since the days when she was carried as a baby in front of her father's saddle.

Springing from the car, Macallister dragged a bridle out of the tonneau, and walking in a quiet matter-of-fact way he went up to the stranger and slipped the bridle on him, talking to him in a soothing voice all the time. Then he led him up to the car and told his daughter what she must do.

"Jean," he said, "that fire will be here in ten minutes and all I've got in the world is in these mares and foals. There's only one thing that can save them, and that is this horse. This is Constantine the Great, the horse that won both the Sydney and Melbourne Derbies and the Melbourne Cup. You'll have to ride him bareback, for there's no time to go and get a saddle, but they say he's very quiet. Now listen to what I've got to tell you.

"As soon as I let the mares and foals out of this paddock, they'll go like mad things all over the bush, and half of them will be crippled or killed in the darkness: but if you can keep ahead of them for the first mile, they'll follow you and you can lead them up to the big bald hill where there's no grass and no timber. When you get them there, try and keep them there — do your best anyhow. They'll be pretty tired by that time and if you keep on riding round and round, and calling out to them in the darkness they may follow you and it may save the lot.

"And now there's another thing. There's that gate at the Two Mile, you'll have no time to stop and open it or the mares will scatter all over the place. Run him right slap into it, and send it flying. It opens in the middle and his weight will smash it like paper. Don't stop for anything and don't look behind you. The mares will follow you through the gate and the main thing is to keep ahead of them the first mile. If there's a horse in the world that can keep ahead of those thoroughbred mares with nothing on their backs, this is the one. I did not want him here, but it looks as if he might save us.

"As soon as I get you away, I'll go up to the house and tell your mother to hide in the river if the fire comes, and then I'll go back to try and save that old crippled woman down in the hut on the flat."

Even as he spoke a red glare showed down at the bend of the river and the mares grew terrified. Swinging the girl on to the big horse's back, he led him towards the gate, patting him on the neck, and talking to him.

"Old man," he said, "you're running for a big stake tonight. Bigger than the Melbourne Cup. There's a hundred thousand pounds of money in these mares and there's my little girl's life. It's up to you to save them, so now go to it like a thoroughbred."

By this time they had reached the gate, the big horse walking quite unconcerned, while the terrified mares crowded behind him.

Giving his daughter a hurried kiss, Macallister threw the gate open, and with the big horse in front, the wild cavalcade swept away into the darkness.

For the first half mile Jean knew nothing but the great swinging strides of the horse beneath her, the dimly seen stretch of track in front, and behind her the roaring of hundreds of hoofs, and the mares whinnying and calling to their foals. If she came off, or if the big horse made a false step in the darkness and came down, she would be trodden flat in an instant by the terrified rush of the mares behind her: but there was a wild exhilaration in the ride that banished all thought of fear. Constantine the Great lay down to work without fear or excitement, for it was nothing new to him to hear the drumming of a field of horses behind him. Some instinct inherited from his Arab ancestors made him reach out and clear in his stride the little waterways that crossed the track. Once or twice in the headlong flight the girl's knee grazed perilously against the trees, and more than once she had to lie flat down on his neck to avoid being swept off by an overhanging branch: but still the great machine-like stride swept him along in front of the mares, and still they followed in close formation at his heels. After a while the pace slackened and Jean was able to sit up and call out to the mares, who knew her voice and answered her with shrill neighs: but the pace was still fast enough to make any delay risky and Jean knew that if she stopped to open the Two Mile gate the mares would probably swing on down the fence into the darkness and smash themselves up in the scrub.

Having got so far in safety, her spirits rose and she amused herself by talking to the big horse as they swept along.

"There's a gate ahead of us," she said, "and you've got to smash it or these mares and foals will be killed. Will you do it for me? Don't jump it, or I'll very likely come off, for I'm not very good at jumping fences barebacked, and if the mares follow you over it, that will be the end of me."

Luckily, the gate was hidden under the shadow of some trees, and the big horse was on it before he saw it.

With no time to jump he gave a snort of defiance and raced straight into it.

Smash! The two by four hardwood battens were splintered like matches under the weight of the blow, and without pause or hesitation he swept on while the mares crowded and crushed through the gap that he had left. So instantaneous had been the smash that Jean had hardly been shifted on her precarious perch, but with each stride that the big horse took she felt something moist on her hands. She was puzzled to think what it could be, but at last she realised that the horse had cut himself rather badly on the gate and that his blood was splashing up on to her hands and clothes. For the first time in that wild ride she felt utterly miserable, but there was nothing that could be done about it so she held her course through the rough timber for the Bald Hill.

Arriving at the hill, she found that an advanced wing of the fire had nearly cut her off, and everything was red flames, smoke, and confusion. In a sort of sanctuary on top of the hill, all sorts of bush animals had gathered, wallabies and kangaroos bewildered with terror racing madly round and round, while rabbits with their fur on fire rushed screaming across the open. A mob of emus, all fear of mankind forgotten, trotted up to her and almost stuck their heads in her face as though asking for guidance. Coming up at their ungainly trot, they had cut the mob of mares in two, and for a moment it looked as though one wing of the mares would lose their heads and race into the scrub; but just as things hung in the balance a foal trotted towards her from the outlying mob, his mother followed him, and in another moment all the mares had gathered together again.

By the light of the burning trees Jean recognised the foal that had so unexpectedly come to her help at a critical moment. "Why," she said, "it's Silas! And he seems to know this horse! Aren't you frightened, Silas?" But Silas, with his small nostrils sniffing the smoke, was quite at his ease, and appeared to think that Providence would hesitate before destroying a gentleman of his quality.

Ringed with smoke and fire, and hampered by terrified wild animals, Jean rode backwards and forwards through the night, keeping the mares together and vainly trying to see what injury her mount had sustained. She dared not get off the horse lest she should never be able to get on again, but as daylight broke she was able to see a big raw gash across his chest from which the blood still welled and, overcome with weariness and excitement, she burst into tears.

A few hours later a big gaunt horse with bloodstained chest and forelegs, and ridden by an inexpressibly weary little girl, led the Limestone mares back to the homestead. Here she found the lucerne paddocks had saved the house from destruction, and after receiving the frantically excited greetings of her father and mother, her first thought was of the injury that her horse had sustained at the gate. After examination her father pronounced it only superficial and it was a thankful girl that tumbled into bed to sleep off the recollections of the night amidst the fire.

When things had settled down a bit in the horse paddock once more, Lady

Susan marched up to the stranger and said, "We have to thank you for saving our lives. Do you mind telling me your name? These English ladies and myself are now of the opinion that you must be a far more important person than you look."

"Well ma'am," he said, "I have a name all right. Such as it is you may have heard it, for they call me Constantine the Great. As for importance, well, I've won some races and I've lost others. I've raced against some of your foals and you want to look after that little fellow you have now, for a gamer bit of stuff I never saw."

When the mares discovered who he was, there was great excitement in hunting over his pedigree, and it was found that he was first cousin to fifteen of them, and was more or less distantly related to every mare in the paddock. It took them several days to hunt out all the relationships.

A few months later the leading newspaper starred the item: "Constantine the Great has come back to work, and appears to be in great fettle except that his chest is disfigured by a scar which he no doubt sustained while playing about in the paddock. It does not give him any trouble and he is certain to add to his already imposing record of wins."

In the Stable

What! You don't like him; well, maybe — we all have our fancies, of course:
Brumby to look at you reckon? Well, no: he's a thoroughbred horse;
Sired by a son of old Panic — look at his ears and his head —
Lop-eared and Roman-nosed, ain't he? — well, that's how the Panics are bred.
Gluttonous, ugly and lazy, rough as a tip-cart to ride,
Yet if you offered a sovereign apiece for the hairs on his hide
That wouldn't buy him, nor twice that; while I've a pound to the good,
This here old stager stays by me and lives like a thoroughbred should:
Hunt him away from his bedding, and sit yourself down by the wall,
Tell you hear how the old fellow saved me from Gilbert, O'Maley and Hall.

Gilbert and Hall and O'Maley, back in the bushranging days,
Made themselves kings of the district — ruled it in old-fashioned ways —
Robbing the coach and the escort, stealing our horses at night,
Calling sometimes at the homesteads and giving the women a fright:

Came to the station one morning — and why they did this no one knows —
Took a brood mare from the paddock — wanting some fun, I suppose —
Fastened a bucket beneath her, hung by a strap round her flank,
Then turned her loose in the timber back of the seven-mile tank.

Go! She went mad! She went tearing and screaming with fear through the
    trees,
While the curst bucket beneath her was banging her flanks and her knees.
Bucking and racing and screaming she ran to the back of the run,
Killed herself there in a gully; by God, but they paid for their fun!
Paid for it dear, for the black boys found tracks, and the bucket, and all,
And I swore that I'd live to get even with Gilbert, O'Maley and Hall.

Day after day then I chased them — 'course they had friends on the sly,
Friends who were willing to sell them to those who were willing to buy.
Early one morning we found them in camp at the Cockatoo Farm
One of us shot at O'Maley and wounded him under the arm:
Ran them for miles in the ranges, till Hall, with his horse fairly beat,
Took to the rocks and we lost him — the others made good their retreat.
It was war to the knife then, I tell you, and once, on the door of my shed,
They nailed up a notice that offered a hundred reward for my head!

Then we heard they were gone from the district, they stuck up a coach in the
    west,
And I rode by myself in the paddocks, taking a bit of a rest,
Riding this colt as a youngster — awkward, half-broken and shy,
He wheeled round one day on a sudden; I looked, but I couldn't see why,
But I soon found out why, for before me, the hillside rose up like a wall,
And there on the top with their rifles were Gilbert, O'Maley and Hall!

'Twas a good three-mile run to the homestead — bad going, with plenty of
    trees —
So I gathered the youngster together, and gripped at his ribs with my knees.
'Twas a mighty poor chance to escape them! It puts a man's nerve to the test
On a half-broken colt to be hunted by the best mounted men in the west.
But the half-broken colt was a racehorse! He lay down to work with a will,
Flashed through the scrub like a clean-skin — by Heavens we *flew* down the
    hill!
Over a twenty-foot gully he swept with the spring of a deer
And they fired as we jumped, but they missed me — a bullet sang close to
    my ear —
And the jump gained us ground, for they shirked it: but I saw as we raced
    through the gap
That the rails at the homestead were fastened — I was caught like a rat in
    a trap.

Fenced with barbed wire was the paddock — barbed wire that would cut like
    a knife —
How was a youngster to clear it that never had jumped in his life?

Bang went a rifle behind me — the colt gave a spring, he was hit;
Straight at the sliprails I rode him — I felt him take hold of the bit;
Never a foot to the right or the left did he swerve in his stride,
Awkward and frightened, but honest, the sort it's a pleasure to ride!
Straight at the rails, where they'd fastened barbed wire on the top of the post,
Rose like a stag and went over, with hardly a scratch at the most;
Into the homestead I darted, and snatched down my gun from the wall,
And I tell you I made them step lively, Gilbert, O'Maley and Hall!

Yes! There's the mark of the bullet — he's got it inside of him yet
Mixed up somehow with his victuals, but bless you he don't seem to fret!
Gluttonous, ugly, and lazy — eats any thing he can bite;
Now, let us shut up the stable, and bid the old fellow goodnight:
Ah! We can't breed 'em, the sort that were bred when we old 'uns were young.
Yes, I was saying, these bushrangers, none of 'em lived to be hung,
Gilbert was shot by the troopers, Hall was betrayed by his friend,
Campbell disposed of O'Maley, bringing the lot to an end.

But you can talk about riding — I've ridden a lot in the past —
Wait till there's rifles behind you, you'll know what it means to go fast!
I've steeplechased, raced, and "run horses", but I think the most dashing of
    all
Was the ride when the old fellow saved me from Gilbert, O'Maley and Hall!

How Gilbert Died

There's never a stone at the sleeper's head,
   There's never a fence beside,
And the wandering stock on the grave may tread
   Unnoticed and undenied,
But the smallest child on the Watershed
   Can tell you how Gilbert died.

For he rode at dusk, with his comrade Dunn
   To the hut at the Stockman's Ford,
In the waning light of the sinking sun
   They peered with a fierce accord.
They were outlaws both — and on each man's head
   Was a thousand pounds reward.

They had taken toll of the country round,
   And the troopers came behind
With a black that tracked like a human hound
   In the scrub and the ranges blind:
He could run the trail where a white man's eye
   No sign of a track could find.

He had hunted them out of the One Tree Hill
   And over the Old Man Plain,
But they wheeled their tracks with a wild beast's skill,
   And they made for the range again.
Then away to the hut where their grandsire dwelt,
   They rode with a loosened rein.

And their grandsire gave them a greeting bold:
   "Come in and rest in peace,
No safer place does the country hold —
   With the night pursuit must cease,
And we'll drink success to the roving boys,
   And to hell with the black police."

But they went to death when they entered there,
   In the hut at the Stockman's Ford,
For their grandsire's words were as false as fair —
   They were doomed to the hangman's cord.
He had sold them both to the black police
   For the sake of the big reward.

In the depth of night there are forms that glide
  As stealthy as serpents creep,
And around the hut where the outlaws hide
  They plant in the shadows deep,
And they wait till the first faint flush of dawn
  Shall waken their prey from sleep.

But Gilbert wakes while the night is dark —
  A restless sleeper, aye,
He has heard the sound of a sheepdog's bark,
  And his horse's warning neigh,
And he says to his mate, "There are hawks abroad,
  And it's time that we went away."

Their rifles stood at the stretcher head,
  Their bridles lay to hand,
They wakened the old man out of his bed,
  When they heard the sharp command:
"In the name of the Queen lay down your arms,
  Now, Dunn and Gilbert, stand!"

Then Gilbert reached for his rifle true
  That close at his hand he kept,
He pointed it straight at the voice and drew,
  But never a flash outleapt,
For the water ran from the rifle breach —
  It was drenched while the outlaws slept.

Then he dropped the piece with a bitter oath,
  And he turned to his comrade Dunn:
"We are sold," he said, "we are dead men both,
  But there may be a chance for one;
I'll stop and I'll fight with the pistol here,
  You take to your heels and run."

So Dunn crept out on his hands and knees
  In the dim, half-dawning light,
And he made his way to a patch of trees,
  And vanished among the night,
And the trackers hunted his tracks all day,
  But they never could trace his flight.

But Gilbert walked from the open door
  In a confident style and rash;
He heard at his side the rifles roar,

And he heard the bullets crash.
But he laughed as he lifted his pistol-hand,
And he fired at the rifle flash.

Then out of the shadows the troopers aimed
At his voice and the pistol sound,
With the rifle flashes the darkness flamed,
He staggered and spun around,
And they riddled his body with rifle balls
As it lay on the blood-soaked ground.

There's never a stone at the sleeper's head
There's never a fence beside,
And the wandering stock on the grave may tread
Unnoticed and undenied,
But the smallest child on the Watershed
Can tell you how Gilbert died.

Under the Shadow of Kiley's Hill

This is the place where they all were bred;
Some of the rafters are standing still;
Now they are scattered and lost and dead,
Every one from the old nest fled,
Out of the shadow of Kiley's Hill.

Better it is that they ne'er came back —
Changes and chances are quickly rung;
Now the old homestead is gone to rack,
Green is the grass on the well-worn track
Down by the gate where the roses clung.

Gone is the garden they kept with care;
Left to decay at its own sweet will,
Fruit trees and flower beds eaten bare,
Cattle and sheep where the roses were,
Under the shadow of Kiley's Hill.

Where are the children that throve and grew
  In the old homestead in days gone by?
One is away on the far Barcoo
Watching his cattle the long year through,
  Watching them starve in the droughts and die.

One in the town where all cares are rife,
  Weary with troubles that cramp and kill,
Fain would be done with the restless strife,
Fain would go back to the old bush life,
  Back to the shadow of Kiley's Hill.

One is away on the roving quest,
  Seeking his share of the golden spoil,
Out in the wastes of the trackless west,
Wandering ever he gives the best
  Of his years and strength to the hopeless toil.

What of the parents? That unkempt mound
  Shows where they slumber united still;
Rough is their grave, but they sleep as sound
Out on the range as on holy ground,
  Under the shadow of Kiley's Hill.

A Bunch of Roses

Roses ruddy and roses white,
  What are the joys that my heart discloses?
Sitting alone in the fading light
Memories come to me here to-night
  With the wonderful scent of the big red roses.

Memories come as the daylight fades
  Down on the hearth where the firelight dozes;
Flicker and flutter the lights and shades,
And I see the face of a queen of maids
  Whose memory comes with the scent of roses.

Visions arise of a scene of mirth,
　And a ballroom belle that superbly poses —
A queenly woman of queenly worth,
And I am the happiest man on earth
　With a single flower from a bunch of roses.

Only her memory lives tonight —
　God in His wisdom her young life closes;
Over her grave may the turf be light,
Cover her coffin with roses white —
　She was always fond of the big white roses.

Such are the visions that fade away —
　Man proposes and God disposes;
Look in the glass and I see to-day
Only an old man, worn and grey,
　Bending his head to a bunch of roses.

In the Droving Days

"Only a pound," said the auctioneer,
"Only a pound; and I'm standing here
Selling this animal, gain or loss.
Only a pound for the drover's horse;
One of the sort that was ne'er afraid,
One of the boys of the Old Brigade;
Thoroughly honest and game, I'll swear,
Only a little the worse for wear;
Plenty as bad to be seen in town,
Give me a bid and I'll knock him down;
Sold as he stands, and without recourse,
Give me a bid for the drover's horse."

Loitering there in an aimless way
Somehow I noticed the poor old grey,
Weary and battered and screwed, of course,
Yet when I noticed the old grey horse,
The rough bush saddle, and single rein

Of the bridle laid on his tangled mane,
Straightway the crowd and the auctioneer
Seemed on a sudden to disappear,
Melted away in a kind of haze,
For my heart went back to the droving days.

Back to the road, and I crossed again
Over the miles of the saltbush plain —
The shining plain that is said to be
The dried-up bed of an inland sea,
Where the air so dry and so clear and bright
Refracts the sun with a wondrous light,
And out in the dim horizon makes
The deep blue gleam of the phantom lakes.

At dawn of day we would feel the breeze
That stirred the boughs of the sleeping trees,
And brought a breath of the fragrance rare
That comes and goes in that scented air;
For the trees and grass and the shrubs contain
A dry sweet scent on the saltbush plain.
For those that love it and understand,
The saltbush plain is a wonderland.
A wondrous country, where nature's ways
Were revealed to me in the droving days.

We saw the fleet wild horses pass,
And the kangaroos through the Mitchell grass,
The emu ran with her frightened brood
All unmolested and unpursued.
But there rose a shout and a wild hubbub
When the dingo raced for his native scrub,
And he paid right dear for his stolen meals
With the drovers' dogs at his wretched heels.
For we ran him down at a rattling pace,
While the pack horse joined in the stirring chase.
And a wild halloo at the kill we'd raise —
We were light of heart in the droving days.

'Twas a drover's horse, and my hand again
Made a move to close on a fancied rein.
For I felt the swing and the easy stride
Of the grand old horse that I used to ride
In drought or plenty, in good or ill,
That same old steed was my comrade still;

The old grey horse with his honest ways
Was a mate to me in the droving days.

When we kept our watch in the cold and damp,
If the cattle broke from the sleeping camp,
Over the flats and across the plain,
With my head bent down on his waving mane,
Through the boughs above and the stumps below
On the darkest night I would let him go
At a racing speed; he would choose his course,
And my life was safe with the old grey horse.
But man and horse had a favourite job,
When an outlaw broke from a station mob,
With a right good will was the stockwhip plied,
As the old horse raced at the straggler's side,
And the greenhide whip such a weal would raise,
We could use the whip in the droving days.

"Only a pound!" and this was the end —
Only a pound for the drover's friend.
The drover's friend that had seen his day,
And now was worthless, and cast away
With a broken knee and a broken heart
To be flogged and starved in a hawker's cart.
Well, I made a bid for a sense of shame
And the memories dear of the good old game.

"Thank you? Guinea! and cheap at that!
Against you there in the curly hat!
Only a guinea, and one more chance,
Down he goes if there's no advance,
Third, and the last time, one! two! three!"
And the old grey horse was knocked down to me.
And now he's wandering, fat and sleek,
On the lucerne flats by the Homestead Creek;
I dare not ride him for fear he'd fall,
But he does a journey to beat them all,
For though he scarcely a trot can raise,
He can take me back to the droving days.

Bush Life

Life, after all, is mostly made up of little things, prosaic and unpicturesque. The squatter, for instance, is supposed (in literature) to ride about over his vast domains on a thoroughbred horse, always at full gallop. In the moving pictures, he is generally shown wearing a red shirt and top boots, as those things lend verisimilitude to an otherwise dull and uninteresting narrative. In real life, he rarely rides in anything but a motor car; and if he appeared in a red shirt and top boots, all the emus on the run would follow him for miles, dancing and cavorting about, wondering what strange animal had got in amongst them.

This article, then, is concerned with the little things of life in the bush, the everyday occurrences which mean so much to the bush people. If we can find therein some humour and some human nature, so much the better. The first picture to be thrown on our screen was roughly sketched in a notebook on a trip to Brewarrina.

"West of Dubbo, the west begins . . . land of vast distances. Behind us the railway line stretches, straight as an arrow across the plains till the rails seem to run together and disappear in the distance. Ahead of us, it runs on, straight as ever, through a shimmer of haze, till it is lost in a lagoon which is not really a lagoon but a mirage. When these western people wish to describe the essence of meanness, they say that a man is too mean to give your dog a drink at his mirage.

"And who shall describe the eerie loneliness of this country? A few sheep, a few galahs, and a few magpies; these are the only living things, other than human, seen in two hundred miles. Travelling through a station of a hundred thousand sheep, one hardly sees any of them. At little dusty wayside stations the people get in and out — long-legged, thin men, sunburnt to a mahogany colour. Women almost as sunburnt, with quick and earnest faces. The lounge lizard and the baby doll have no place in this life. Two women meet on the platform, get into the carriage, and start a conversation. Of what will they speak? Will they talk about trips to Sydney, about fashions, or about their families? Not a bit of it. One says to the other, 'Have you had the mice yet?' And there we get the keynote of bush life. Nature, resenting human invasion, keeps up a sort of guerrilla warfare, using such weapons as plagues of mice, grasshoppers, caterpillars, and in some places even kangaroos and emus. The bushman and his wife can never go to sleep on the job.

"'Have we had the mice?' says her friend. 'My dear, the place is just a mass of mice. We have to hang everything up by wire hooks to the trees away from the mice. I pulled back the bedclothes to put the baby to sleep and there was a nest of mice in the bed.'

"'How are the flies with you this season?'

"'Pretty bad. We have had to crutch everything and the boys get so tired after working in the yards all the week that they won't play tennis on Sundays. We get tired too. We've been making jam all the week. We have millions of grapes and figs, but the bees and the hornets have come down in droves to suck the juice out of the fruit and we're terrified of getting stung. If you like to send over, we can give you a couple of clothes baskets full of grapes and figs and we would never miss them.'

"This is Nature in the west, giving with one hand, and taking with the other.

"The train rattles on. The sun sinks lower in the west, shedding a coloured light on the dark silver of the myall trees and the homely grey of the old man saltbush. In this light the krui bush and the emu bush become things of beauty, for they seem to reflect the rays of the sun. Through the carriage windows the breeze brings in a scent of pine. Is there anything more beautiful than the plains in a good season?

"The train stops at a little township, and two passengers get in, one obviously a city man and the other a shy, silent, country youth with hands calloused by lifting sheep whose fleeces are full of thistles and burr. Country and City are face to face.

"The city man asks him: 'Do you happen to know anything about a place called Gongolgon?' (Pronounced Gon-*gol*-gon)

"The answer comes in the true back block drawl, 'Yairs! I know Gongolgon all right. I come from near Gongolgon.'

"'Good. Then perhaps you can give me some information. My company has lent some money on an hotel there — the Woolpack Hotel — but the man has left it, and I want to know how it is getting on. It's the best hotel in Gongolgon, isn't it?'

"'Oh, yairs! It's the best hotel in Gongolgon all right. There is only one hotel in Gongolgon.'

"'But I mean it's in a good position — in the main street and all that?'

"'Oh, yairs! There is only one street in Gongolgon.'

"'Well, have you seen it lately? Do you know how the place is looking?'

"'Well, I wouldn't say it is *too* good.'

"'Not too good? What do you mean by not too good?'

"'Oh, the swagmen has been campin' there and they burned all the floors and the fences an' the counters, an' all that for firewood. And some chap come along and carted away a lot of the bricks at night. I s'pose he was building somethin'.'

"'Carted away the bricks! Then is everything gone?'

"'Oh no, everything isn't gone. The *foundations* is there all right. They'd come in handy if you wanted to build another pub.'

"That ended the dialogue. Who shall say that the bush holds no surprises, no breaks in its monotony?"

A land of makeshifts, a land of discomforts rather than of absolute dangers — such was the bush in the earlier days. The Americans fought Indians in open warfare, a picturesque business with great glory for those who survived.

Our people had their troubles with the blacks, but it was never a war, just a beating-off of treacherous attacks. Nobody gained any glory by it, and the man who shot a black stood more chance of getting a gaol sentence than any decoration for valour. Hardships and discomforts were borne with a grin and were never told as exploits — they were told as jokes. Take, for instance, the case of a kangaroo-shooting gang who were caught in a flood between two rivers. It rained and rained and rained. Day by day the space of dry land available to them grew less and less. Their food ran out. No bread, no meat, no tea, no tobacco. Their outlook seemed to be a choice between drowning and starvation. Then one of the rivers fell suddenly, as Queensland rivers do, and a horseman got through to them. As he rode up, they hailed him: "Have you had your lunch yet?"

"No," he said. "I'm just going to have it. I've got some with me."

"Oh," they said, "have some of ours."

"What have you got?"

"We've got stumpy and mushrooms."

("Stumpy" was native bear. They had been living for the best part of a week on native bear and mushrooms!)

Does anyone remember Mark Twain's book, *The Mississippi Pilot*, in which he told of the steamboat racing on the Mississippi, where the stokers worked up such a fierce draught that every time a nigger put a log of wood on the furnace he went up the chimney with it? We also had our river piloting, grotesque rather than glorious. The American steamers went along with uniformed stewards, bands playing, and leadsmen calling "by the deep five" and "mark twain", the latter being a leadsman's cry from which the great writer took his name. Compare this with steam boating on the Darling before the railways cut out the river trade. The description is written by an eyewitness.

"Tied up to a tree at the foot of a Chinaman's garden is the steamer *Wandering Jew*, waiting for the river to rise. She is built of slabs nailed together and her builders seem to have determined to put into her as many different kinds of wood, and as many different lengths, colours and thicknesses of timber as possible. In shape, she is a good deal like the ace of diamonds, with paddle wheels sticking out on either side; her hold is floored with the odds and ends of slabs left over from her construction and grass is growing in her empty hold. But her captain refuses to be downhearted. He speaks in true nautical fashion of meeting 'other vessels' on his voyages, and says that he has a chart of the river showing all the snags; but that trees are constantly falling into the river and forming new snags which make navigation dangerous.

"He says that his boat can do three knots an hour against the current; but has made as much as fourteen knots when coming down with a flood. The deckhand, who is also the fireman, says that he fires her with logs. 'Sometimes they send the wrong lengths aboard,' he says, 'and then I have to cut 'em up myself. I'm a fireman,' he says, 'not a wood-and-water joey.'"

In such a life there is nothing picturesque, nothing poetical. But this boat had been burnt to the water's edge three times and there rise in the memory the verses about Jim Bludso, the American river captain, whose boat caught fire; and how he said he would "hold her nose agin the bank till the last galoot's ashore"; and how he stuck to his job till they were all landed; and then "Bludso's ghost went up alone in the smoke of the *Prairie Belle*."

Perhaps if we considered the life of this Darling river captain, we might also find something picturesque. The long, drowsy days when the river was full and the boat found her own way downriver, her wool-laden barges towing behind her; the anxious trips when the river was low and unsuspected snags lay ready to rip the bottom out of her; and the call of the floods when the *Wandering Jew* put out into a boundless waste of waters, all banks covered and all landmarks gone, in the hope of saving some settlers marooned lower down the river. They are all gone now — the *Wandering Jew*, her old captain who took himself so seriously, and the deck hand who objected to being a wood-and-water joey. Some old timer, sitting by the river, may close his eyes and fancy that he sees again the smoke of the *Wandering Jew* coming round the bend and that he hears again the coughing of her rusty horizontal engine. These things are just a tradition, a part of our history. In this manner did the men of the past lay the foundations for the national structure, building better than they knew. Water! What had the Australian of the interior to do with water? And yet, in this curious country, it is surprising to find the part played by water. Here again comes in the element of the unexpected which runs through all bush life. The Dawson River in Queensland, for instance, is a normal river enough, runs in the usual way for the most part; and yet, on occasions, it comes down in such fashion that it is four miles wide and has to be crossed in boats. By the time that the boat has reached the centre of the river there is nothing to be seen but the trees and the flood. The voyager is out of sight of land, a long way inland from the Queensland coast. Nor does the unexpectedness end here. Sometimes the river is backed up by other rivers, also struggling to find their way to the sea, and the current actually runs the wrong way, up-river instead of down. Who shall predict anything, or lay down any dogmatic rules, for a country where the beasts have beaks, the cherries grow with their stones outside, the foxes fly in the air, and the rivers run the wrong way!

A couple of hundred years hence, perhaps, someone will write the history of these early days, a lot of it incredible, or, at the least, difficult of understanding. But when that date arrives, time will have mellowed the past. The man who carted away the Gongolgon Hotel, brick by brick, will be as romantic as a Highland raider; the hard-bitten captain and deck hand of the *Wandering Jew* will rank with the early Vanderbilts who ran a ferry in New York; and there will be a terrific demand for samples of old colonial curios — beds with strips of greenhide in the place of springs, and crudely carved stockwhip handles made of the scented myall wood. Then, and then only, will the bush people come into their own.

Last Week

Oh, the new chum went to the backblock run,
But he should have gone there last week.
He tramped ten miles with a loaded gun,
But of turkey or duck he saw never a one,
For he should have been there last week,
   They said,
There were flocks of 'em there last week.

He wended his way to a waterfall,
And he should have gone there last week.
He carried a camera, legs and all,
But the day was hot, and the stream was small,
For he should have gone there last week,
   They said,
They drowned a man there last week.

He went for a drive, and he made a start,
Which should have been made last week,
For the old horse died of a broken heart;
So he footed it home and he dragged the cart —
But the horse was all right last week,
   They said,
He trotted a match last week.

So he asked the bushies who came from far
To visit the town last week,
If they'd dine with him, and they said, "Hurrah!"
But there wasn't a drop in the whisky jar —
"You should have been here last week,"
   He said,
"I drank it all up last week!"

Conroy's Gap

This was the way of it, don't you know —
   Ryan was "wanted" for stealing sheep,
And never a trooper, high or low,
   Could find him — catch a weasel asleep!
Till Trooper Scott, from the Stockman's Ford —
   A bushman, too, as I've heard them tell —
Chanced to find him drunk as a lord
   Round at the Shadow of Death Hotel.

D' you know the place? It's a wayside inn,
   A low grog-shanty — a bushman trap,
Hiding away in its shame and sin
   Under the shelter of Conroy's Gap —
Under the shade of that frowning range,
   The roughest crowd that ever drew breath —
Thieves and rowdies, uncouth and strange,
   Were mustered round at the Shadow of Death.

The trooper knew that his man would slide
   Like a dingo pup, if he saw the chance;
And with half a start on the mountain side
   Ryan would lead him a merry dance.
Drunk as he was when the trooper came,
   To him that did not matter a rap —
Drunk or sober, he was the same,
   The boldest rider in Conroy's Gap.

"I want you, Ryan," the trooper said,
   "And listen to me, if you dare resist,
So help me heaven, I'll shoot you dead!"
   He snapped the steel on his prisoner's wrist,
And Ryan, hearing the handcuffs click,
   Recovered his wits as they turned to go,
For fright will sober a man as quick
   As all the drugs that the doctors know.

There was a girl in that rough bar
   Went by the name of Kate Carew,
Quiet and shy as the bush girls are,
   But ready-witted and plucky, too.
She loved this Ryan, or so they say,

And passing by, while her eyes were dim
With tears, she said in a careless way,
  "The Swagman's round in the stable, Jim."

Spoken too low for the trooper's ear,
  Why should she care if he heard or not?
Plenty of swagmen far and near,
  And yet to Ryan it meant a lot.
That was the name of the grandest horse
  In all the district from east to west
In every show ring, on every course
  They always counted the Swagman best.

He was a wonder, a raking bay —
  One of the grand old Snowdon strain —
One of the sort that could race and stay
  With his mighty limbs and his length of rein.
Born and bred on the mountain side,
  He could race through scrub like a kangaroo,
The girl herself on his back might ride,
  And the Swagman would carry her safely through.

He would travel gaily from daylight's flush
  Till after the stars hung out their lamps,
There was never his like in the open bush,
  And never his match on the cattle camps.
For faster horses might well be found
  On racing tracks, or a plain's extent,
But few, if any, on broken ground
  Could see the way that the Swagman went.

When this girl's father, old Jim Carew,
  Was droving out on the Castlereagh
With Conroy's cattle, a wire came through
  To say that his wife couldn't live the day.
And he was a hundred miles from home,
  As flies the crow, with never a track,
Through plains as pathless as ocean's foam,
  He mounted straight on the Swagman's back.

He left the camp by the sundown light,
  And the settlers out on the Marthaguy
Awoke and heard, in the dead of night,
  A single horseman hurrying by.
He crossed the Bogan at Dandaloo,

And many a mile of the silent plain
That lonely rider behind him threw
  Before they settled to sleep again.

He rode all night and he steered his course
  By the shining stars with a bushman's skill,
And every time that he pressed his horse
  The Swagman answered him gamely still.
He neared his home as the east was bright,
  The doctor met him outside the town:
"Carew! How far did you come last night?"
  "A hundred miles since the sun went down."

And his wife got round, and an oath he passed,
  So long as he or one of his breed
Could raise a coin, though it took their last
  The Swagman never should want a feed.
And Kate Carew, when her father died,
  She kept the horse and she kept him well:
The pride of the district far and wide,
  He lived in style at the bush hotel.

Such was the Swagman; and Ryan knew
  Nothing about could pace the crack;
Little he'd care for the man in blue
  If once he got on the Swagman's back.
But how to do it? A word let fall
  Gave him the hint as the girl passed by;
Nothing but "Swagman — stable-wall;
  Go to the stable and mind your eye."

He caught her meaning, and quickly turned
  To the trooper: "Reckon you'll gain a stripe
By arresting me, and it's easily earned;
  Let's go to the stable and get my pipe,
The Swagman has it." So off they went,
  And soon as ever they turned their backs
The girl slipped down, on some errand bent
  Behind the stable, and seized an axe.

The trooper stood at the stable door
  While Ryan went in quite cool and slow,
And then (the trick had been played before)
  The girl outside gave the wall a blow.
Three slabs fell out of the stable wall —

'Twas done 'fore ever the trooper knew —
And Ryan, as soon as he saw them fall,
  Mounted the Swagman and rushed him through.

The trooper heard the hoofbeats ring
  In the stable yard, and he slammed the gate,
But the Swagman rose with a mighty spring
  At the fence, and the trooper fired too late,
As they raced away and his shots flew wide
  And Ryan no longer need care a rap,
For never a horse that was lapped in hide
  Could catch the Swagman in Conroy's Gap.

And that's the story. You want to know
  If Ryan came back to his Kate Carew;
Of course he should have, as stories go,
  But the worst of it is, this story's true:
And in real life it's a certain rule,
  Whatever poets and authors say
Of high-toned robbers and all their school,
  These horse thief fellows aren't built that way.

Come back! Don't hope it — the slinking hound,
  He sloped across to the Queensland side,
And sold the Swagman for fifty pound,
  And stole the money, and more beside.
And took to drink, and by some good chance
  Was killed — thrown out of a stolen trap.
And that was the end of this small romance,
  The end of the story of Conroy's Gap.

Big Kerrigan

The first big person I ever met was, naturally, a schoolmaster. To all small boys there is something superhuman about their first school-master, and I was a very small boy, only about eight years old at the time.

The school was situated in a little hamlet called Binalong, where the mail coach used to stop to change horses, and where the gold escort from the Lambing Flat diggings used to create a sensation once a week as it went clattering through the town, with two armed troopers riding in the front and another armed trooper sitting with his carbine across his knees on the box seat alongside the coachman.

It had been a great bushranging district, and the house where Gilbert the bushranger was shot, and the grave of Gilbert in the police paddock, were the two show places of the town. In the warm summer evenings the station hands and house servants would sit out on the wood heap and sing, to the wailings of a concertina, songs about "Dunn, Gilbert, and Ben Hall", "The Wild Colonial Boy", and "Bold Jack Donahoo", and there were any amount of men in the district who would have had a crack at the escort only for the armed guard.

Every morning I had to walk a mile or so up the paddock, freezing with cold in the winter or sweating with heat in the summer, catch my pony, and ride him the four miles into school. Our schoolmaster, Moore by name and Irish to the roots of his teeth, was supposed by us boys to have "fit in the Fenian rebellion", which was all to the good so far as we were concerned. It was a great Irish district and some of my schoolmates had parents who had been "sent out" for participating in some similar festivity.

Our schoolmaster and the little wiry Irish police trooper shared the sover-eignty of the hamlet between them and they both had a consuming passion for game cocks. Micky Tracey, son of the poundkeeper, said that he had "sneaked up on them wanst, at the back of the police station so they were, and they fighting game cocks agin each other, and the cocks with steel spurs on".

We could hardly believe that two men who between them represented law, and literature, and the Government, backed up by the black tracker, would be guilty of such an enormity. But we got an even worse shock later on. One fine day the priest, who drove twenty miles to hold mid-week service, drove his Abbott waggonette and pair of fast ponies into the school yard and went inside, as we supposed, to talk politics and higher mathematics with the teacher. Of course we children swarmed all over his trap and, after pulling out bags of horse feed, surplices, etc., we heard something cackle and, lo and behold, there was a game cock, eyeing us with haughty indifference from his confined quarters in a fruit case!

Well, that priest went into a burning house to save a woman's life, and perhaps the bird was only brought out for comparison and, so to speak, educational purposes. *Honi soit qui mal y pense*.

Then the world, and civilisation, hit us with a bang. The great Southern Railway, connecting Sydney and Melbourne, was built right through the town, and for miles to the north and miles to the south were nothing but torn earth and navvies' camps, and blasts going off, and the clang of temporary rails. Fettlers, gangers, dobbin drivers and construction men all swarmed into our little town, and on a pay Friday not Monte Carlo itself had anything on us when it came to drink and gambling. The navvies didn't consider that they were properly intoxicated till they lost all power of speech or movement, and they used to stagger homewards along the road, bearing bottles, till they fell gloriously in the dust.

I used to train my pony to jump over their prostrate figures on the road home, altogether ignoring, as children are apt to do, the painful results that would occur if the navvy got up while the pony was in the air over him. "Cornish wrastlers", English fighting men, step-dancers and singers from the music halls followed in the wake of the navvies' camps, and in the twinkling of an eye we were civilised. Beards, bush ballads and elastic-sided boots all went out of fashion together, and the railway brought us our newspapers every day, instead of the mail coach bringing them once a week.

It was in connection with one of these navvies, however, that my hero worship received its first shock. There is a slang saying, very common throughout Australia, "Why go crook of a Monday?" It probably arises from the fact that people are not at their best to face work and worry on Monday after the relaxation of Sunday. Anyway, it was on a Monday that Trooper O'Mara, wearing his uniform, a revolver and a worried expression, came into the little slab schoolroom and started a whispered colloquy with the teacher — or at least they whispered for a while and then, growing excited, they raised their voices. And thus it was that we learnt that "Big Kerrigan", a celebrated navvy who could lift an anvil and was the champion "wrastler" of a dozen railway camps, had been drinking steadily through Friday, Saturday, and Sunday and was now at large suffering from delirium tremens.

" 'Tis down by the crick he is," said the trooper, "and him wid an axe. He must be locked up or he'll murder somebody or maybe kill himself. I call on you, Mr Moore, in the Queen's name, to assist me to arrest this man."

Here were our two famous men — O'Mara, who, as we believed, had "taken" several bushrangers single-handed, and the teacher who had fit in the Fenian rebellion — faced at last with a chance to show their stuff. Bound together as they were by the ties of cock fighting, each must support the other to the death.

To our dismay, the teacher showed every sign of being a conscientious objector. "I'll not go, O'Mara," he said. " 'Tis your job to arrest drunks. 'Tis my job to teach the childerrun. Ye've been carrying that revolver a long time, let us see do ye know how to use it. Ye're an armed trooper of the Queen.

Go on and do your job!"

"Yes, and if I shoot him, where'll we be? The railway camps will wreck the town, and when I tell them that I called on ye for assistance and ye wouldn't come, they'll hang the pair of us. Come on! Let ye back up what I say, and if we can coax him into the shed at the back of the court house I could maybe handcuff his arms round the big upright — if so be as he didn't walk away with the whole thing. I've just shifted me turkeys out of it, anyhow."

For one brief moment, the teacher hesitated. Then, like Caesar jumping the Rubicon, he crossed the room, seized his hat and, taking me by the hand, he set out after the trooper. It has since occurred to me that he took me because I was a magistrate's son and would add a sort of tone to the inquest, if any. Having no orders to the contrary, the other children followed like a small pack of hounds after their master, and thus we set out to arrest Big Kerrigan.

All we knew of his movements was that he had gone down along the creek and he might have left the creek and gone away up into the scrub in the police paddock, or he might have fallen down one of the prospectors' holes that still remained unfilled and unfenced at unexpected and irregular intervals along the flat. But there are always ways of finding things in the bush, and they mostly depend upon birds. A magpie will find you a snake, a crow will find you a dead man and a spurwing plover will locate any other sort of trouble. Sure enough, we heard the plovers shrieking and saw them circling over a clump of big trees at a bend of the creek, and there we found Big Kerrigan.

And even as I saw him, the whole glamour of the adventure dropped away from me. This poor crazed mammoth, with foam on his lips and stark terror in his eyes, dodging in a sort of shuffling run from tree to tree, occasionally swinging his axe to threaten imaginary pursuers, and shouting, "They're after me, they're after me!" Remember, I was only eight years old, and the horror of the thing made such an impression on me that never since then have I had anything but detestation for those who would sell liquor to a drunken man. But the problem before us was what to do with Kerrigan. A delirium tremens patient of Herculean strength and armed with an axe is a handful for anybody.

Luckily, the trooper was a Master of Arts when it came to dealing with drunks. Slipping his revolver round under his coat "lest the sight of it might annoy him", he issued his battle orders to the teacher. "I'll go up an' speak wid him," he said. "And if I can get him to come along wid me, do ye close in on his other side, an' we'll just coax him along. I'll not try to put the handcuffs on him. They'd hobble a horse, but they wouldn't go round them wrists of his."

. We children stood breathless as he walked up within five yards of the giant with the axe. "Kerrigan! Kerrigan!" he said. Slowly the fear-crazed eyes of the maniac focused themselves on the trooper, and Kerrigan, trembling like a frightened horse, stood leaning on his axe. "O'Mara," he said, the words bubbling out from the foam on his lips, "ye'll not take me. I can bate ye, I can bate any bastard of a polisman."

"So ye can," said O'Mara cheerfully, "or any two of 'em. But I'm not wantin' to take ye. I've got nothin' agin ye. But ye're not fit to be out here wid no hat and the ants all over ye. Come along wid me, and I'll look after ye."

For a while, things hung in the balance. A look of suspicion came into his eyes and we expected Kerrigan to spring at the policeman and smash him to pieces with the axe. "What d'ye want with me?" he said.

"The ganger told me to get ye to come up to my house and give ye a nip of brandy and a wash, and he'll send in for ye. The plate-layin' is all gone to hell, and you away drinkin'. See, now, let one of the childer carry the axe for ye, and I'll walk one side of ye and Mr Moore here will walk the other and we'll keep them off ye. They'll never come near ye, with us here. See, now, give one of the childer the axe to carry and we'll go up and get a nip of brandy."

And thus was the arrest of Kerrigan effected. Without a word he handed over the axe and, with the trooper on one arm and the teacher on the other, the procession set out for the police station. Now and again Kerrigan relapsed into frenzy and threw his Herculean arms about, sending the trooper and the teacher sprawling in the dust. But the two Irishmen had their blood up and they closed in on him again, hanging onto his arms as killers hang onto the jaws of a whale.

Arrived at the station, a strong nip of brandy reduced the giant to a state of coma, during which his arms were secured round the centre post of the shed by a steel chain. He woke up at intervals during the night, and roared like a volcano, and every time that he did so the dispossessed turkeys on top of the roof gobbled frantically; the fowls woke up and started a cackling chorus like the frogs of Aristophanes; all the dogs in the blacks' camp rushed about barking madly; and Kiley's bull, in his paddock across the road, rumbled his disapproval in a style which indicated that, unless somebody did something pretty soon, he would have to come down and do it himself.

Thus did my teacher justify his claim to be considered my first great man. True, he had at first shrunk back when adventure called, but look how he behaved afterwards!

It was my fate, in later years, to meet many great men — Lord Roberts, Lord French, Lord Kitchener, Rudyard Kipling and Winston Churchill. Would any of them have done any better?

from *Illalong Children*

Those Names

The shearers sat in the firelight, hearty and hale and strong,
After the hard day's shearing, passing the joke along:
The "ringer" that shore a hundred, as they never were shorn before,
And the novice who, toiling bravely, had tommyhawked half a score,
The tar boy, the cook, and the slushy, the sweeper that swept the board,
The picker-up, and the penner, with the rest of the shearing horde.
There were men from the inland stations where the skies like a furnace glow,
And men from the Snowy River, the land of the frozen snow;
There were swarthy Queensland drovers who reckoned all land by miles,
And farmers' sons from the Murray, where many a vineyard smiles.
They started at telling stories when they wearied of cards and games,
And to give these stories a flavour they threw in some local names,
And a man from the bleak Monaro, away on the tableland,
He fixed his eyes on the ceiling, and he started to play his hand.

He told them of Adjintoothbong, where the pine-clad mountains freeze,
And the weight of the snow in summer breaks branches off the trees,
And, as he warmed to the business, he let them have it strong —
Nimitybelle, Conargo, Wheeo, Bongongolong;
He lingered over them fondly, because they recalled to mind
A thought of the old bush homestead, and the girl that he left behind.
Then the shearers all sat silent till a man in the corner rose;
Said he, "I've travelled aplenty but never heard names like those,
Out in the western districts, out on the Castlereagh
Most of the names are easy — short for a man to say.
"You've heard of Mungrybambone and the Gundabluey pine,
Quobbotha, Girilambone, and Terramungamine,
Quambone, Eunonyhareenha, Wee Waa, and Buntijo —"
But the rest of the shearers stopped him, "For the sake of your jaw, go slow,
If you reckon those names are short ones out where such names prevail,
Just try and remember some long ones before you begin the tale."

And the man from the western district, though never a word he said,
Just winked with his dexter eyelid, and then he retired to bed.

Come-by-Chance

As I pondered very weary o'er a volume long and dreary —
For the plot was void of interest — 'twas that Postal Guide, in fact,
There I learnt the true location, distance, size, and population
Of each township, town, and village in the radius of the Act.

And I learnt that Puckawidgee stands beside the Murrumbidgee,
And that Booleroi and Bumble get their letters twice a year,
Also that the post inspector, when he visited Collector,
Closed the office up instanter, and re-opened Dungalear.

But my languid mood forsook me, when I found a name that took me,
Quite by chance I came across it — "Come-by-Chance" was what I read;
No location was assigned it, not a thing to help one find it,
Just an "N" which stood for northward, and the rest was all unsaid.

I shall leave my home, and forthward wander stoutly to the northward
Till I come by chance across it, and I'll straightway settle down,
For there can't be any hurry, nor the slightest cause for worry
Where the telegraph don't reach you nor the railways run to town.

And one's letters and exchanges come by chance across the ranges,
Where a wiry young Australian leads a pack horse once a week,
And the good news grows by keeping, and you're spared the pain of weeping
Over bad news when the mailman drops the letters in the creek.

But I fear, and more's the pity, that there's really no such city,
For there's not a man can find it of the shrewdest folk I know,
"Come-by-Chance", be sure it never means a land of fierce endeavour,
It is just the careless country where the dreamers only go.

Though we work and toil and hustle in our life of haste and bustle,
All that makes our life worth living comes unstriven for and free;
Man may weary and importune, but the fickle goddess Fortune
Deals him out his pain or pleasure careless what his worth may be.

All the happy times entrancing, days of sport and nights of dancing,
Moonlit rides and stolen kisses, pouting lips and loving glance:
When you think of these be certain you have looked behind the curtain,
You have had the luck to linger just a while in "Come-by-Chance".

Black Swans

As I lie at rest on a patch of clover
In the western park when the day is done,
I watch as the wild black swans fly over
With their phalanx turned to the sinking sun;
And I hear the clang of their leader crying
To a lagging mate in the rearward flying,
And they fade away in the darkness dying,
Where the stars are mustering one by one.

Oh! ye wild black swans, 'twere a world of wonder
For a while to join in your westward flight,
With the stars above and the dim earth under,
Through the cooling air of the glorious night.
As we swept along on our pinions winging,
We should catch the chime of a church-bell ringing,
Or the distant note of a torrent singing,
Or the far-off flash of a station light.

From the northern lakes with the reeds and rushes,
Where the hills are clothed with a purple haze,
Where the bellbirds chime and the songs of thrushes
Make music sweet in the jungle maze,
They will hold their course to the westward ever,
Till they reach the banks of the old grey river,
Where the waters wash, and the reed beds quiver
In the burning heat of the summer days.

Oh! ye strange wild birds, will ye bear a greeting
To the folk that live in that western land?
Then for every sweep of your pinions beating,
Ye shall bear a wish to the sunburnt band,
To the stalwart men who are stoutly fighting
With the heat and drought and dust storm smiting,
Yet whose life somehow has a strange inviting,
When once to the work they have put their hand.

Facing it yet! Oh, my friend stout-hearted,
What does it matter for rain or shine,
For the hopes deferred and the gain departed?
Nothing could conquer that heart of thine.
And thy health and strength are beyond confessing

As the only joys that are worth possessing.
May the days to come be as rich in blessing
As the days we spent in the auld lang syne.

I would fain go back to the old grey river,
To the old bush days when our hearts were light,
But, alas! those days they have fled for ever,
They are like the swans that have swept from sight.
And I know full well that the strangers' faces
Would meet us now in our dearest places;
For our day is dead and has left no traces
But the thoughts that live in my mind tonight.

There are folk long dead, and our hearts would sicken —
We would grieve for them with a bitter pain,
If the past could live and the dead could quicken,
We then might turn to that life again.
But on lonely nights we would hear them calling,
We should hear their steps on the pathways falling,
We should loathe the life with a hate appalling
In our lonely rides by the ridge and plain.

In the silent park is a scent of clover,
And the distant roar of the town is dead,
And I hear once more as the swans fly over
Their far-off clamour from overhead.
They are flying west by their instinct guided,
And for man likewise is his fate decided,
And griefs apportioned and joys divided
By a mighty power with a purpose dread.

The Amateur Gardener

The first step in amateur gardening is to sit down and consider what good you are going to get by it. If you are only a tenant by the month, as most people are, it is obviously not much use your planting a fruit orchard or an avenue of oak trees, which will take years to come to maturity. What you want is something that will grow quickly, and will stand transplanting for when you move it would be a sin to leave behind you all the plants on which you have spent so much labour and so much patent manure. We knew a man once who was a bookmaker by trade — and a leger bookmaker at that — but he had a passion for horses and flowers, and when he "had a big win", as he occasionally did, it was his custom to have movable wooden stables built on skids put up in the yard, and to have tons of the best soil that money could buy carted into the garden of the premises which he was occupying. Then he would keep splendid horses in the stables, grow rare roses and show-bench chrysanthemums in the garden and the landlord passing by would see the garden in a blaze of colour, and would promise himself that he would raise the bookmaker's rent next quarter day. However, when the bookmaker "took the knock", as he invariably did at least twice a year, it was his pleasing custom to move without giving any notice. He would hitch two carthorses to the stables, and haul them away at night. He would dig up not only the roses, trees, and chrysanthemums that he had planted, but would also cart away the soil he had brought in; in fact, he used to shift the garden bodily. He had one garden that he shifted to nearly every suburb in Sydney in turn, and he always argued that change of air was invaluable for chrysanthemums. Be this as it may, the proposition is self-evident that the would-be amateur gardener should grow flowers not for posterity, nor for his landlord, nor for his creditors, but for himself.

Being determined then to go in for gardening on commonsense principles, and having decided on the class of shrubs that you mean to grow, the next thing is to consider what sort of a chance you have of growing them. If your neighbour keeps game fowls it may be taken for granted that before long they will pay you a visit, and you will see the rooster scratching your pot plants out by the roots as if they were so much straw, just to make a nice place to lie down and fluff the dust over himself. Goats will also stray in from the street, and bite the young shoots off, selecting the most valuable plants with a discrimination that would do credit to a professional gardener; and whatever valuable plant a goat bites is doomed. It is therefore useless thinking of growing any delicate or squeamish plants. Most amateur gardeners maintain a lifelong struggle against the devices of Nature, and when the forces of man and the forces of Nature come into conflict Nature will win every time. Nature has decreed that certain plants shall be hardy, and therefore suitable to suburban amateur gardens, but the suburban amateur gardener persists in trying to grow quite other plants, and in despising those marked out by Nature for his use. It is to correct this tendency that this article is written.

The greatest standby to the amateur gardener should undoubtedly be the blue-flowered shrub known as plumbago. This homely but hardy plant will grow anywhere. It naturally prefers a good soil and a sufficient rainfall, but if need be it will worry along without either. Fowls cannot scratch it up, and even a goat turns away dismayed from its hard-featured branches. The flower is not strikingly beautiful nor ravishingly scented, but it flowers nine months out of the year, and though smothered with street dust and scorched by the summer sun you will find that faithful old plumbago plugging along undismayed. A plant like this should be encouraged and made much of, but the misguided amateur gardener as a rule despises it. The plant known as the churchyard geranium is also one marked out by Providence for the amateur, as is also cosmea, a plant that comes up year after year when once planted. In creepers, bignonia and lantana will hold their own under difficulties perhaps as well as any that can be found. In trees, the Port Jackson fig is a patriotic plant to grow, and it is a fine plant to provide exercise, as it sheds its leaves unsparingly, and requires to have the whole garden swept up every day. Your aim as a student of Nature should be to encourage the survival of the fittest. In grasses, too, the same principle holds good. There is a grass called nut grass, and another called Parramatta grass, either of which will hold its own against anything living or dead. The average gardening manual gives you recipes for destroying these grasses. Why should you destroy them in favour of a sickly plant that needs constant attention? No. The Parramatta grass is the selected of Nature, and who are you to interfere with Nature?

Having thus decided to go in for strong, simple plants that will hold their own, and a bit over, you must get your implements of husbandry. A spade is the first thing, but the average ironmonger will show you an unwieldy weapon only meant to be used by navvies. Don't buy it. Get a small spade, about half-size — it is nice and light and doesn't tire the wrist, and with it you can make a good display of enthusiasm, and earn the hypocritical admiration of your wife. After digging for half an hour or so, you can get her to rub your back with any of the backache cures advertised in this journal and from that moment you will have no further need for the spade.

Besides a spade, a barrow is about the only other thing needed, and anyhow it is almost a necessity for removing cases of whisky into the house. A rake is useful sometimes as a weapon, when your terrier dog has bailed up a cat, and will not attack it till the cat is made to run. And talking of terrier dogs, an acquaintance of ours has a dog that does all his gardening. The dog is a small elderly terrier, whose memory is failing somewhat, so as soon as the terrier has planted a bone in the garden the owner slips over and digs it up and takes it away. When the terrier goes back and finds the bone gone, he distrusts his own memory, and begins to think that perhaps he has made a mistake, and has dug in the wrong place; so he sets to work and digs patiently all over the garden, turning over acres of soil in his search for the missing bone. Meanwhile, the man saves himself a lot of backache.

The sensible amateur gardener, then, will not attempt to fight with Nature but will fall in with her views. What more pleasant than to get out of bed at 11.30 on a Sunday morning, and look out of your window at a lawn waving with the feathery plumes of Parramatta grass, and to see beyond it the churchyard or stinking geranium flourishing side by side with the plumbago and the Port Jackson fig? The garden gate blows open, and the local commando of goats, headed by an aged and fragrant patriarch (locally known as De Wet from the impossibility of capturing him), rush in; but their teeth will barely bite through the wiry stalks of the Parramatta grass, and the plumbago and the fig tree fail to attract them; and before long they scale the fence by standing on one another's shoulders, and disappear into the next-door garden, where a fanatic is trying to grow show roses. After the last goat has scaled your neighbour's fence, and only De Wet is left in your garden, your little dog discovers him, and De Wet beats a hurried retreat, apparently at full speed, with the little dog exactly one foot behind him in frantic pursuit. We say apparently at full speed, because old experience has taught that De Wet can run as fast as a greyhound when he likes; but he never exerts himself to go any faster than is necessary to just keep in front of whatever dog is after him; in fact, De Wet once did run for about a hundred yards with a greyhound after him, and then he suddenly turned and butted the greyhound cranksided, as Uncle Remus would say. Hearing the scrimmage, your neighbour comes onto his verandah, and sees the chase going down the street. "Ha! that wretched old De Wet again!" he says. "Small hope your dog has of catching him! Why don't you get a garden gate like mine, so as he won't get in?" "No; he can't get in at your gate," is the reply, "but I think his commando are in your back garden now." The next thing is a frantic rush by your neighbour, falling downstairs in his haste, and the sudden reappearance of the commando skipping easily back over the fence, and through your gate into the street again, stopping to bite some priceless pot plants of your neighbour's as they come out. A horse gets in, but his hoofs make no impression on the firm turf of the Parramatta grass, and you get quite a hearty laugh by dropping a chair on him out of the first floor window, and seeing him go tearing down the street. The game fowls of your other neighbour come fluttering into your garden, and scratch and chuckle and fluff themselves under your plumbago bush; but you don't worry. Why should you? They can't hurt it: and besides, you know well enough that the small black hen and the big yellow hen, who have disappeared from the throng, are even now laying their daily eggs for you at the back of the thickest bush. Your little dog rushes frantically up and down the front bed of your garden barking and racing, and tearing up the ground, because his rival little dog who lives down the street is going past with his master, and each pretends that he wants to be at the other — as they have pretended every day for the past three years. But the performance he goes through in the garden doesn't disturb you. Why should it? By following the directions in this article you have selected plants that he cannot hurt. After breakfasting at 12 noon, you stroll out, and, perhaps, smooth with your foot or with your small spade, the inequalities made by the hens; you gather up casually the eggs that they have laid; you whistle to your little dog, and go out for a stroll with a light heart. That is the true way to enjoy amateur gardening.

Investigating Flora

'Twas in scientific circles
   That the great Professor Brown
Had a world-wide reputation
   As a writer of renown.
He had striven finer feelings
   In our natures to implant
By his *Treatise on the Morals*
   Of the Red-eyed Bulldog Ant.
He had hoisted an opponent
   Who had trodden unawares
On his *Reasons for Bare Patches*
   On the Female Native Bears.
So they gave him an appointment
   As instructor to a band
Of the most attractive females
   To be gathered in the land.

'Twas a "Ladies' Science Circle" —
   Just the latest social fad
For the Nicest People only,
   And to make their rivals mad.
They were fond of "science rambles"
   To the country from the town —
A parade of female beauty
   In the leadership of Brown.
They would pick a place for luncheon
   And catch beetles on their rugs;
The Professor called 'em "optera" —
   They called 'em "nasty bugs".
Well, the thing was bound to perish
   For no lovely woman can

Feel the slightest real interest
    In a club without a Man —
The Professor hardly counted
    He was crazy as a loon,
With a countenance suggestive
    Of an elderly baboon.
But the breath of Fate blew on it
    With a sharp and sudden blast,
And the "Ladies' Science Circle"
    Is a memory of the past.

There were two-and-twenty members,
    Mostly young and mostly fair,
Who had made a great excursion
    To a place called Dontknowwhere,
At the crossing of Lost River,
    On the road to No Man's Land.
There they met an old selector,
    With a stockwhip in his hand,
And the sight of so much beauty
    Sent him slightly "off his nut";
So he asked them, smiling blandly,
    "Would they come down to the hut?"
"I am come," said the Professor,
    In his thin and reedy voice,
"To investigate your flora,
    Which I hear is very choice."

The selector stared dumbfounded,
    Till at last he found his tongue:
"To investigate my Flora!
    Oh, you howlin' Brigham Young!
Why, you've two-and-twenty wimmen —
    Reg'lar slap-up wimmen, too!
And you're after little Flora!
    And a crawlin' thing like you!
Oh, you Mormonite gorilla!
    Well, I've heard it from the first
That you wizened little fellers
    Is a hundred times the worst!
But a dried-up ape like you are,
    To be marchin' through the land
With a pack of lovely wimmen —
    Well, I cannot understand!"

"You mistake," said the Professor,
    In a most indignant tone —
While the ladies shrieked and jabbered
    In a fashion of their own —
"You mistake about these ladies,
    I'm a lecturer of theirs;
I am Brown, who wrote the *Treatise
    On the Female Native Bears*!
When I said we wanted flora,
    What I meant was native flowers."
"Well, you *said* you wanted *Flora*,
    And I'll swear you don't get ours!
But here's Flora's self a-comin',
    And it's time for you to skip,
Or I'll write a treatise on you,
    And I'll write it with the whip!
Now, I want no explanations;
    Just you hook it out of sight,
Or you'll charm the poor girl some'ow!"
    The Professor looked in fright:
She was six feet high and freckled,
    And her hair was turkey-red.
The Professor gave a whimper,
    And threw down his bag and fled,
And the Ladies' Science Circle,
    With a simultaneous rush,
Travelled after its Professor,
    And went screaming through the bush!

At the crossing of Lost River,
    On the road to No Man's Land,
Where the grim and ghostly gum trees
    Block the view on every hand,
There they weep and wail and wander,
    Always seeking for the track,
For the hapless old Professor
    Hasn't sense to guide 'em back;
And they clutch at one another,
    And they yell and scream in fright
As they see the gruesome creatures
    Of the grim Australian night;
And they hear the mopoke's hooting,
    And the dingo's howl so dread,
And the flying foxes' jabber
    From the gum trees overhead;

While the weird and wary wombats,
    In their subterranean caves,
Are a-digging, always digging,
    At those wretched people's graves;
And the pike-horned Queensland bullock,
    From his shelter in the scrub,
Has his eye on the proceedings
    Of the Ladies' Science Club.

The Cat

Few know anything about domestic animals — about their inner life and the workings of their minds. Take, for instance, the common roof-tree cat. Most people think that the cat is an unintelligent animal, fond of ease, and caring little for anything but mice and milk. But a cat has really more character than most human beings, and gets a great deal more satisfaction out of life. Of all the animal kingdom, the cat has the most many-sided character. He — or she — is an athlete, a musician, an acrobat, a Lothario, a grim fighter, a sport of the first water. All day long, the cat loafs about the house and takes things easy, and sleeps by the fire, and allows himself to be pestered by the attentions of silly women and annoyed by children. To pass the time away he sometimes watches a mouse hole for an hour or two — just to keep himself from dying of ennui, and people get the idea that this sort of thing is all that life holds for the cat. But watch him as the shades of evening fall, and you see the cat as he really is.

When the family sits down to tea, the cat usually puts in an appearance to get his share, and he purrs noisily and rubs himself against the legs of the family, and all the time he is thinking of a fight or a love affair that is coming off that evening. If there is a guest at table the cat is particularly civil to him, because the guest is likely to have the best of what food is going. Sometimes, instead of recognising his civility with something to eat, the guest stoops down and strokes the cat, and says, "Poor pussy! Poor pussy!" The cat soon gets tired of that — he puts up his claw and quietly but firmly rakes the guest in the leg.

"Ow!" says the guest, "the cat stuck his claw into me!" The family is delighted. It remarks, "Isn't it sweet of him? Isn't he intelligent? *He wants you to give him something to eat.*"

The guest dare not do what he would like to do — kick the cat through the window — so with tears of rage and pain in his eyes, he affects to be very much amused, and sorts out a bit of fish from his plate and gives it to the cat. The cat gingerly receives it, with a look in his eyes as much as to say: "Another time, my friend, you won't be so dull of comprehension," and purrs maliciously as he carries the bit of fish away to a safe distance from the guest's boot before eating it. A cat isn't a fool — not by a long way.

When the family has finished tea, and gathers round the fire to enjoy the hours of indigestion together, the cat slouches casually out of the room and disappears. Life, true life, now begins for him. He saunters down his own backyard, springs to the top of the fence with one easy bound, drops lightly down the other side, trots across a right-of-way to a vacant allotment, and skips to the roof of an empty shed. As he goes, he throws off the effeminate look of civilisation; his gait becomes lithe and panther-like; he looks quickly, keenly, from side to side, and moves noiselessly, for he has many enemies — dogs, cabmen with whips, and small boys with stones. Arrived on the top of the shed, the cat arches his back and rakes his claws once or twice through the soft bark of the old roof, then wheels round and stretches himself a few times, just to see that every muscle is in full working order; and then, dropping his head nearly to his paws, sends across a league of backyards his call to his kindred — his call to love, or war, or sport.

Before long they come — gliding, graceful shadows, approaching circuitously, and halting occasionally to look round and reconnoitre — tortoiseshell, tabby, and black, all domestic cats, but all transformed for the nonce into their natural state. No longer are they the hypocritical, meek creatures who an hour ago were cadging for fish and milk. They are now ruffling, swaggering blades with a Gascon sense of their dignity. Their fights are grim, determined battles, and a cat will be clawed to ribbons before he'll yield. Even the young lady cats have this inestimable superiority over human beings that they can fight among themselves, and work off the jealousy, hatred and malice of their lives in a sprawling, yelling combat on a flat roof. All cats fight, and all keep themselves more or less in training while they are young. Your cat may be the acknowledged lightweight champion of his district — a Griffo of the feline ring! Just think how much more he gets out of his life than you do out of yours — what a hurricane of fighting and love-making his life is — and blush for yourself. You have had one little love affair, and never a good, all-out fight in your life!

And the sport they have, too! As they get older and retire from the ring they go in for sport more systematically, and the suburban backyards that are to us but dullness indescribable, are to them hunting grounds and trysting places where they may have more sport and adventure than ever had King Arthur's knights or Robin Hood's merry men. Grimalkin decides to go and kill a canary in a neighbouring verandah. Consider the fascination of it — the stealthy reconnaissance from the top of the fence; the care to avoid waking the house dog; the noiseless approach and the hurried dash upon the verandah, and the fierce clawing at the fluttering bird till the mangled body is dragged through the bars of the cage; the exultant retreat with the spoil and the growling over the feast that follows. Not the least entertaining part of it is the demure satisfaction of arriving home in time for breakfast and hearing the house-mistress say, "Tom must be sick; he seems to have no appetite."

It is always levelled as a reproach against cats that they are more fond of their home than of the people in it. Naturally, the cat doesn't like to leave his country, the land where he has got all his friends, and where he knows every landmark. Exiled in a strange land, he would have to learn a new geography, would have to find out all about another tribe of dogs, would have to fight and make love to an entirely new nation of cats. Life isn't long enough for that sort of thing and so, when the family moves, the cat, if allowed, will stay at the old house and attach himself to the new occupiers. He will give them the privilege of boarding him while he enjoys life in his own way. He is not going to sacrifice his whole career for the doubtful reward which fidelity to his old master or mistress might bring.

And if people know so little about cats, how much less do they know about the dog? This article was started as an essay on the dog, and the cat was only incidentally to be referred to, but there was so much to say about cats that they have used up all the space, and a fresh start must be made to deal with the dog — the friend of man.

Any Other Time

All of us play our very best game —
   Any other time.
Golf or billiards, it's all the same —
   Any other time.
Lose a match and you always say,
"Just my luck! I was 'off' to-day!
I could have beaten him quite halfway —
   Any other time!"

After a fiver you ought to go —
   Any other time.
Every man that you ask says "Oh,
   Any *other* time.
Lend you a fiver! I'd lend you two,

But I'm overdrawn and my bills are due,
Wish you'd ask me — now, mind you do —
    Any other time!"

Fellows will ask you out to dine —
    Any other time.
"Not tonight, for we're twenty-nine —
    Any other time.
Not tomorrow, for cook's on strike —
Not next day, I'll be out on the bike —
Just drop in whenever you like —
    Any other time!"

Seasick passengers like the sea —
    Any other time.
"Something . . . I ate . . . disagreed . . . with me!
    Any other time
Ocean-trav'lling is . . . simply bliss,
Must be my . . . liver . . . has gone amiss . . .
Why, I would laugh . . . at a sea . . . like this —
    Any other time."

Most of us mean to be better men —
    Any other time:
Regular upright characters then —
    Any other time.
Yet somehow as the years go by
Still we gamble and drink and lie,
When it comes to the last we'll want to die —
    Any other time!

The Story of Mongrel Grey

This is the story the stockman told,
    On the cattle camp, when the stars were bright;
The moon rose up like a globe of gold
    And flooded the plain with her mellow light.
We watched the cattle 'till dawn of day
And he told me the story of Mongrel Grey.

"He was a knock-about station hack,
    Spurred and walloped, and banged and beat;
Ridden all day with a sore on his back,
    Left all night with nothing to eat.
That was a matter of everyday —
Common occurrence to Mongrel Grey.

"Pr'aps we'd have sold him, but someone heard
    He was bred out back on a flooded run,
Where he learnt to swim like a water bird,
    Midnight or midday were all as one.
In the flooded ground he could find his way,
Nothing could puzzle old Mongrel Grey.

" 'Tis a special gift that some horses learn,
    When the floods are out they will splash along
In girth-deep water, and twist and turn
    From hidden channel and billabong.
Never mistaking the road to go,
For a man may guess — but the horses *know*.

"I was camping out with my youngest son
    — Bit of a nipper just learnt to speak —
In an empty hut on the lower run,
    Shooting and fishing in Conroy's Creek.
The youngster toddled about all day,
And with our horses was Mongrel Grey.

"All of a sudden the flood came down
    Fresh from the hills with the mountain rain,
Roaring and eddying, rank and brown,
    Over the flats and across the plain.
Rising and falling — fall of night —
Nothing but water appeared in sight!

"'Tis a nasty place when the floods are out,
    Even in daylight, for all around
Channels and billabongs twist about,
    Stretching for miles in the flooded ground.
And to move was a hopeless thing to try
In the dark, with the water just racing by.

"I had to try it. I heard a roar,
    And the wind swept down with the blinding rain;
And the water rose till it reached the floor
    Of our highest room, and 'twas very plain
The way the water was sweeping down
We must shift for the highlands at once, or drown.

"Off to the stable I splashed, and found
    The horses shaking with cold and fright;
I led them down to the lower ground,
    But never a yard would they swim that night!
They reared and snorted and turned away,
And none would face it but Mongrel Grey.

"I bound the child on the horse's back,
    And we started off with a prayer to Heaven,
Through the rain and the wind and the pitchy black,
    For I knew that the instinct God has given
To guide His creatures by night and day
Would lead the footsteps of Mongrel Grey.

"He struck deep water at once and swam —
    I swam beside him and held his mane —
Till we touched the bank of the broken dam
    In shallow water — then off again,
Swimming in darkness across the flood,
Rank with the smell of the drifting mud.

"He turned and twisted across and back,
    Choosing the places to wade or swim,
Picking the safest and shortest track,
    The pitchy darkness was clear to him.
Did he strike the crossing by sight or smell?
The Lord that led him alone could tell!

"He dodged the timber whene'er he could,
    But the timber brought us to grief at last;
I was partly stunned by a log of wood,
    That struck my head as it drifted past;

And I lost my grip of the brave old grey,
And in half a second he swept away.

"I reached a tree, where I had to stay,
  And did a perish for two days hard;
And lived on water — but Mongrel Grey,
  He walked right into the homestead yard
At dawn next morning, and grazed around,
With the child on top of him safe and sound.

"We keep him now for the wife to ride,
  Nothing too good for him now of course;
Never a whip on his fat old hide,
  For she owes the child to that old grey horse.
And not Old Tyson himself could pay,
The purchase money of Mongrel Grey."

Prelude

I have gathered these stories afar,
  In the wind and the rain,
In the land where the cattle camps are,
  On the edge of the plain.
On the overland routes of the west,
  When the watches were long,
I have fashioned in earnest and jest
  These fragments of song.

They are just the rude stories one hears
  In sadness and mirth,
The records of wandering years,
  And scant is their worth.
Though their merits indeed are but slight,
  I shall not repine,
If they give you one moment's delight,
  Old comrades of mine.

Lost

"He ought to be home," said the old man, "without there's something amiss.
He only went to the Two-mile — he ought to be back by this.
He *would* ride the Reckless filly, he *would* have his wilful way;
And, here, he's not back at sundown — and what will his mother say?

"He was always his mother's idol, since ever his father died;
And there isn't a horse on the station that he isn't game to ride.
But that Reckless mare is vicious, and if once she gets away
He hasn't got strength to hold her — and what will his mother say?"

The old man walked to the sliprail, and peered up the dark'ning track,
And looked and longed for the rider that would never more come back;
And the mother came and clutched him, with sudden, spasmodic fright:
"What has become of my Willie? Why isn't he home tonight?"

Away in the gloomy ranges, at the foot of an ironbark,
The bonnie, winsome laddie was lying stiff and stark;
For the Reckless mare had smashed him against a leaning limb,
And his comely face was battered, and his merry eyes were dim.

And the thoroughbred chestnut filly, the saddle beneath her flanks,
Was away like fire through the ranges to join the wild mob's ranks;
And a broken-hearted woman and an old man worn and grey
Were searching all night in the ranges till the sunrise brought the day.

And the mother kept feebly calling, with a hope that would not die,
"Willie! where are you, Willie?" But how can the dead reply;
And hope died out with the daylight, and the darkness brought despair,
God pity the stricken mother, and answer the widow's prayer!

Though far and wide they sought him, they found not where he fell;
For the ranges held him precious, and guarded their treasure well.
The wattle blooms above him, and the bluebells blow close by,
And the brown bees buzz the secret, and the wild birds sing reply.

But the mother pined and faded, and cried, and took no rest,
And rode each day to the ranges on her hopeless, weary quest.
Seeking her loved one ever, she faded and pined away,
But with strength of her great affection she still sought every day.

"I know that sooner or later I shall find my boy," she said.
But she came not home one evening, and they found her lying dead,
And stamped on the poor pale features, as the spirit homeward pass'd,
Was an angel smile of gladness — she had found the boy at last.

Sitting in Judgment

A SHOW RING SKETCH

The scene is an Australian country show ring — a circular enclosure of about four acres extent — with a spiked batten fence round it, and a listless crowd of back-country settlers hanging around the fence. Back of these there are the sheds for produce, and the machinery sections, where steam threshers and earth scoops are humming, and buzzing, and thundering unnoticed. Crowds of sightseers wander along the cattle stalls and gape at the fat bullocks; side shows are flourishing, a blasé goose is drawing marbles out of a tin canister, and a boxing showman is showing his muscles outside his tent while his partner urges the youth of the district to come in and be thumped for the edification of the audience.

Suddenly a gate opens at the end of the show ring, and horses, cattle, dogs, vehicles, motor cars, and bicyclists crowd into the arena. It is called a general parade, but it might better be described as general chaos.

Trotting horses and ponies, in harness, go whirling round the ring, every horse and every driver fully certain that every eye is fixed on them; the horses — the vainest creatures in the world — arch their necks, and lift their feet up, whizzing past in bewildering succession, till the onlookers get giddy at the constant thud, thud, thud of the hoofs and the rustle of the wheels.

Inside the whirling circle of vehicles, blood stallions are standing on their hind legs, and screaming defiance at all comers; great shaggy-fronted bulls, with dull vindictive eyes, pace along, looking as though they were trying to remember who it was that struck them last. A showground bull always seems to be nursing a grievance.

Mixed up with the stallions and bulls are dogs and donkeys, the dogs being led by attendants, who are apparently selected on the principle that the larger the dog, the smaller the custodian should be, while the donkeys are the only creatures absolutely unmoved by their surroundings, for they sleep peaceably as they walk along, occasionally waking up to utter melodious hoots.

In the centre of the ring a few lady riders, stern-featured women for the most part, are being "judged" by a trembling official, who dares not look any of them in the face, but hurriedly and apologetically examines the horses and saddles, whispers his award to the stewards, and runs at top speed to the official stand, which he reaches in safety just as the award is made known to the competitors.

The defeated ladies immediately begin to "perform," i.e., to ask the universe at large whether anyone ever heard the like of that! But the stewards slip away like shadows, and they are left "performing" to empty benches, so they ride haughtily round the ring, glaring defiance at the spectators.

All the time that the parade is going on, stewards and committee men are wandering about among the competitors trying to find the animals to be judged. The clerk of the ring — a huge man mounted on a small cob — gallops about, roaring out in a voice like a bull: "This way for the fourteen-stone 'acks! Come on, you twelve-'and ponies!" and by degrees various classes get judged, and disperse grumbling. Then the bulls begin to file out with their grievances still unsettled, the lady riders are persuaded to withdraw, and the clerk of the ring sends a sonorous bellow across the ground: "Where's the jumpin' judges?"

From the official stand comes a brisk, dark-faced, wiry little man; he has been a steeplechase rider and a trainer in his time; long experience of that tricky animal, the horse, has made him reserved and slow to express an opinion; he mounts the table, and produces a notebook; from the bar of the booth comes a large, hairy, red-faced man, a man whose face shows absolute self-content. He is a noted show judge, because he refuses, as a rule, to listen to anybody else's opinion, and when he does listen to it, he scornfully contradicts it, as a matter of course. The third judge is a local squatter, who has never judged before, and is overwhelmed with a sense of his own importance.

They seat themselves on a raised platform in the centre of the ring, and hold consultation. The small dark man produces his notebook.

"I always keep a scale of points," he says. "Give 'em so many points for each fence. Then give 'em so many for make, shape, and quality, and so many for the way they jump."

The fat man looks infinite contempt. "I never want any scale of points," he says. "One look at the 'orses is enough for me. A man that judges by points ain't a judge at all, I reckon. What do you think?" he goes on, turning to the squatter. "Do you use points?"

"Never," says the squatter, firmly; which, as he has never judged before in his life, is not at all surprising.

"Well, we'll each go our own way," says the little man. "I'll keep points. Send 'em in."

"Number one: Conductor!" roars the ring steward in a voice like thunder, and a long-legged grey horse comes trotting into the ring and sidles about uneasily. His rider points him for the first jump, and goes at it at a terrific pace. Nearing the fence the horse makes a wild spring, and clears it by feet, while the crowd yell applause; at the second jump he races right close under the obstacle, props dead, and rises in the air with a leap like a goat, while the crowd yell their delight again, and say, "My oath! Ain't he clever?" At the third fence he shifts about uneasily as he comes near it and finally darts at it at an angle, clearing about thirty feet quite unnecessarily, and again the hurricane of cheers breaks out. "Don't he fly 'em?" says one man, waving his hat. At the last fence he makes his spring yards too soon, and, while his forelegs get over all right, his hind legs drop on the rail with a sounding rap, and he leaves a little tuft of hair sticking in the fence.

"I like to see 'em feel their fences," says the fat man. "I had a bay 'orse once, and he felt every fence ever he jumped; shows their confidence."

"I think he'll feel that last one for awhile," says the little dark man. "He hit it pretty hard. What's this now?"

"Number two: Homeward Bound!" And an old solid chestnut horse comes out, and canters up to each jump, clearing them coolly and methodically, always making his spring at the correct distance from the fence. The crowd are not struck by the performance, and the fat man says, "No pace!" but surreptitiously makes two strokes to indicate number two on the cuff of his shirt.

"Number eleven: Spite!" A leggy, weedy chestnut brute, half racehorse, half nondescript, ridden by a terrified amateur, who goes at the fence with a white set face. The horse races up to the fence, and stops dead, among the jeers of the crowd. The rider lets daylight into him with his spurs, and rushes him at the fence again, and this time he gets over.

Round he goes, clouting some fences with his front legs, others with his hind legs. The crowd jeer, but the fat man, from a sheer spirit of opposition, says, "That would be a good horse if he was rode better." And the squatter says, "Yes, he belongs to a young feller just near me. I've seen him jump splendidly out in the bush, over brush fences."

The little dark man says nothing, but makes a note in his book.

"Number twelve: Gaslight!" "Now, you'll see a horse," says the fat man. "I've judged this 'orse in twenty different shows, and gave him first prize every time!"

Gaslight turns out to be a fiddle-headed, heavy-shouldered brute, whose long experience of jumping in shows where they give points for pace, as if the affair were a steeplechase, has taught him to get the business over as quickly as he can. He goes thundering round the ring, pulling double, and standing off his fences in a style that would infallibly bring him to grief if following hounds across roads or through broken timber.

"Now," says the fat man, "that's a 'unter, that is. What I say is, when you come to judge at a show, pick out the 'orse that you would soonest be on if Ned Kelly was after you, and there you have the best 'unter." The little man makes no reply, but makes his usual scrawl in the book, while the squatter hastens to agree with the fat man. "I like to see a bit of pace myself," he ventures to remark.

The fat man sits on him heavily. "You don't call that pace, do you?" he says. "He was only going dead slow."

Various other competitors come in and do their turn round the ring, some propping and bucking over the jumps, others rushing and tearing at their fences, none jumping as a hunter ought to do. Some get themselves into difficulties by changing their feet or misjudging their distance, and are loudly applauded by the crowd for their "cleverness" in getting themselves out of difficulties which, if they had any cleverness, they would not have got into.

A couple of rounds narrow the competitors down to a few, and the task of deciding is then entered upon.

"I have kept a record," says the little man, "of how they jump each fence, and I give them points for style of jumping, and for their make and shape and hunting qualities. The way I bring it out is that Homeward Bound is the best, with Gaslight second."

"Homeward Bound!" says the fat man. "Why, the pace he went wouldn't head a duck. He didn't go as fast as a Chinaman could trot with two baskets of stones. I want to have three of 'em in to have a look at 'em." Here he looks surreptitiously at his cuff, and seeing a note, "No. II", mistakes it for "number eleven", and says: "I want number eleven to go another round."

This order is shouted across the ground, and the leggy, weedy chestnut with the terrified amateur up, comes sidling and snorting out into the ring. The fat man looks at him with scorn.

"What is that fiddle-headed brute doing in the ring?" he says.

"Why," says the ring steward, "you said you wanted him."

"Well," says the fat man, "if I said I wanted him, I *do* want him. Let him go the round."

The terrified amateur goes at the fences with the rashness of despair, and narrowly escapes being clouted off on two occasions. This puts the fat man in a quandary, because, as he has kept no record, he has got all the horses jumbled up in his head, but he has one fixed idea, viz., to give first prize to Gaslight; as to what is to come second he is open to argument. From sheer contrariness he says that number eleven would be "all right if he were rode better", and the squatter agrees. The little man is overruled, and the prizes go — Gaslight, first; Spite, second; Homeward Bound, third.

The crowd hoot loudly as Spite's rider comes round with the second ribbon, and the small boys suggest to the judge in shrill tones that he ought to boil his head. The fat man stalks majestically into the steward's stand, and on being asked how he came to give Spite the second prize, remarks oracularly: "I judge the 'orse; I don't judge the rider."

This silences criticism, and everyone adjourns to have a drink.

Over the flowing bowl the fat man says, "You see, I don't believe in this nonsense about points. I can judge 'em without that."

The scene closes with twenty dissatisfied competitors riding away from the ring, vowing they will never bring another horse there in their lives, and one, the winner, saying:

"Bly me, I knew it would be all right with old Billy judging. 'E *knows* this 'orse."

The Amateur Rider

Him going to ride for us! *Him* — with the pants and the eyeglass and all.
Amateur! don't he just look it — it's twenty to one on a fall.
Boss must be gone off his head to be sending our steeplechase crack
Out over fences like these with an object like that on his back.

Ride! Don't tell *me* he can ride. With his pants just as loose as balloons,
How can he sit on his horse? And his spurs like a pair of harpoons;
Ought to be under the Dog Act, he ought, and be kept off the course.
Fall! why, he'd fall off a cart, let alone off a steeplechase horse.

Yessir! the 'orse is all ready — I wish you'd have rode him before;
Nothing like knowing your 'orse, sir, and this chap's a terror to bore;
Battleaxe always could pull, and he rushes his fences like fun —
Stands off his jump twenty feet, and then springs like a shot from a gun.

Oh, he can jump 'em all right, sir, you make no mistake, 'e's a toff;
Clouts 'em in earnest, too, sometimes, you mind that he don't clout you off —
Don't seem to mind how he hits 'em, his shins is as hard as a nail,
Sometimes you'll see the fence shake and the splinters fly up from the rail.

All you can do is to hold him and just let him jump as he likes,
Give him his head at the fences, and hang on like death if he strikes;
Don't let him run himself out — you can lie third or fourth in the race —
Until you clear the stone wall, and from that you can put on the pace.

Fell at that wall once, he did, and it gave him a regular spread,
Ever since that time he flies it — he'll stop if you pull at his head,
Just let him race — you can trust him — he'll take first-class care he don't
   fall,
And I think that's the lot — but remember, *he must have his head at the wall.*

Well, he's down safe as far as the start, and he seems to sit on pretty neat,
Only his baggified breeches would ruinate anyone's seat —
They're away — here they come — the first fence, and he's head over heels
   for a crown!
Good for the new chum, he's over, and two of the others are down!

Now for the treble, my hearty — By Jove, he can ride, after all;
Whoop, that's your sort — let him fly them! He hasn't much fear of a fall.
Who in the world would have thought it? And aren't they just going a pace?
Little Recruit in the lead there will make it a stoutly run race.

Lord! But they're racing in earnest — and down goes Recruit on his head,
Rolling clean over his boy — it's a miracle if he ain't dead.
Battleaxe, Battleaxe yet! By the Lord, he's got most of 'em beat —
Ho! did you see how he struck, and the swell never moved in his seat?

Second time round, and, by Jingo! he's holding his lead of 'em well;
Hark to him clouting the timber! It don't seem to trouble the swell.
Now for the wall — let him rush it. A thirty-foot leap, I declare —
Never a shift in his seat, and he's racing for home like a hare.

What's that that's chasing him — Rataplan — regular demon to stay!
Sit down and ride for your life now! Oh, good, that's the style — come away!
Rataplan's certain to beat you, unless you can give him the slip;
Sit down and rub in the whalebone now — give him the spurs and the whip!

Battleaxe, Battleaxe, yet — and it's Battleaxe wins for a crown;
Look at him rushing the fences, he wants to bring t'other chap down.
Rataplan never will catch him if only he keeps on his pins;
Now! the last fence! and he's over it! Battleaxe, Battleaxe wins!

Well, sir, you rode him just perfect — I knew from the first you could ride.
Some of the chaps said you couldn't, an' I says just like this a' one side:
Mark me, I says, that's a tradesman — the saddle is where he was bred.
Weight! you're all right, sir, and thank you; and them was the words that I
    said.

Mulga Bill's Bicycle

'Twas Mulga Bill, from Eaglehawk, that caught the cycling craze;
He turned away the good old horse that served him many days;
He dressed himself in cycling clothes, resplendent to be seen;
He hurried off to town and bought a shining new machine;
And as he wheeled it through the door, with air of lordly pride,
The grinning shop assistant said, "Excuse me, can you ride?"

"See here, young man," said Mulga Bill, "from Walgett to the sea,
From Conroy's Gap to Castlereagh, there's none can ride like me.
I'm good all round at everything, as everybody knows,
Although I'm not the one to talk — I *hate* a man that blows.
But riding is my special gift, my chiefest, sole delight;
Just ask a wild duck can it swim, a wildcat can it fight.
There's nothing clothed in hair or hide, or built of flesh or steel,
There's nothing walks or jumps, or runs, on axle, hoof, or wheel,
But what I'll sit, while hide will hold and girths and straps are tight:
I'll ride this here two-wheeled concern right straight away at sight."

'Twas Mulga Bill, from Eaglehawk, that sought his own abode,
That perched above the Dead Man's Creek, beside the mountain road.
He turned the cycle down the hill and mounted for the fray,
But ere he'd gone a dozen yards it bolted clean away.
It left the track, and through the trees, just like a silver streak,
It whistled down the awful slope towards the Dead Man's Creek.

It shaved a stump by half an inch, it dodged a big white-box:
The very wallaroos in fright went scrambling up the rocks,
The wombats hiding in their caves dug deeper underground,
As Mulga Bill, as white as chalk, sat tight to every bound.
It struck a stone and gave a spring that cleared a fallen tree,
It raced beside a precipice as close as close could be;
And then as Mulga Bill let out one last despairing shriek
It made a leap of twenty feet into the Dead Man's Creek.

'Twas Mulga Bill, from Eaglehawk, that slowly swam ashore:
He said, "I've had some narrer shaves and lively rides before;
I've rode a wild bull round a yard to win a five-pound bet,
But this was the most awful ride that I've encountered yet.
I'll give that two-wheeled outlaw best; it's shaken all my nerve
To feel it whistle through the air and plunge and buck and swerve.
It's safe at rest in Dead Man's Creek, we'll leave it lying still;
A horse's back is good enough henceforth for Mulga Bill."

'Twas Mulga Bill, from Eaglehawk, that caught the cycling craze;
He turned away the good old horse that served him many days;

Mulga Bill's Bicycle, p. 256

And now by coach and mailman's bag it goes from town to town,
And Conroy's Gap and Conroy's Creek have marked it "further down".

The Travelling Post Office, p. 257

The Travelling Post Office

The roving breezes come and go, the reed beds sweep and sway,
The sleepy river murmurs low, and loiters on its way,
It is the land of lots o' time along the Castlereagh.

The old man's son had left the farm, he found it dull and slow,
He drifted to the great north-west where all the rovers go.
"He's gone so long," the old man said, "he's dropped right out of mind,
But if you'd write a line to him I'd take it very kind;
He's shearing here and fencing there, a kind of waif and stray,
He's droving now with Conroy's sheep along the Castlereagh.
The sheep are travelling for the grass, and travelling very slow;
They may be at Mundooran now, or past the Overflow,
Or tramping down the black soil flats across by Waddiwong,
But all those little country towns would send the letter wrong,
The mailman, if he's extra tired, would pass them in his sleep,
It's safest to address the note to 'Care of Conroy's sheep',
For five and twenty thousand head can scarcely go astray,
You write to 'Care of Conroy's sheep along the Castlereagh'."

By rock and ridge and riverside the western mail has gone,
Across the great Blue Mountain Range to take that letter on.
A moment on the topmost grade while open fire doors glare,
She pauses like a living thing to breathe the mountain air,
Then launches down the other side across the plains away
To bear that note to "Conroy's sheep along the Castlereagh".

And now by coach and mailman's bag it goes from town to town,
And Conroy's Gap and Conroy's Creek have marked it "further down".
Beneath a sky of deepest blue where never cloud abides,
A speck upon the waste of plain the lonely mailman rides.
Where fierce hot winds have set the pine and myall boughs asweep
He hails the shearers passing by for news of Conroy's sheep.
By big lagoons where wildfowl play and crested pigeons flock,
By campfires where the drovers ride around their restless stock,
And past the teamster toiling down to fetch the wool away
My letter chases Conroy's sheep along the Castlereagh.

Rio Grande's Last Race

Now this was what Macpherson told
   While waiting in the stand;
A reckless rider, over-bold,
The only man with hands to hold
   The rushing Rio Grande.

He said, "This day I bid goodbye
   To bit and bridle rein,
To ditches deep and fences high,
For I have dreamed a dream, and I
   Shall never ride again.

"I dreamt last night I rode this race
   That I to-day must ride,
And cant'ring down to take my place
I saw full many an old friend's face
   Come stealing to my side.

"Dead men on horses long since dead,
   They clustered on the track;
The champions of the days long fled,
They moved around with noiseless tread —
   Bay, chestnut, brown, and black.

"And one man on a big grey steed
   Rode up and waved his hand;
Said he, 'We help a friend in need,
And we have come to give a lead
   To you and Rio Grande.

" 'For you must give the field the slip,
   So never draw the rein,
But keep him moving with the whip,
And if he falter — set your lip
   And rouse him up again.

" 'But when you reach the big stone wall,
   Put down your bridle hand
And let him sail — he cannot fall —
But don't you interfere at all;
   You trust old Rio Grande.'

"We started, and in front we showed,
  The big horse running free:
Right fearlessly and game he strode,
And by my side those dead men rode
  Whom no one else could see.

"As silently as flies a bird,
  They rode on either hand;
At every fence I plainly heard
The phantom leader give the word,
  'Make room for Rio Grande!'

"I spurred him on to get the lead,
  I chanced full many a fall;
But swifter still each phantom steed
Kept with me, and at racing speed
  We reached the big stone wall.

"And there the phantoms on each side
  Drew in and blocked his leap;
'Make room! make room!' I loudly cried,
But right in front they seemed to ride —
  I cursed them in my sleep.

"He never flinched, he faced it game,
  He struck it with his chest,
And every stone burst out in flame,
And Rio Grande and I became
  As phantoms with the rest.

"And then I woke, and for a space
  All nerveless did I seem;
For I have ridden many a race,
But never one at such a pace
  As in that fearful dream.

"And I am sure as man can be
  That out upon the track,
Those phantoms that men cannot see
Are waiting now to ride with me,
  And I shall not come back.

"For I must ride the dead men's race,
  And follow their command;
'Twere worse than death, the foul disgrace

If I should fear to take my place
   Today on Rio Grande."

He mounted, and a jest he threw,
   With never sign of gloom;
But all who heard the story knew
That Jack Macpherson, brave and true,
   Was going to his doom.

They started, and the big black steed
   Came flashing past the stand;
All single-handed in the lead
He strode along at racing speed,
   The mighty Rio Grande.

But on his ribs the whalebone stung,
   A madness it did seem!
And soon it rose on every tongue
That Jack Macpherson rode among
   The creatures of his dream.

He looked to left and looked to right,
   As though men rode beside;
And Rio Grande, with foam-flecks white,
Raced at his jumps in headlong flight
   And cleared them in his stride.

But when they reached the big stone wall,
   Down went the bridle hand,
And loud we heard Macpherson call,
"Make room, or half the field will fall!
   Make room for Rio Grande!"

"He's down! he's down!" And horse and man
   Lay quiet side by side!
No need the pallid face to scan,
We knew with Rio Grande he ran
   The race the dead men ride.

Here's Luck

(A TOAST AT A HUNT CLUB DINNER)

It chanced one day I watched a steeplechase,
  And one horse singled out and led them all
Across the fences at a rattling pace
  Until he hit a fence and took a fall.
His rider laughed and muttered with a smile —
"Well, anyhow, I led 'em for a while."

And this the text is for my theme tonight —
  A moral that the wisest men have sung:
Our life is very short — and swift the flight
  Of time — so, comrades, go it while young.
And when old age comes on you'll find it good
To think you made the running while you could.

There's nothing now too solid or too high
  For some of you to take and chance a spill;
But we must funk the fences bye and bye,
  When limbs grow stiff and hands have lost their skill.
In wintry age we'll seek the hearthstone's blaze;
So let us make the most of youth's bright days.

So now, my friends, good luck and may you keep
  Stout hearts and true and honest kindly mirth,
When drawing nearer to the last great leap
  That lands us on the other side of earth,
Where many a gallant horseman and brave steed
Has gone before to give us all a lead.

The History of a Jackaroo in Five Letters

No. 1

Letter from Joscelyn de Greene, of Wiltshire, England, to college friend

Dear Gus,

The Governor has fixed things up for me at last. I am not to go to India, but to Australia. It seems the Governor met some old Australian swell named Moneygrub at a dinner in the City. He has thousands of acres of land and herds of sheep, and I am to go out and learn the business of sheep raising. Of course it is not quite the same as going to India; but some really decent people do go out to Australia sometimes, I am told, and I expect it won't be so bad. In India one generally goes into the Civil Service, nothing to do and lots of niggers to wait on you but the Australian Civil Service no fellow can well go into — it is awful low business, I hear. I have been going in for gun and revolver practice so as to be able to hold my own against the savages and the serpents in the woods of Australia. Mr Moneygrub says there isn't much fighting with the savages nowadays; but, he says, the Union shearers will give me all the fight I want. What is a Union shearer, I wonder? My mother has ordered an extra large artist's umbrella for me to take with me for fear of sunstroke, and I can hold it over me while watching the flocks. She didn't half like my going until Mr Moneygrub said that they always dressed for dinner at the head station, and that a Church of England clergyman visits there twice a month. I am only to pay a premium of £500 for the experience, and Mr Moneygrub says I'll be able to make that out of scalps in my spare time. He says there is a Government reward for scalps. I don't mind a brush with the savages, but if he thinks I'm going to scalp my enemies he is mistaken. Anyhow, I sail next week, so no more from yours, outward bound,
Joscelyn de Greene.

No. 2

Letter from Moneygrub and Co., London, to the manager of the company's Drybone station, Paroo River, Australia

Dear Sir,

We beg to advise you of having made arrangements to take a young gentleman named Greene as colonial experiencer, and he will be consigned to you by the next boat. His premium is £500, and you will please deal with him in the usual way. Let us know when you have vacancies for any more colonial experiencers, as several are now asking about it, and the premiums are forthcoming. You are on no account to employ Union shearers this year; and you must cut expenses as low as you can. Would it not be feasible to work the station with the colonial experience men and Chinese labour? &c., &c., &c.

No. 3

Letter from Mr Robert Saltbush, of Frying Pan station, to a friend

Dear Billy,

Those fellows over at Drybone station have been at it again. You know it joins us, and old Moneygrub, who lives in London, sends out an English bloke every now and again to be a jackaroo. He gets £500 premium for each one, and the manager puts the jackaroo to boundary ride a tremendous great paddock at the back of the run, and he gives him a week's rations and tells him never to go through a gate, because so long as he only gets lost in the paddock he can always be found somehow, but if he gets out of the paddock, Lord knows whether he'd ever be seen again. And there these poor English devils are, riding round the fences and getting lost and not seeing a soul until they go near mad from loneliness; and then they run away at last, and old Macgregor, the manager, he makes a great fuss and goes after them with a whip, but he takes care to have a stockman pick their tracks up and take them to the nearest township, and then they go on the spree and never come back, and old Moneygrub collars the £500 and sends out another jackaroo. It's a great game. The last one they had was a fellow called Greene. They had him at the head station for a while, letting him get pitched off the station horses. He said: "They're awfully beastly horses in this country, by Jove; they're not content with throwing you off, but they'd kick you afterwards if you don't be careful." When they got full up of him at the head station they sent him out to the big paddock to an old hut full of fleas, and left him there with his tucker and two old screws of horses. The horses, of course, gave him the slip, and he got lost for two days looking for them, and his meat was gone bad when he got home. He killed a sheep for tucker, and how do you think he killed it? He shot it! It was a ram, too, one of Moneygrub's best rams, and there will be the deuce to pay when they find out. About the fourth day a swagman turned up, and he gave the swaggie a gold watch chain to show him the way to the nearest town, and he is there now — on the spree, I believe. He had a fine throat for whisky, anyhow, and the hot climate has started him in earnest. Before he left the hut and the fleas, he got a piece of raddle and wrote on the door: "Hell. S.R.O.", whatever that means. I think it must be some sort of joke. The brown colt I got from Ginger is a clinker, a terror to kick, but real fast. He takes a lot of rubbing out for half a mile, &c., &c., &c.

No. 4

*Letter from Sandy Macgregor, manager of Drybone station,
to Messrs Moneygrub & Co., London*

Dear Sirs,

I regret to have to inform you that the young gentleman, Mr Greene, whom you sent out, has seen fit to leave his employment and go away to the township. No doubt he found the work somewhat rougher than he had been used to, but if young gentlemen are sent out here to get experience they must expect to rough it like other bushmen. I hope you will notify his friends of the fact: and if you have applications for any more colonial experiencers we now have a vacancy for one. There is great trouble this year over the shearing, and a lot of grass will be burnt unless some settlement is arrived at. &c., &c., &c.

No. 5

Extract from evidence of Senior Constable Rafferty, taken at an inquest before Lushington, P.M. for the North-east by South Paroo district, and a jury

I am a senior constable, stationed at Walloopna beyant. On the 5th instant, I received information that a man was in the horrors at Flanagan's hotel. I went down and saw the man, whom I recognise as the deceased. He was in the horrors: he was very bad. He had taken all his clothes off, and was hiding in a fowl house to get away from the devils which were after him. I went to arrest him, but he avoided me, and escaped over a paling fence on to the Queensland side of the border, where I had no power to arrest him. He was foaming at the mouth and acting like a madman. He had been on the spree for several days. From enquiries made, I believe his name to be Greene, and that he had lately left the employment of Mr Macgregor, at Drybone. He was found dead on the roadside by the carriers coming into Walloopna. He had evidently wandered away from the township, and died from the effects of the sun and the drink.

Verdict of jury: "That deceased came to his death by sunstroke and exposure during a fit of delirium tremens caused by excessive drinking. No blame attached to anybody." Curator of intestate estates advertises for next of kin of J. Greene, and nobody comes forward. Curtain!

Jim Carew

Born of a thoroughbred English race,
   Well-proportioned and closely knit,
Neat of figure and handsome face,
   Always ready and always fit,
Hard and wiry of limb and thew,
That was the ne'er-do-well Jim Carew.

One of the sons of the good old land —
   Many a year since his like was known;
Never a game but he took command,
   Never a sport but he held his own;
Gained at his college a triple blue —
Good as they make them was Jim Carew.

Came to grief — was it card or horse?
   Nobody asked and nobody cared;
Ship him away to the bush of course,
   Ne'er-do-well fellows are easily spared;
Only of women a tolerable few
Sorrowed at parting with Jim Carew.

Gentleman Jim on the cattle camp,
   Sitting his horse with an easy grace;
But the reckless living has left its stamp
   In the deep drawn lines of that handsome face,
And a harder look in those eyes of blue:
Prompt at a quarrel is Jim Carew.

Billy the Lasher was out for gore —
   Twelve-stone navvy with chest of hair,
When he opened out with a hungry roar,
   On a ten-stone man it was hardly fair;
But his wife was wise if his face she knew
By the time you were done with him, Jim Carew.

Gentleman Jim in the stockmen's hut
   Works with them, toils with them, side by side;
As to his past — well, his lips are shut.
   "Gentleman once," say his mates with pride;
And the wildest Cornstalk can ne'er outdo
In feats of recklessness, Jim Carew.

What should he live for? A dull despair!
   Drink is his master and drags him down,
Water of Lethe that drowns all care.
   Gentleman Jim has a lot to drown,
And he reigns as king with a drunken crew,
Sinking to misery, Jim Carew.

Such is the end of the ne'er-do-well —
   Jimmy the Boozer, all down at heel;
But he straightens up when he's asked to tell
   His name and race, and a flash of steel
Still lightens up in those eyes of blue —
"I am, or — no, I *was* — Jim Carew."

Castlebar

Bidding good morrow to all our cares,
   Riding along with a joyful heart,
Little we reck of the world's affairs,
   All that we ask is a decent start.
Though the jumps are big and the distance far
We will get to the finish on Castlebar.

Little Blue Peter goes sailing by;
   Little Blue Peter may stand or fall,
For his rider reckons no man can die
   Till his day comes round — so he chances all!
And away to the front where the good ones are
Go Little Blue Peter and Castlebar.

Bay and chestnut and brown and black,
   I hear in the timber their hoof beats drum,
As I clear the fence on the Prospect track
   I turn in the saddle and watch them come.
But the chestnut horse with the big white star,
Why isn't he following Castlebar?

Dear little woman with eyes of blue,
  With lissom figure and easy grace,
I turn in the saddle and long for you
  As the field sweeps on at a rattling pace.
But I know that away on the heights afar
Your heart is following Castlebar.

As Long As Your Eyes Are Blue

Wilt thou love me, sweet, when my hair is grey,
  And my cheeks shall have lost their hue?
When the charms of youth shall have passed away,
  Will your love as of old prove true?
For the looks may change, and the heart may range,
  And the love be no longer fond;
Wilt thou love with truth in the years of youth
  And away to the years beyond?

Oh, I love you, sweet, for your locks of brown
  And the blush on your cheek that lies —
But I love you most for the kindly heart
  That I see in your sweet blue eyes —
For the eyes are signs of the soul within,
  Of the heart that is leal and true,
And mine own sweetheart, I shall love you still,
  Just as long as your eyes are blue.

For the locks may bleach, and the cheeks of peach
  May be reft of their golden hue;
But mine own sweetheart, I shall love you still,
  Just as long as your eyes are blue.

By the Grey Gulf-water

Far to the northward there lies a land,
  A wonderful land that the winds blow over,
And none may fathom nor understand
  The charm it holds for the restless rover;
A great grey chaos — a land half made,
  Where endless space is and no life stirreth;
And the soul of a man will recoil afraid
  From the sphinx-like visage that Nature weareth.
But old Dame Nature, though scornful, craves
  Her dole of death and her share of slaughter;
Many indeed are the nameless graves
  Where her victims sleep by the Grey Gulf-water.

Slowly and slowly those grey streams glide,
  Drifting along with a languid motion,
Lapping the reed beds on either side,
  Wending their way to the Northern Ocean.
Grey are the plains where the emus pass
  Silent and slow, with their staid demeanour;
Over the dead men's graves the grass
  Maybe is waving a trifle greener.
Down in the world where men toil and spin
  Dame Nature smiles as man's hand has taught her;
Only the dead men her smiles can win
  In the great lone land by the Grey Gulf-water.

For the strength of man is an insect's strength,
  In the face of that mighty plain and river,
And the life of a man is a moment's length
  To the life of the stream that will run for ever.
And so it cometh they take no part
  In small-world worries; each hardy rover
Rideth abroad and is light of heart,
  With the plains around and the blue sky over.
And up in the heavens the brown lark sings
  The songs that the strange wild land has taught her;
Full of thanksgiving her sweet song rings —
  And I wish I were back by the Grey Gulf-water.

Father Riley's Horse

'Twas the horse thief, Andy Regan, that was hunted like a dog
   By the troopers of the upper Murray side,
They had searched in every gully — they had looked in every log,
   But never sight or track of him they spied,
Till the priest at Kiley's Crossing heard a knocking very late
   And a whisper "Father Riley — come across!"
So his Rev'rence in pyjamas trotted softly to the gate
   And admitted Andy Regan — and a horse!

"Now, it's listen, Father Riley, to the words I've got to say,
   For it's close upon my death I am tonight.
With the troopers hard behind me I've been hiding all the day
   In the gullies keeping close and out of sight.
But they're watching all the ranges till there's not a bird could fly,
   And I'm fairly worn to pieces with the strife,
So I'm taking no more trouble, but I'm going home to die,
   'Tis the only way I see to save my life.

"Yes, I'm making home to mother's, and I'll die o' Tuesday next
   An' be buried on the Thursday — and, of course,
I'm prepared to meet my penance, but with one thing I'm perplexed
   And it's — Father, it's this jewel of a horse!
He was never bought nor paid for, and there's not a man can swear
   To his owner or his breeder, but I know,
That his sire was by Pedantic from the Old Pretender mare
   And his dam was close related to The Roe.

"And there's nothing in the district that can race him for a step,
   He could canter while they're going at their top:
He's the king or all the leppers that was ever seen to lep,
   A five-foot fence — he'd clear it in a hop!
So I'll leave him with you, Father, till the dead shall rise again,
   'Tis yourself that knows a good 'un; and, of course,
You can say he's got by Moonlight out of Paddy Murphy's plain
   If you're ever asked the breeding of the horse!

"But it's getting on to daylight and it's time to say goodbye,
   For the stars above the east are growing pale.
And I'm making home to mother — and it's hard for me to die!
   But it's harder still, is keeping out of gaol!
You can ride the old horse over to my grave across the dip

Where the wattle bloom is waving overhead.
Sure he'll jump them fences easy — you must never raise the whip
    Or he'll rush 'em! — now, goodbye!" and he had fled!

So they buried Andy Regan, and they buried him to rights,
    In the graveyard at the back of Kiley's Hill;
There were five-and-twenty mourners who had five-and-twenty fights
    Till the very boldest fighters had their fill.
There were fifty horses racing from the graveyard to the pub,
    And their riders flogged each other all the while.
And the lashin's of the liquor! And the lavin's of the grub!
    Oh, poor Andy went to rest in proper style.

Then the races came to Kiley's — with a steeplechase and all,
    For the folk were mostly Irish round about,
And it takes an Irish rider to be fearless of a fall,
    They were training morning in and morning out.
But they never started training till the sun was on the course
    For a superstitious story kept 'em back,
That the ghost of Andy Regan on a slashing chestnut horse,
    Had been training by the starlight on the track.

And they read the nominations for the races with surprise
    And amusement at the Father's little joke,
For a novice had been entered for the steeplechasing prize,
    And they found that it was Father Riley's moke!
He was neat enough to gallop, he was strong enough to stay!
    But his owner's views of training were immense,
For the Reverend Father Riley used to ride him every day,
    And he never saw a hurdle nor a fence.

And the priest would join the laughter: "Oh," said he, "I put him in,
    For there's five and twenty sovereigns to be won.
And the poor would find it useful, if the chestnut chanced to win,
    And he'll maybe win when all is said and done!"
He had called him Faugh-a-ballagh, which is French for "clear the course",
    And his colours were a vivid shade of green:
All the Dooleys and O'Donnells were on Father Riley's horse,
    While the Orangemen were backing Mandarin!

It was Hogan, the dog poisoner — aged man and very wise,
    Who was camping in the racecourse with his swag,
And who ventured the opinion, to the township's great surprise,
    That the race would go to Father Riley's nag.
"You can talk about your riders — and the horse has not been schooled,

And the fences is terrific, and the rest!
When the field is fairly going, then ye'll see ye've all been fooled,
    And the chestnut horse will battle with the best.

"For there's some has got condition, and they think the race is sure,
    And the chestnut horse will fall beneath the weight,
But the hopes of all the helpless, and the prayers of all the poor,
    Will be running by his side to keep him straight.
And it's what's the need of schoolin' or of workin' on the track,
    Whin the saints are there to guide him round the course!
I've prayed him over every fence — I've prayed him out and back!
    And I'll bet my cash on Father Riley's horse!"

Oh, the steeple was a caution! They went tearin' round and round,
    And the fences rang and rattled where they struck.
There was some that cleared the water — there was more fell in and drowned,
    Some blamed the men and others blamed the luck!
But the whips were flying freely when the field came into view,
    For the finish down the long green stretch of course,
And in front of all the flyers — jumpin' like a kangaroo,
    Came the rank outsider — Father Riley's horse!

Oh, the shouting and the cheering as he rattled past the post!
    For he left the others standing, in the straight;
And the rider — well they reckoned it was Andy Regan's ghost,
    And it beat 'em how a ghost would draw the weight!
But he weighed it, nine stone seven, then he laughed and disappeared,
    Like a banshee (which is Spanish for an elf),
And old Hogan muttered sagely, "If it wasn't for the beard
    They'd be thinking it was Andy Regan's self!"

And the poor of Kiley's Crossing drank the health at Christmastide
    Of the chestnut and his rider dressed in green.
There was never such a rider, not since Andy Regan died,
    And they wondered who on earth he could have been.
But they settled it among 'em, for the story got about,
    'Mongst the bushmen and the people on the course,
That the Devil had been ordered to let Andy Regan out
    For the steeplechase on Father Riley's horse!

An Outback Marriage

CHAPTER VI

A COACH ACCIDENT

The coach from Tarrong railway station to Emu Flat, and then on to Donohoe's Hotel, ran twice a week. Pat Donohoe was mailman, contractor and driver, and his admirers said that Pat could hit his five horses in more places at once than any other man on the face of the earth. His coach was horsed by the neighbouring squatters, through whose stations the road ran; and any horse that developed homicidal tendencies, or exhibited a disinclination to work, was at once handed over to the mailman to be licked into shape. The result was that, as a rule, Pat was driving teams composed of animals that would do anything but go straight, but under his handling they were generally persuaded, after a day or two, to settle down to their work.

On the day when Hugh and Mrs Gordon read Mr Grant's letter at Kuryong, the train deposited at Tarrong, a self-reliant young lady of about twenty, accompanied by nearly a truck-full of luggage — solid leather portmanteaux, canvas-covered bags, iron boxes, and so on — which produced a great sensation among the rustics. She was handsome enough to be called a beauty, and everything about her spoke of exuberant health and vitality. Her figure was supple, and she had the clear pink and white complexion which belongs to cold climates.

She seemed accustomed to being waited on, and watched without emotion the guard and the solitary railway official — porter, station-master, telegraph-operator and lantern-man, all rolled into one — haul her hundredweights of luggage out of the train. Then she told the perspiring station-master, etc, to please have the luggage sent to the hotel, and marched over to that building in quite an assured way, carrying a small handbag. Three commercial travellers, who had come up by the same train, followed her off the platform, and the most gallant of the three winked at his friends, and then stepped up and offered to carry her bag. The young lady gave him a pleasant smile, and handed him the bag; together they crossed the street, while the other commercials marched disconsolately behind. At the door of the hotel she took the bag from her cavalier, and there and then, in broad Australian daylight, rewarded him with twopence — a disaster which caused him to apply to his firm for transfer to some foreign country at once. She marched into the bar, where Dan, the landlord's son, was sweeping, while Mrs Connellan, the landlady, was wiping glasses in the midst of a stale fragrance of overnight beer and tobacco smoke.

"I am going to Kuryong," said the young lady, "and I expected to meet Mr Gordon here. Is he here?"

Mrs Connellan looked at her open-eyed. Such an apparition was not often seen in Tarrong. Mr and Mrs Connellan had only just "taken the pub", and

*Miss Grant's arrival at Kuryong homestead caused great
excitement among the inhabitants.*

An Outback Marriage, p. 278

Or there were sheep to inspect, or fences to look at — an excuse for an excursion was never lacking.

An Outback Marriage, p. 283

what with trying to keep Connellan sober and refusing drinks to tramps, loafers and blackfellows, Mrs Connellan was pretty well worn out. As for making the hotel pay, that idea had been given up long ago. It was against Mrs Connellan's instincts of hospitality to charge anyone for a meal or a bed, and when any great rush of bar trade took place it generally turned out to be "Connellan's shout", so the hotel was not exactly a gold-mine. In fact, Mrs Connellan had decided that the less business she did, the more money she would make; and she rather preferred that people should not stop at her hotel. This girl looked as if she would give trouble; might even expect clean beds and clean sheets when there were none within the hotel, and might object to fleas, of which there were plenty. So the landlady pulled herself together, and decided to speed the parting guest as speedily as possible.

"Mr Gordon couldn't git in," she said. "The cricks (creeks) is all up. The coach is going down to Kiley's Crossing today. You had better go with that."

"How soon does the coach start?"

"In an hour or two. As soon as Pat Donohoe, the mailman, has got a horse shod. Come in and have a wash, and fix yourself up till breakfast is ready. Where's your bag?"

"My luggage is at the railway station."

"I'll send Dan over for it. Dan, Dan, Dan!"

" 'Ello," said Dan's voice, from the passage, where, with the wild-eyed servant-girl, he had been taking stock of the new arrival.

"Go over to the station and git this lady's bag. Is there much to carry?"

"There are only four portmanteaux and three bags, and two boxes and a hat-box, and a roll of rugs; and please be careful of the hat-box."

"You'd better git the barrer, Dan."

"Better git the bloomin' bullock dray," growled Dan, quite keen to see this aggregation of luggage; and foreseeing something to talk about for the next three months. "She must ha' come up to start a store, I reckon," said Dan; and off he went to struggle with boxes for the next half-hour or so.

Over Mary Grant's experiences at the Tarrong Hotel we will not linger. The dirty water, peopled by wriggling animalculae, that she poured out of the bedroom jug; the damp, cloudy, unhealthy-smelling towel on which she dried her face; the broken window through which she could hear herself being discussed by loafers in the yard; all these things are matters of course in bush townships, for the Australian, having a soul above details, does not shine at hotel-keeping. The breakfast was enlivened by snatches of song from the big, good-natured bush girl who waited at table, and who "fancied" her voice somewhat, and marched into the breakfast-room singing in an ear-splitting soprano:

"It's a vilet from me —"

(*spoken*) "What you'll have, there's chops, steaks, and bacon and eggs" — "Chops, please."

(*singer continues*) "Sainted mother's —"

(*spoken*) "Tea or coffee" — "Tea, please."

(singer finishes) — "grave."

While she ate, Miss Grant had an uneasy feeling that she was being stared at; all the female staff and hangers-on of the place having gathered round the door to peer in at her and to appraise to the last farthing her hat, her tailor-made gown, and her solid English walking-shoes, and to indulge in wild speculation as to who or what she could be. A Kickapoo Indian in full war-paint, arriving suddenly in a little English village, could not have created more excitement than she did at Tarrong. After breakfast she walked out on the verandah that ran round the little one-storey weatherboard hotel, and looked down the mile and a-half of road, with little galvanised-iron-roofed cottages at intervals of a quarter of a mile or so, that constituted the town-ship. She watched Conroy, the policeman, resplendent in breeches and polished boots, swagger out from the court-house yard, leading his horse to water. The town was waking to its daily routine; Garry, the butcher, took down the clumsy board that passed for a window-shutter, and McDermott, the carter, passed the hotel, riding a huge rough-coated draught horse, bare-backed. Everyone gave him a "Mornin', Billy!" as he passed, and he returned the greeting as he did every morning of his life. A few children loitered past to the little school-house, staring at her as though she were some animal.

She was in a hurry to get away — English people always are — but in the bright lexicon of the bush there is no such word as hurry. Tracey, the black-smith, had not by any means finished shoeing the coach horse yet. So Mrs Connellan made an attempt to find out who she was, and why she was going to Kuryong.

"You'll have a nice trip in the coach," she said. "Lier (lawyer) Blake's going down. He's a nice feller."

"Yes?" Miss Grant politely responded.

"Father Kelly, too. He's good company."

"Yes?"

"Are you staying long at Kuryong?"

"Some time, I expect."

"Are you going to teach the children?"

"No, I'm going to live there. My father owns Kuryong. My father is Mr Grant."

Mrs Connellan was simply staggered at this colossal treasure-trove, this majestic piece of gossip that had fallen on her like rain from Heaven. Mr Grant's daughter! Going out to Kuryong! What a piece of news! Hardly knowing what she did, she shuffled out of the room, and interrupted the singing waitress who was wiping plates, and had just got back to "It's a vilet" when Mrs Connellan burst in on her.

"Maggie! Maggie! Do you know who that is? Grant's daughter! The one that used to be in England. She must be going to Kuryong to live, with all that luggage. What'll the Gordons say? The old lady won't like it, will she? This'll be a bit of news, won't it?" And she went off to tell the cook, while Maggie darted to the door to meet Dan, and tell him.

Dan told the station-master when he went back for the next load, and when he had finished carting the luggage he got on a horse and went round telling everybody in the little town. The station-master told the ganger of the four navvies who went by on their trolly down the line to work. At the end of their four-mile length they told the ration-carrier of Eubindal station, who happened to call in at their camp for a drink of tea. He hurried off to the head-station with the news, and on his way told three teamsters, an inspector of selections, and a black boy belonging to Mylong station, whom he happened to meet on the road. Each of them told everybody that they met, pulling up and standing in their stirrups to discuss the matter in all its bearings, in the leisurely style of the bush; and wondering what she had come out for, whether the Gordons would get the sack from Kuryong, whether she would marry Hugh Gordon, whether she was engaged already, whether she was good-looking, how much money she had, and how much old Grant would leave her. In fact, before twenty-four hours were over, all the district knew of her arrival; which possibly explains how news travels in Africa among the Kaffirs, who are supposed to have a signalling system that no one has yet fathomed; but the way it gets round in Australia is just as wonderful as among the Kaffirs, in fact, for speed and thoroughness of information we should be inclined to think that our coloured brethren run a bad second.

At last, however, Tracey had finished shoeing the coach horse, and Miss Grant, with part of her luggage, took a seat on the coach behind five of Donohoe's worst horses, next to a well-dressed, powerfully built man of about five-and-twenty. He looked and talked like a gentleman, and she heard the coachman address him as "Mr Blake". She and he shared the box-seat with the driver, and just at the last moment the local priest hurried up and climbed on the coach. In some unaccountable way he had missed hearing who the young lady was, and for a time he could only look at her back hair and wonder.

It was not long before, in the free and easy Australian style, the passengers began to talk to each other as the coach bumped along its monotonous road — up one hill, through an avenue of dusty, tired-looking gumtrees, down the other side through a similar avenue, up another hill precisely the same as the last, and so on.

Blake was the first to make advances. "Not much to be seen on this sort of journey, Miss Grant," he said.

The young lady looked at him with serious eyes. "No," she said, "we've only seen two houses since we left the town. All the rest of the country seems to be a wilderness."

Here the priest broke in. He was a broth of a boy from Maynooth, just the man to handle the Doyle and Donohoe congregation.

"It's the big stations is the roon of the country," he said. "How is the country to go ahead wid all the good land locked up? There's Kuryong on ahead here would support two hundred fam'lies, and what does it employ now? Half a dozen shepherds, widout a rag to their back."

"I am going to Kuryong," said the girl; and the priest was silent.

By four in the afternoon they reached Kiley's River, running yellow and froth-covered with melting snow. The coachman pulled his horses up on the bank, and took a good, long look at the bearings. As they waited, the Kuryong vehicle came down on the other side of the river.

"There's Mr Gordon," said the coachman. "I don't think he'll try it. I reckon it's a trifle deep for me. Do you want to get across particular, Mr Blake?"

"Yes, very particularly, Pat. I've told Martin Donohoe to meet me down here with some witnesses in a cattle-stealing case."

"What about you, Father Kelly?"

"I'm go'n on to Tim Murphy's dyin' bed. Put 'em into the wather, they'll take it aisy."

The driver turned to the third passenger. "It's a bit dangerous-like, Miss. If you like to get out, it's up to you to say so. The coach might wash over. There's a settler's place up the river a mile. You can go and stay there till the river goes down, and Mr Gordon'll come and meet you."

"Thanks, I'll go on," said the lady.

Preparations for crossing the river were soon made. Anything that would spoil by getting wet, or that would float out of the coach, was lifted up and packed on the roof. The passengers stood up on the seats. Then Pat Donohoe put the whip on his leaders, and calling to his two wheelers, old-seasoned veterans, he put them at it.

Snorting and trembling, the leaders picked their way into the yellow water, the coach bumping over the rubble of the crossing-place. Hugh Gordon, watching from the far-side of the river, saw the coach dip and rock and plunge over the boulders. On it came till the water was actually lapping into the body of the coach, roaring and swirling round the horses' legs, up to their flanks and bellies, while the driver called out to them and kept them straight with voice and reins. Every spring he had a similar crossing, and he knew almost to an inch at what height it was safe to go into the river. But this time, as ill-luck would have it, the off-side leader was a young, vicious, thorough-bred colt, who had been handed over to him to be cured of a propensity for striking people with his fore-feet. As the horses worked their way into the river, the colt, with the courage of his breeding, pulled manfully, and breasted the current fearlessly. But suddenly a floating log drifted down, and struck him on the front legs. In an instant he reared up, and threw himself heavily sideways against his mate, bringing him to his knees; then the two of them, floundering and scrambling, were borne away with the current, dragging the coach after them. In a few yards they were off the causeway; the coach, striking deep water, settled like a boat, and turned over on its side, with the leaders swimming for their lives. As for the wheelers, they were pulled down with the vehicle, and were almost drowning in their harness.

Cool as a cucumber, Blake had turned to the girl. "Can you swim?" he said. And she answered him as coolly, "Yes, a little."

"Well, put your hands on my shoulders, and leave everything to me." Just then the coach settled over with one final surge, and they were in the water.

Away they went with the roaring current, the girl clinging fast to his shoulders, while he gave his whole attention to dodging the stumps and snags that were showing their formidable teeth above water. For a while she was able to hold on. Then, with a sickening sense of helplessness, she felt herself torn from him, and whirled away like a leaf. The rank smell of the muddy water was in her nostrils, the fear of death in her heart. She struggled to keep afloat. Suddenly a blood-streaked face appeared, and Blake, bleeding from a cut on the forehead, caught her with a strong grip and drew her to him. A few more seconds of whirling chaos, and she felt land under her feet, and Blake half-carrying her to the bank. They had been swept on to one of the many sand-banks which ran out into the stream, and were safe.

Half-hysterical, she sat down on a huge log, and waited while Blake ran upstream to give help to the coachman. While the two had been battling in the water, the priest had stayed with the coachman to cut the horses free, till at last all four got clear of the wreck, and swam ashore. Then the men followed them, drifting down the current and fighting their way to shore at about the same place.

Hugh Gordon drove the waggonette down to pick up the party when they landed. The scene on the bank would have made a good picture. The horses, dripping with water and shaking with cold, were snorting and staring, while the coachman was trying to fix up some gear out of the wreck, so that he could ride one of them. The priest, his broad Irish face ornamented by a black clay pipe, was tramping up and down in his wet clothes. Blake was helping Miss Grant to wring the water out of her clothes, and she was somewhat incoherently trying to thank him. As Hugh drove up, Blake looked up and caught his eye, and there flashed between the two men an unmistakable look of hostility. Then Hugh jumped from the waggonette, and walked up to Miss Grant, holding out his hand.

"I'm Hugh Gordon," he said. "We only got your father's letter today, or I would have been down to meet you. I hope you are not hurt. Jump into the trap, and I'll run down to the Donohoes', and get you some dry things." Then, turning to Blake, he said somewhat stiffly, "Will you get in, Mr Blake?"

"Thanks," said Blake, equally stiffly, "I can ride one of the mail horses. It's no distance. I won't trouble you."

But the girl turned and put her hand into Blake's, and spoke with the air of a queen.

"I am very much obliged to you — more than I can tell you. You have saved my life. If ever I can do anything to repay you I will."

"Oh, nonsense," said Blake, "that's nothing. It was only a matter of dodging the stumps. You'd better get on now to Donohoe's Hotel, and get Mrs Donohoe to find some dry things for you."

The mere fact of his refusing a lift showed that there was some hostility between himself and Hugh Gordon; but the priest, who had climbed into the

Kuryong vehicle as a matter of course, settled the matter off-hand.

"Get in the trap," he said. "Get in the trap, man. What's the use for two of ye to ride the mail horses, and get your death o' cold? Get in the trap!"

"Of course I'll give you a lift," said Hugh. "Jump in, and let us get away before you all get colds. What will you do about the coach and the luggage, Pat?"

"I'll borry them two old draught horses from Martin Donohoe, and they'll haul it out. Bedad, some o' that luggage'll be washed down to the Murrumbidgee before night; but the most of it is strapped on. Push along, Mr Gordon, and tell Martin I'm coming."

With some reluctance Blake got into the waggonette; before long they were at Donohoe's Hotel, and Mary Grant was soon rigged out in an outfit from Mrs Donohoe's best clothes — a pale-green linsey bodice and purple skirt — everything, including Mrs Donohoe's boots, being about four sizes too big. But she looked by no means an unattractive little figure, with her brown eyes and healthy colour showing above the shapeless garments.

She came into the little sitting-room laughing at the figure she cut, sat down, and drank scalding tea, and ate Mrs Donohoe's cakes, while talking with Father Kelly and Blake over the great adventure.

When she was ready to start she got into the waggonette alongside Hugh, and waved good-bye to the priest and Blake and Mrs Donohoe, as though they were old friends. She had had her first touch of colonial experience.

CHAPTER VIII

AT THE HOMESTEAD

Miss Grant's arrival at Kuryong homestead caused great excitement among the inhabitants. Mrs Gordon received her in a motherly way, trying hard not to feel that a new mistress had come into the house; she was anxious to see whether the girl exhibited any signs of her father's fiery temper and imperious disposition. The two servant-girls at the homestead — great herculean, good-natured bush girls, daughters of a boundary-rider, whose highest ideal of style and refinement was Kuryong drawing-room — breathed hard and stared round-eyed, like wild fillies, at the unconscious intruder. The station-hands — Joe the wood-and-water boy, old Alfred the groom, Bill the horse-team driver, and Harry Warden the married man, who helped with sheep, mended fences, and did station-work in general — all watched for a sight of her. They exchanged opinions about her over their smoke at night by the huge open fireplace in the men's hut, where they sat in a semicircle, toasting their shins at the blaze till their trousers smoked again, each man with a pipe of black tobacco going full swing from tea till bed-time. But the person who felt the most intense excitement over the arrival of the heiress was Miss Harriott.

For all her nurse's experience, Ellen Harriott was not a woman of the world.

Except for the period of her hospital training, she had passed all her life shut up among the mountains. Her dream-world was mostly constructed out of high-class novels, and she united a shrewd wit and a clever brain to a dense ignorance of the real world, that left her like a ship without a rudder. She was, like most bush-reared girls, a great visionary — many a castle-in-the-air had she built while taking her daily walk by the river under the drooping willows. The visions, curiously enough, always took the direction of magnificence. She pictured herself as a leader of society, covered with diamonds, standing at the head of a broad marble staircase and receiving Counts by the dozen (*vide* Ouida's novels, read by stealth); or else as a rich man's wife who dispensed hospitality regally, and was presented at Court, and set the fashion in dress and jewels. At the back of all her dreams there was always a man — a girl's picture is never complete without a man — a strong, masterful man, whose will should crush down opposition, and whose abilities should make his name — and incidentally her name — famous all over the world. She herself, of course, was always the foremost figure, the handsomest woman, the best-dressed, the most admired; for Ellen Harriott, though only a girl, and a friendless governess at Kuryong, was not inclined to put herself second to anyone. Having learnt from her father's papers that he was of an old family, she considered herself anybody's equal. Her brain held a crazy enough jumble of ideas, no doubt; but given a strong imagination, no experience, and omnivorous reading, a young girl's mind is exactly the place where fantastic ideas will breed and multiply. She went about with Mrs Gordon to the small festivities of the district, and was welcomed everywhere, and deferred to by the local settlers; she had yet to know what a snub meant; so the world to her seemed a very easy sort of place to get along in. The coming of the heiress was as light over a trackless ocean. Here was someone who had seen, known, and done all the things which she herself wished to see, know, and do; someone who had travelled on the Continent, tobogganed in Switzerland, ridden in Rotten Row, voyaged in private yachts, hunted in the shires; here was the world at last come to her door — the world of which she had read so much and knew so little.

On the second morning after Miss Grant's arrival, that young lady turned up at breakfast in a tailor-made suit with short skirt and heavy boots, and announced her intention of "walking round the estate"; but as Kuryong — though only a small station, as stations go — was, roughly, ten miles square, this project had to be abandoned. Then she asked Hugh if he would have the servants mustered. He told her that the two servants were in the kitchen, but it turned out that she wanted to interview all the station-hands, and it had to be explained that the horse-driver was six miles out on the run with his team, drawing in a load of bark to roof the hay shed, and that Harry Warden was down at the drafting yards, putting in a new trough to hold an arsenical solution, through which the sheep had to tramp to cure their feet; and that everybody else was away out on some business or other. But the young lady stuck to her point, and had the groom and the wood-and-water boy paraded, they being the only two available. The groom was an English importation, and earned her approval by standing in a rigid and deferential attitude, and saying "Yes, Miss," and "No, Miss," when spoken to; but the wood-and-water boy stood with his arms akimbo and his mouth open, and when she asked him how he liked being on the station he said, "Oh, it's not too bad," accompanying his remark with a sickly grin that nearly earned him summary dismissal.

The young lady returned to the house in rather a sharp temper, and found Hugh standing by a cart, which had just got back with her shipwrecked luggage.

"Well, Miss Grant," he said, "the things are pretty right. The water went down in an hour or so, and the luggage on the top only got a little wetting — just a wave now and again. How have you been getting on?"

"Not at all well," she laughed. "I don't understand the people here. I will get you to take me round before I do another thing. It is so different from England. Are you sure my clothes are all right?"

"I can't be sure, of course, but you can unpack them as soon as you like."

It was not long before the various boxes were opened. Ellen Harriott was called in to assist, and the two girls had a real good afternoon, looking at and talking over clothes and jewellery. The things had come fairly well out of the coach disaster. When an English firm makes a water-tight cover for a bag or box, it *is* water-tight; even the waters of Kiley's River had swept over the canvas of Miss Grant's luggage in vain. And when the sacred boxes were opened, what a treasure-trove was unveiled!

The noblest study of mankind is man, but the most fascinating study of womankind is another woman's wardrobe, and the Australian girl found something to marvel at in the quality of the visitor's apparel. Dainty shoes, tailor-made jackets, fashionable short riding-habits, mannish-looking riding-boots, silk undergarments, beautiful jewellery; all were taken out of their packages and duly admired. As each successive treasure was produced, Ellen Harriott's eyes grew rounder with astonishment; and when, out of a travelling bag, there appeared a complete dressing-table outfit of silverware — silver-backed hair-brushes, silver manicure set, silver handglass, and so forth — she drew a long breath of wonder and admiration.

It was her first sight of the vanities of the world, the things that she had only dreamed of. The outfit was not anything extraordinary from an English point of view, but to the bush-bred girl it was a revelation.

"What beautiful things!" she said. "Now, when you go visiting to a country-house in England, do you always take things like these, all these riding-boots and things?"

"Oh, yes. You wouldn't ride without them."

"And do you take a maid to look after them?"

"Well, you must have a maid."

"And when you travel on the Continent, do you always take a maid?"

"I always took one."

"What is Paris like? Isn't it just a dream? Did you go to the opera? — Have you been on the Riviera? — Oh, do tell me about those places — is it like you read about in books? — all beautiful, well-dressed women and men with nothing to do — and did you go to Monte Carlo?"

This was all poured out in a rush of words; but in Mary's experience the Continent was merely a place where the Continentals got the better of the English, and she said so.

"Travelling is so mixed up with discomfort, that it loses half its plumage," she said. "I'll tell you all I can about Paris some other time. Now you tell me," she went on, folding carefully a silk blouse and putting it in a drawer, "are there any neighbours here? Will anyone come to call?"

"I'm afraid you'll find it very dull here," said Ellen. "There are no neighbours at all except Poss and Binjie, two young fellows on the next station. The people in town are just the publicans and the storekeeper, and all the selectors around us are a very wild lot. Very few strangers come that we can have in the house. They are nearly all cattle and sheep buyers, and they are either too nervous to say a word, or they talk horses. They always come just after mealtime, too, and we have to get everything laid on the table again — sometimes we have ten meals a day in this house. And the swagmen come all day long, and Mrs Gordon or I have to go and give them something to eat; there's plenty to do, always. So you see, there are plenty of strangers, but no neighbours."

"What about Mr Blake?" said Miss Grant. "Isn't he a neighbour?"

It would have needed a much quicker eye than Mary's to catch the half-involuntary movement Ellen Harriott made when Blake's name was mentioned. She flashed a look of inquiry at the heiress that seemed to say, "What interest do you take in Mr Blake? What is he to you?"

Then the long eyelashes shut down over the dark eyes again, and with an air of indifference she said, "Oh, Mr Blake? Of course I know him. I dance with him sometimes at the show balls, and all that. I have been out for a ride with him, too. I think he's nice, but Hugh and Mrs Gordon won't ask him here because he belongs to the selectors, and his mother was a Miss Donohoe. He takes up their cases — and wins them, too. But he never comes here. He always stays down at the hotel when he comes out this way."

"I intend to ask him here," said Miss Grant. "He saved my life."

Again the long eyelashes dropped to hide the sparkle of the eyes.

"Of course, if you like to ask him —"

"Do you think he'd come?"

"Yes, I'm sure he would. If you like to write and ask him, Peter could ride down to Donohoe's today with a note."

From which it would seem that one, at any rate, of the Kuryong household was not wholly indifferent to Mr Blake.

CHAPTER XIII
THE RIVALS

For the next couple of weeks, affairs at Kuryong flowed on in usual station style. A saddle-horse was brought in for Miss Grant, and out of her numerous boxes that young lady produced a Bond Street outfit that fairly silenced criticism. She rode well too, having been taught in England, and she, Poss, Binjie and Hugh had some great scampers after kangaroos, half-wild horses, or anything else that would get up and run in front of them. She was always so fresh, cheerful, and ready for any excitement that the two boys became infatuated in four days, and had to be hunted home on the fifth, or they would have both proposed. Some days she spent at the homestead housekeeping, cooking, and giving out rations to swagmen — the wild, half-crazed travellers who came in at sundown for the dole of flour, tea and sugar, which was theirs by bush custom. Some days she spent with the children, and with them learnt a lot of bush life. It being holiday-time, they practically ran wild all over the place, spending whole days in long tramps to remote parts in pursuit of game. They had no "play", as that term is known to English children. They didn't play at being hunters. They were hunters in real earnest, and their habits and customs had come to resemble very closely those of savage tribes that live by the chase.

With them Mary had numberless new experiences. She got accustomed to seeing the boys climb big trees by cutting steps in the bark with a tomahawk, going out on the most giddy heights after birds' nests, or dragging the possum from his sleeping-place in a hollow limb. She learned to hold a frenzied fox terrier at the mouth of a hollow log, ready to pounce on the kangaroo rat which had taken refuge there, and which flashed out as if shot from a catapult on being poked from the other end with a long stick. She learned to mark the hiding-place of the young wild ducks that scuttled and dived, and hid themselves with such supernatural cunning in the reedy pools. She saw the native companions, those great, solemn, grey birds, go through their fantastic and intricate dances, forming squares, pirouetting, advancing, and retreating with the solemnity of professional dancing-masters. She lay on the river-bank with the children, gun in hand, breathless with excitement, waiting for the rising of the duck-billed platypus — that quaint combination of fish, flesh and fowl — as he dived in the quiet waters, a train of small bubbles marking his track. She fished in deep pools for the great, sleepy, hundred-pound cod-fish that sucked down bait and hook, holus-bolus, and then were hauled in with hardly any resistance, and lived for days contentedly, tethered to the bank by a line through their gills.

In these amusements time passed pleasantly enough, and by the time school-work was resumed Mary Grant had become one of the family.

Of Hugh she at first saw little. His work took him out on the run all day long, looking after sheep in the paddocks, or perhaps toiling day after day in the great, dusty drafting-yards. In the cool of the afternoon the two girls would often canter over the four miles or so of timbered country to the yards, and wait till Hugh had finished his day's work. As a rule, Poss or Binjie, perhaps both, were in attendance to escort Miss Harriott, with the result that Hugh and Mary found themselves paired off to ride home together. Before long he found himself looking forward to these rides with more anxiety than he cared to acknowledge, and in a very short time he was head over ears in love with her.

Any man, being much alone with any woman in a country house, will fall in love with her; but a man such as Hugh Gordon, ardent, imaginative, and very young, meeting every day a woman as beautiful as Mary Grant, was bound to fall a victim. He soon became her absolute worshipper. All day long, in the lonely rides through the bush, in the hot and dusty hours at the sheep-yards, through the pleasant, lazy canter home in the cool of the evening, his fancies were full of her — her beauty and her charm. It was happiness enough for him to be near her, to feel the soft touch of her hand, to catch the faint scent that seemed to linger in her hair. After the day's work they would stroll together about the wonderful old garden, and watch the sunlight die away on the western hills, and the long strings of wild fowl hurrying down the river to their nightly haunts. Sometimes he would manage to get home for lunch, and afterwards, on the pretext of showing her the run, would saddle a horse for her, and off they would go for a long ride through the mountains. Or there were sheep to inspect, or fences to look at — an excuse for an excursion was never lacking.

For the present he made no sign; he was quite contented to act as confidant and adviser, and many a long talk they had together over the various troubles that beset the manager of a station.

It would hardly be supposed that a girl could give much advice on such matters, and at first her total ignorance of the various difficulties amused him; but when she came to understand them better, her cool common-sense compelled his admiration. His temperament was nervous and excitable, and he let things fret him. She took everything in a cheery spirit, and laughed him out of his worries. One would not expect to find many troubles in rearing sheep and selling their wool; but the management of any big station is a heavy task, and Kuryong would have driven Job mad.

The sheep themselves, to begin with, seem always in league against their owners. Merinos, though apparently estimable animals, are in reality dangerous monomaniacs, whose sole desire is to ruin the man that owns them. Their object is to die, and to do so with as much trouble to their owners as they possibly can. They die in the droughts when the grass, roasted to a dull white by the sun, comes out by the roots and blows about the bare paddocks; they die in the wet, when the long grass in the sodden gullies breeds "fluke" and "bottle" and all sorts of hideous complaints. They get burnt in bush fires from sheer malice, refusing to run in any given direction, but charging round and round in a ring till they are calcined. They get drowned by refusing to leave flooded country, though hunted with frenzied earnestness.

It was not the sheep so much as the neighbours whose depredations were drawing lines on Hugh Gordon's face. "I wouldn't care," he confided to Miss Grant, "if they only took a beast or two. But the sheep are going by hundreds. We mustered five hundred short in one paddock this month. And there isn't a Doyle or a Donohoe cow but has three calves at least, and two of each three belong to us."

He dared not prosecute them. No local jury would convict in face of the hostility that would be aroused. They had made "alibis" a special study; the very judges were staggered by the calmness and plausibility with which they got themselves out of difficulties.

A big station with a lot of hostile neighbours is like a whale with the killers round it; it is open to attack on all sides, and cannot retaliate. A match dropped carelessly in a patch of grass sets miles of country in a blaze. Hugh, as he missed the stock, and saw fences cut and grass burnt, could only grind his teeth and hope that a lucky chance would put some of the enemy in his power. To Mary it seemed incredible that in the nineteenth century people should be able to steal sheep without suffering for it; and Hugh soon saw that she was a true daughter of William Grant, as far as fighting was concerned. She listened with set teeth to all stories of depredation and trespass, and they talked over many a plan together. But though they became quite friendly their intimacy seemed to make no progress. To her he was rather the employee than the friend. In fact he did not get on half so far as did Gavan Blake, who came up to Kuryong occasionally, and made himself so agreeable that already his name was being coupled with that of the heiress. Ellen Harriott always spoke to Blake when he came to the station, and gave no sign of jealousy at his attentions to Mary Grant; but she was waiting and watching, as one who has been a nurse learns to do. And things were in this state when an unexpected event put an altogether different complexion on affairs.

from *An Outback Marriage*

The Lost Leichhardt

An English scientific society is fitting out a pioneering party to search for
traces of the lost explorer Leichhardt.

Another search for Leichhardt's tomb,
  Though fifty years have fled
Since Leichhardt vanished in the gloom,
  Our one Illustrious Dead!

But daring men from Britain's shore,
  The fearless bulldog breed,
Renew the fearful task once more,
  Determined to succeed.

Rash men, that know not what they seek,
  Will find their courage tried.
For things have changed on Cooper's Creek
  Since Ludwig Leichhardt died.

Along where Leichhardt journeyed slow
  And toiled and starved in vain;
These rash excursionists must go
  Per Queensland railway train.

Out on those deserts lone and drear
  The fierce Australian black
Will say — "You show it pint o' beer,
  It show you Leichhardt track!"

And loud from every squatter's door
  Each pioneering swell
Will hear the wild pianos roar
  The strains of "Daisy Bell".

The watchers in those forests vast
  Will see, at fall of night,
Commercial travellers bounding past
  And darting out of sight.

About their path a fearful fate
  Will hover always near.
A dreadful scourge that lies in wait —
  The Longreach Horehound Beer!

And then, to crown this tale of guilt,
   They'll find some scurvy knave,
Regardless of their quest, has built
   A pub on Leichhardt's grave!

Ah, yes! Those British pioneers
   Had best at home abide,
For things have changed in fifty years
   Since Ludwig Leichhardt died.

Camouflage

Beside the bare and beaten track of travelling flocks and herds
The woodpecker went tapping on, the postman of the birds,
"I've got a letter here," he said, "that no one's understood,
Addressed as follows: 'To the bird that's like a piece of wood.'

"The soldier bird got very cross — it wasn't meant for her;
The spurwing plover had a try to stab me with a spur;
The jackass laughed, and said the thing was written for a lark.
I think I'll chuck this postman job and take to stripping bark."

Then all the birds for miles around came in to lend a hand;
They perched upon a broken limb as thick as they could stand,
And just as old man eaglehawk prepared to have his say
A portion of the broken limb got up and flew away.

Then, casting grammar to the winds, the postman said, "That's him!
The boobook owl — he squats himself along a broken limb,
And pokes his beak up like a stick; there's not a bird, I vow,
Can tell you which is boobook owl and which is broken bough.

"And that's the thing he calls his nest — that jerry-built affair —
A bunch of sticks across a fork; I'll leave his letter there.
A cuckoo wouldn't use his nest, but what's the odds to him —
A bird that tries to imitate a piece of leaning limb!"

Preparing for Premiers

SCENE: Office of High Official in charge of Colonial affairs in London. High Official discovered glaring at table covered with lists of visiting potentates, programmes of amusements, lists of precedence, cablegrams, &c., &c. A waste-paper basket full of K.C.M.G. ribbons and orders stands by the table. On the table a handbag full of Privy Councillorships. High Official rings bell angrily. To him enters subordinate official, the Honourable Somebody, a very tired-looking youth.

HIGH OFFICIAL: "Look here, this is a nice state of things. I'm only just back from Monte Carlo, and I've got to set to work and clear up all this business. Now, have you got a list of the people we are responsible for?"

TIRED YOUTH: "Ya-a-as."

HIGH OFFICIAL: "Well, who *is* there? There's the Indian Viceroy, of course, and the Premier of Canada — we know all about *them*. And then there's the chappie from China, my brother-in-law, *he's* all right. But what about these Australian brutes? How many are there? Two, I suppose — Premier of South Australia and Premier of North Australia — eh? there must be a North Australia if there's a South Australia! Where's your list — how many are there?"

TIRED YOUTH: "There's seven."

HIGH OFFICIAL: "*Seven*! Good God, are the whole population Premiers over there? There's not seven places for them to be Premiers of! You must have made a mistake. Get the map!"
(*They get the map and pore over it discontentedly.*)

HIGH OFFICIAL (*triumphantly*): "There you are! What did I tell you! There's only five colonies, even if each place has a Premier, which I don't believe. There's Queensland, New South Wales, Victoria, South Australia and West Australia. Now, how the devil do you make seven out of that?"

TIRED YOUTH: "*I* don't know. One of the clerks made out the beastly list."

HIGH OFFICIAL: "Which clerk?"

TIRED YOUTH: "I don't know. How should I know one beastly clerk from another?"

HIGH OFFICIAL: "Well, you must find out. Seven! There must be two frauds among 'em. Nice we'll look if we let two infernal pickpockets loose among those Indian Rajahs all over diamonds. How are you going to identify 'em when they come? There's one fellow I could swear to, anyhow — a big, hairy, orang-outang of a man about seven feet high. He was here before. I'll swear to *him* anywhere. What was his name again? Gibbs or Gibson, or something like that."

TIRED YOUTH: "Dibbs, I think. Always reminded me of money, I know."

HIGH OFFICIAL: "Well, perhaps it was, but I *think* it was Gibbs. Anyhow, is *he* coming?"

TIRED YOUTH: "I don't know. How should I know? I suppose he is."

HIGH OFFICIAL (*at his wits' end*): "Well, for goodness sake send someone here that does know. You'll get me into nice trouble, going on like this. Send for a clerk that knows about it, and, meanwhile, we'll have a go at this list of precedence."
(*Tired youth rings bell for clerk, and returns to table to look over list of precedence.*)

HIGH OFFICIAL: "See here, the truth's this. We've got orders from headquarters to soap these confounded self-governing colonies all we can. But, if we send their Premiers in to a function before the Indian Princes — my goodness, the Indians will stick 'em in the back with a *tulwar*, or something. Then there's the Indian, China, Straits Settlement, African, and Crown colonies' lot. Which is to come first, and which last? Have you any idea?"

TIRED YOUTH: "*I* don't know. There's a clerk knows all these things."
(*Enter clerk.*)

HIGH OFFICIAL: "Look here, is there any table of precedence in the office?"

CLERK: "Yes, my Lord."

HIGH OFFICIAL: "Thank God! Who made it out?"

CLERK: "Lord Titmarsh, when he was in office, my Lord."

HIGH OFFICIAL: "Bless him and praise him! See that it is followed with literal accuracy; literal accuracy, you understand — and I'll take all the credit if it goes right, and Titmarsh can take all the blame if it goes wrong. So far, so good. Now there's another thing. How many Premiers are coming from Australia?"

CLERK: "Seven, my Lord!"

HIGH OFFICIAL (*to tired youth*): "See! He's made the same mistake you did. If I wasn't here to look after you fellows you'd run the empire to the devil. Seven, indeed!" (To Clerk): "Do you know, sir, there are only five colonies in Australia? Look at the map."

CLERK: "Yes, my Lord; but there's a Premier of Tasmania and a Premier of New Zealand."

HIGH OFFICIAL: "Oh, good gracious! They say America is mostly colonels; this place appears to be mostly Premiers. Now, what do you know about 'em? How are you going to be sure that some fraud doesn't pass himself off as a Premier — some anarchist, with a bomb in his trousers pocket, and blow us all kite-high?"

CLERK: "We have photographs of them all, sir, and a private and confidential cipher report from the Governor of each colony as to their political leanings."

HIGH OFFICIAL: "Let's have a look. Who's this fat, bald-headed man, that looks like a tallow-merchant?"

CLERK: "The Hon. G. H. Reid, my Lord, Premier of New South Wales."

HIGH OFFICIAL (*angrily*): "There you go again! I tell you a man named Gibbs is Premier of New South Wales — great, long, hairy man, quite different from this fellow. I met Gibbs often. This is a fraud, I'll take my oath. Don't he look it — look at his face, all jowl and jelly."

CLERK: "There has been a change of Ministry, my Lord, and this is the present Premier."

HIGH OFFICIAL: "Well, he's not much to look at, anyhow. What does his Governor say about him? Who *is* his Governor, anyhow? Hampden — Oh, I was in the House with Hampden. Dry sort of fellow, not such a fool as he looked. What does he say about him? Let's have a look. (*Reads report mumblingly.*) Truckles to Labor Party . . . time server . . . not last long . . . change may be for the worse . . . no force of character . . . afraid of the Labor Party . . . dare not take K.C.M.G. . . . better be bought with a P.C.-ship. I like that — a P.C.-ship indeed for a ruffian like this — an anarchist without the courage of his villainy. We bought Gibbs with a K.C.M.G. Let this ruffian have a K.C.M.G. or nothing."

TIRED YOUTH (*waking to interest in proceedings*): "I read those reports. There's one chappie there rather a good sort. All the rest are awful rotters. Read his report. Nelson I think was the name." (*High official mumbles over Nelson's report.*) "Fights Labor Party. . . fearless . . . can't last long . . . has worked well for Imperialistic ideas . . . very courageous man . . . will support Anglo-Japanese treaty. Ah! that's the sort of man. What's *he* to get?"

TIRED YOUTH: "Headquarters say they are *all* to get P.C.-ships."

HIGH OFFICIAL: "All! Good heavens. Well, if we can't degrade that man Reid in any way, see that he gets the suite of rooms in the worst part of the hotel, and give him a hard seat at all functions. And, by the by, what about taking them round? Who's to do it? *You'll* have to do it: I've got the Canadian and Indian lot to look after."

TIRED YOUTH: "Oh, I'll send one of the clerks and get them tickets for everything that is going in the way of concerts and public receptions and so on. I suppose they can't go to anything really select."

HIGH OFFICIAL (*very slowly and deliberately*): "I should think not. Take 'em to the British Museum and the waxworks, and see that the name of some unattached lord or other is always associated with theirs. It will be put in their cables, and help to damn Reid in the eyes of his friends — and that's about all, isn't it?"

TIRED YOUTH: "And supposing they kick up a row, don't you know, if they're not asked to any of the really swaggah things?"

HIGH OFFICIAL: "My dear boy, if they try anything of that sort on, have them bayoneted by the soldiers the moment they show their noses at the gate. Fill up these P.C. forms, and see that you don't fill 'em up wrong. And now I'm off to the Club. Just be decently civil to these people, but don't go too far, because, you know, by this time next year they will probably be back in their shops selling sugar — I'm certain that man Reid sells sugar, by the look of him. *Au revoir!*"

Cable item: All preparations have been made for the reception of the Australian Premiers in London, and they will be the principal items of the Jubilee.

Behind the Scenes

The actor struts his little hour,
    Between the limelight and the band;
The public feel the actor's power,
    Yet nothing do they understand
Of all the touches here and there
    That make or mar the actor's part,
They never see, beneath the glare,
    The artist striving after art.

To them it seems a labour slight
    Where nought of study intervenes;
You see it in another light
    When once you've been behind the scenes.

For though the actor at his best
    Is, like a poet, born not made,
He still must study with a zest
    And practise hard to learn his trade.
So, whether on the actor's form
    The stately robes of Hamlet sit,
Or as Macbeth he rave and storm,
    Or plays burlesque to please the pit,

'Tis each and all a work of art,
    That constant care and practice means —
The actor who creates a part
    Has done his work behind the scenes.

A Nervous Governor-General

We read in the press that Lord Northcote is here
　　To take up Lord Tennyson's mission.
'Tis pleasant to find they have sent us a Peer,
　　And a man of exalted position.
It's his business to see that the Radical horde
　　From loyalty's path does not swerve us;
But his tastes, and the task, don't seem quite in accord
　　For they say that His Lordship is nervous.

Does he think that wild animals walk in the street,
　　Where the wary marsupial is hopping?
Does he think that the snake and the platypus meet
　　And "bail up" the folk who go shopping?
And that boomerangs fly round the scared passer-by
　　Who has come all this way to observe us.
While the blackfellow launches a spear at his eye?
　　— No wonder His Lordship is nervous.

Does he think that with callers he'll be overtasked,
　　From a baronet down to a barber?
Does he dream of the number of times he'll be asked
　　"What he thinks of our Beautiful Harbour?"
Does he sadly reflect on the sorrows that ding
　　Round his task? (From such sorrows preserve us!)
He must hear John See speak and O'Sullivan sing,
　　— It's enough to make any man nervous.

Does he think he'll be waked in the dead of the night
　　From Melbourne to go willy-nilly,
To live at the Federal Capital site
　　At Tumut or Wagra-go-billy?
Well, the Melbournites *may* let the Capital go
　　(Here we wink with one eye, please observe us!)
But not in a hurry! By no means! Oh, no!
　　He has not the least need to be nervous!

The Wind's Message

There came a whisper down the Bland between the dawn and dark,
Above the tossing of the pines, above the river's flow;
It stirred the boughs of giant gums and stalwart ironbark;
It drifted where the wild ducks played amid the swamps below;
It brought a breath of mountain air from off the hills of pine,
A scent of eucalyptus trees in honey-laden bloom;
And drifting, drifting far away along the southern line
It caught from leaf and grass and fern a subtle strange perfume.

It reached the toiling city folk, but few there were that heard —
The rattle of their busy life had choked the whisper down;
And some but caught a fresh-blown breeze with scent of pine that stirred
A thought of blue hills far away beyond the smoky town;
And others heard the whisper pass, but could not understand
The magic of the breeze's breath that set their hearts aglow,
Nor how the roving wind could bring across the Overland
A sound of voices silent now and songs of long ago.

But some that heard the whisper clear were filled with vague unrest;
The breeze had brought its message home, they could not fixed abide;
Their fancies wandered all the day towards the blue hills' breast,
Towards the sunny slopes that lie along the riverside,
The mighty rolling western plains are very fair to see,
Where waving to the passing breeze the silver myalls stand,
But fairer are the giant hills, all rugged though they be,
From which the two great rivers rise that run along the Bland.

Oh! rocky range and rugged spur and river running clear,
That swings around the sudden bends with swirl of snow-white foam,
Though we, your sons, are far away, we sometimes seem to hear
The message that the breezes bring to call the wanderers home.
The mountain peaks are white with snow that feeds a thousand rills,
Along the river banks the maize grows tall on virgin land,
And we shall live to see once more those sunny southern hills,
And strike once more the bridle track that leads along the Bland.

Captain Glossop

Captain's own story of *Emden* fight — Thank God, we didn't start the war
— The sailor talks to the point — English and Australians work together —
Discipline in the Silent Service — A little affair in Mexico.

November 1914. *En route* for the Great War as a correspondent. We
have two battalions of Infantry on board. A topsy-turvy force this,
for the Brigadier, General MacLaurin, has never seen any active service, while the ranks are full of English ex-service men, wearing as many
ribbons as prize bulls. These English ex-service men, by the way, volunteered
to a man when the war broke out, and the Australian ranks were full of
Yorkshiremen, Cockneys, and Cousin Jacks. Every one of them had the fixed
idea of getting a transfer or clearing out and rejoining his old regiment as soon
as he got to England. Who can blame them? It is the English way. Any one
of them would sooner be shot as a private in the Coldstream Guards than get
a decoration in a nameless Australian force. By the end of the war, we ourselves had a tradition.

Fortunately, this expedition was halted in Egypt for training, so they had
to stick to the show whether they liked it or not. When we talk about the
glories of Gallipoli we should give credit to the fifty per cent or so of
Yorkshiremen, Cousin Jacks, Cockneys, etc, who did their share in it.

At sea. Leaving Australia. Among the officers there are many bemedalled
men. When any debatable question comes up, they pout their chests at
MacLaurin and say they never did it that way in their old regiments. For
instance, one hero named Lieutenant Magee was ranching in Mexico, when
Pancho Villa came along and commandeered all his men and horses. Being
left on his beam ends, so to speak, Magee was wondering what he would do
next, when Villa said, "Why not come along with us? Do you know anything
about fighting?" It so happened that Magee had done some voluntary artillery
work, and Villa said, "You are the very man I want. I have just captured two
guns and I have nobody that can work them."

Magee had a great time working those two guns, shooting at all and
sundry, until one day he went down to headquarters and found nobody there
but the General and his staff. All the troops had cleared out and joined some
other general. Knowing that all captured officers were invariably shot, Magee
hopped on to a horse and never stopped going till he reached the coast.

"What did you do with the guns, Magee?" I asked.

"I left them in the middle of the road. I expect they are there yet."

Another officer, a Major MacNaughton, had served in a crack Highland
regiment, and had led the troops up the heights of Dargai or some other
inaccessible and dangerous place. He persisted in wearing a Highland bonnet
in defiance of an order that no equipment was to be worn other than that laid
down by the Australian regulations. MacLaurin, however, was by way of

being a bit of a Highlander himself, and a born, natural soldier. For instance, he took hold of that rough outfit and made the troops stand to attention when another transport was going past.

A New Zealand transport came close alongside, with the men cheering, beating tin pans, and yelling out, "Hello Digger."

Not a word out of our lot, not a move of a muscle: and the New Zealanders went off saying: "You b——! You're too flash to speak to us, are you?" By and by, it seeped into the intelligence of the officers commanding the various transports that this was the correct thing to do; and before we got to Egypt they were all doing it. MacLaurin put Magee under arrest for being late on parade; and, having occasion to send for MacNaughton, he said, "How dare you appear before me improperly dressed? Go and put your cap on, and don't let me see you wearing that thing again."

This, from a man who had never seen any service, to the hero of a hundred fights! MacLaurin straightened everything up, and these two officers became his admirers. Magee said, "When I first joined this outfit I thought that this Brigadier was just about able to take a salute. Now I prophesy that he will command a division before the war is over."

Unfortunately, MacLaurin and his brigade major were both killed by a shell almost as soon as they landed on Gallipoli.

Among our personnel was a gigantic lieutenant named Massie, an international cricketer, strong and rugged as an ironbark tree. By some freak of fortune he had been made adjutant of his battalion though he knew no more about military routine than he knew about flying. His first question was, "How am I to mount guard, when we haven't got any horses?" But by sheer personality and common sense, he managed to make a success of his job. He had a string of officers after him all day long, with troubles and questions.

"They've taken the table out of our orderly room, Jack."

"I caught a fellow cutting some rope out of the rigging to dry his washing on, Jack."

"A chap's hat blew overboard, Jack. How do I get him another?"

Luckily the brigade adjutant was a regular, Lieutenant King, of the King's Liverpool regiment, and by doing the three men's work this King managed to keep the show going; aided largely by the English ex-service men, who love a regular officer but felt it below their dignity to be bossed by volunteers.

It was through friendship with Massie that I got in touch with a celebrity — the man who commanded an Australian warship in the first fight fought under the Australian flag. It is not often that we get from the silent navy an account of a fight from the lips of the man who fought it.

November 15th. Colombo. Arrived in Colombo to find everybody in a wild state of excitement over the sinking of the *Emden* by the *Sydney*. We can hardly believe that Australia's first naval engagement could have been such a sensational win, for our people are not sea-going people and our navy — which some of us used to call a pannikin navy — was never taken very seriously. And now we have actually sunk a German ship!

Colombo harbour is a wonderful sight with warships, transports, merchantmen, Japanese, Russian, English and Australian ships. There is the Russian man-of-war, *Askold*, reported sunk in the Russo-Japanese War, also reported sunk by the *Emden*, and that she sank the *Emden* in this war; *Abouki* (Japanese), *Hampshire* (English), and, best of all, alongside the long breakwater the four funnels — the two centre funnels with white streaks round them — of the *Sydney*. It sort of wakes us up to the idea that we have a country.

Our troops are not allowed ashore lest in their exhilaration they should take Colombo to pieces. The Colombo streets are full of New Zealand Tommies and officers, hundreds of them. They are a fine lot of men, well turned out, and with black boots like the English ammunition boot. They are not enjoying the war, for their General is even a worse "nark" than ours. They are not allowed beer or cigarettes on board their transports. Fancy going to war without beer or cigarettes! Their General is named Godley, but they call him ungodly. Their ranks, like ours, contain a large proportion of men who are not New Zealanders at all, but are soldiers of fortune who have joined up in search of adventure. One of these men says that Godley was not to blame for the beer and cigarette order; that it was done by the New Zealand public, whom he describes as a lot of "narrow-minded, persecuting, canting, Scotch hypocrites". This comes of cutting off a man's tobacco.

General Godley, by the way, afterwards proved himself a very fine soldier, and made a great name for the New Zealanders at Gallipoli. All over the world it is the same — the rougher the general, the better the troops.

The gigantic Massie offers to take me off to interview Glossop, the hero of the *Sydney-Emden* fight. Massie's people are of considerable importance in Sydney and he has entertained Glossop at his house; so, he says that if I go with him and listen to what Glossop says I may get some stuff that the other correspondents wouldn't get. This Massie is about six feet two in height, broad in proportion, and he must be all brains. Any man that can make a success as adjutant of a raw battalion, without any previous experience whatever, can do anything.

We find Glossop in mufti, having a drink by himself, a typical English sailor man, not a bit excited by the fact that he has "woke up to find himself famous": to him the whole affair is a matter of range of guns, weight of metal, speed of ship, and of course a good deal of luck.

"Well, Massie, I had a lot of luck, didn't I?" he says. "Fancy her coming to Cocos just when we were right on the spot, and fancy just having the luck to be on that side of the convoy. If I'd been on the other side, then I wouldn't have got the job. Of course I had the speed of her and the guns of her, but if our people hadn't served the guns properly or if she'd dropped a shell into our engine-room, we might have been sent to the bottom instead of her. You can work out a fight on paper, and one shell will upset the whole calculation.

"She had no idea that there was any vessel of her own power in that part of the Pacific, and she came out looking for a fight — and she got it. She must have got a surprise when she found she had to fight the *Sydney*; and I got a surprise, too, I can tell you. When we were about ten thousand five hundred yards apart I turned nearly due north so as to run parallel with her, and I said to the gunnery lieutenant that we had better get a thousand yards closer before we fired. I knew the *Emden*'s four-point-one guns would be at their extreme limit at ten thousand yards, and I got a shock when she fired a salvo at ten thousand five hundred and two of the shells came aboard us. That's modern gunnery for you. Fancy one ship, rolling about in the sea, hitting another ship — also rolling about in the sea — six miles away! She must have elevated her guns and fired in the air, for we were technically out of range; but it was great gunnery.

"Her first salvo was five guns, of which two shells came aboard us. One shell burst and carried away the after-control, wounding all the men, including Lieutenant Hampden, but no one was killed. The other shell passed within six inches of the gunnery lieutenant and killed a man working a range finder, but it never burst. There was luck again for me — I was in that control room and if the shell had burst I suppose I would have been a goner.

"There was a boy of about sixteen in the control working a telescope. When the shell landed he was stunned by the concussion and was lying under the body of the man that was killed. As soon as he came to himself he threw the man's body off him and started looking for his telescope. 'Where's my bloody telescope?' was all he said. That's the Australian Navy for you.

"The whole thing didn't last forty minutes, but it was a busy forty minutes. She tried to get near enough to torpedo us, but she could only do seventeen knots and we could do twenty-seven, so we scuttled out of range. The *Emden* had a captured collier called the *Buresk* hanging about, trying to get near enough to ram us, and I had to keep a couple of guns trained on this collier all the time. We hit the *Emden* about a hundred times in forty minutes, and fourteen of her shells struck us but most of them were fired beyond her range and the shells hit the side and dropped into the water without exploding. When the *Emden* made for the beach we went after the collier, but we found the Germans had taken the sea-cocks out of her so we had to let her sink. They were game men, I'll say that for them.

"Then we went back to the *Emden* lying in the shallow water and signalled her 'Do you surrender?' She answered by flag-wagging in Morse 'We have no signal book and do not understand your signal.' I asked several times but could get no answer and her flag was still flying, so I fired two salvos into her and then they hauled their flag down. I was sorry afterwards that I gave her those two salvos, but what was I to do? If they were able to flag-wag in Morse, they were surely able to haul a flag down. We understood there was another German warship about and I couldn't have the *Emden* firing at me from the beach while I was fighting her mate.

"We waited off all night with lights out for this vessel, but she never showed up, and then we sent boats ashore to the *Emden*. My God, what a sight! Her captain had been out of action ten minutes after the fight started from lyddite fumes, and everybody on board was demented — that's all you could call it, just fairly demented — by shock, and fumes, and the roar of shells bursting among them. She was a shambles. Blood, guts, flesh, and uniforms were all scattered about. One of our shells had landed behind a gun shield, and had blown the whole gun crew into one pulp. You couldn't even tell how many men there had been. They must have had forty minutes of hell on that ship, for out of four hundred men a hundred and forty were killed and eighty wounded and the survivors were practically madmen. They crawled up to the beach and they had one doctor fit for action; but he had nothing to treat them with — they hadn't even got any water. A lot of them drank salt water and killed themselves. They were not ashore twenty-four hours, but their wounds were fly-blown and the stench was awful — it's hanging about the *Sydney* yet. I took them on board and got four doctors to work on them and brought them up here.

"I've seen my first naval engagement, Massie; and all I can say is, thank God we didn't start the war."

We left Captain Glossop to handle his very turbulent lot of prisoners and went back to our ships. The next night a message came that the *Sydney*, with the German prisoners on board, would pass us at sea about two o'clock in the morning. The Brigadier ordered that all ranks should parade and stand at attention as she went past: an order that started a lot of grumbling among the recruits until a Yorkshire ex-sergeant-major said, "Tha'll be proud, laad, some day to say that tha' did it. Yesterday ye were nowt but a handful o' blacks; but the world's talkin' about ye today."

Under the tropic night the ghost of a warship glided by and all ranks on our transport fell in and stood at attention until she had passed out of sight. A formality, perhaps, but it might have satisfied even Mr Kipling that we were growing up.

from *Happy Dispatches*

Waltzing Matilda

CARRYING A SWAG

Oh there once was a swagman camped in the billabongs,
Under the shade of a Coolibah tree;
And he sang as he looked at the old billy boiling,
"Who'll come a-waltzing Matilda with me."

Who'll come a-waltzing Matilda, my darling,
Who'll come a-waltzing Matilda with me.
Waltzing Matilda and leading a water-bag,
Who'll come a-waltzing Matilda with me.

Up came the jumbuck to drink at the waterhole,
Up jumped the swagman and grabbed him in glee;
And he sang as he put him away in his tucker-bag,
"You'll come a-waltzing Matilda with me!"

Who'll come a-waltzing Matilda, my darling,
Who'll come a-waltzing Matilda with me.
Waltzing Matilda and leading a water-bag,
Who'll come a-waltzing Matilda with me.

Up came the squatter a-riding his thoroughbred;
Up came policemen — one, two, and three.
"Whose is the jumbuck you've got in the tucker-bag?
You'll come a-waltzing Matilda with we."

Who'll come a-waltzing Matilda, my darling,
Who'll come a-waltzing Matilda with me.
Waltzing Matilda and leading a water-bag,
Who'll come a-waltzing Matilda with me.

Up sprang the swagman and jumped in the waterhole,
Drowning himself by the Coolibah tree;
And his voice can be heard as it sings in the billabongs,
"Who'll come a-waltzing Matilda with me."

Who'll come a-waltzing Matilda, my darling,
Who'll come a-waltzing Matilda with me.
Waltzing Matilda and leading a water-bag,
Who'll come a-waltzing Matilda with me.

Index of Titles

Index of First Lines of Verse

Acknowledgments

SLIPCASE: Henry Lawson (Mitchell Library, State Library of NSW) and A. B. Paterson (National Library of Australia).

COVER: A. B. Paterson. National Library of Australia.

Facing p32: *Bushman's home — Victoria c1885*. National Library of Australia.
Facing p33: *Foster Tree Stump Church*. South Gippsland Shire Historical Society.
Facing p48: *Wool shearers at Currawillinghi*. National Library of Australia.
Facing p49: *Interior of wool-shearing shed, West Talgai station, Queensland*. National Library of Australia.
Facing p128: *New South Wales Mounted Rifles crossing the Orange River, South Africa, 1901*. Australian War Memorial.
Facing p129: *Light Horse on the Philistine Plain, Palestine, 1918*. Australian War Memorial.
Facing p144: *Recruiting Office, Melbourne*. Australian War Memorial.
Facing p145: *Australian Troops at Lone Pine, Gallipoli, August 1915*. Australian War Memorial.
Facing p176: *Travelling cattle, Kosciusko*. Tyrell Collection, reproduced courtesy of the Trustees of the Museum of Applied Arts and Sciences.
Facing p177: CHARLES KERRY *Mustering cattle*. Tyrell Collection, reproduced courtesy of the Trustees of the Museum of Applied Arts and Sciences.
Facing p192: CHARLES KERRY *Grandstand, Randwick, Sydney*. Tyrell Collection, reproduced courtesy of the Trustees of the Museum of Applied Arts and Sciences.
Facing p193: *Horseracing*. La Trobe Collection, State Library of Victoria.
Facing p256: CHARLES KERRY *A Modern Australian Shearer*. Tyrell Collection, reproduced courtesy of the Trustees of the Museum of Applied Arts and Sciences.
Facing p257: CHARLES KERRY *A Country Mail Coach c1890*. La Trobe Collection, State Library of Victoria.
Facing p272: *'Bush Life': Staff outside the Victoria River Downs Station*. Mortlock Library of South Australiana, State Library of S.A.
Facing p273: CHARLES KERRY *Travelling Sheep*. Tyrell Collection, reproduced courtesy of the Trustees of the Museum of Applied Arts and Sciences.